Praise for *Lo*
Voice to Fi...

"Sometimes it's hard to understand why God takes things away. Mark losing his singing voice is one of those unanswerable questions. However, I've walked with Mark, from his final show in Hawaii to him bringing hope to the people of Haiti, and God has never let him go. Mark's voice has never been more important."

—Bart Millard, MercyMe

"I grew up singing background vocals and stage-managing for my sister, Rebecca St. James, and we did countless shows with Audio Adrenaline. I remember standing side stage with my mouth on the floor at their ingenuity, passion, and performance. Mark's presence onstage truly inspired me. I've been fortunate to become close friends with Mark, and I have to say that what he's done post–Audio Adrenaline has been even more impacting for me. Stories like his remind me of God's relentless creativity in weaving together imperfect stories for greater redemption."

—Joel Smallbone, For King & Country

"I have had the privilege of touring with Mark multiple times throughout the years. We've worked on records and written songs together, and I have had the honor of doing a lot of life with Mark. He is the genuine article. I believe he is truly a man after God's own heart. He has held steadfast on that course no matter what storms life has thrown at him. He is full of wisdom, and I am thankful that he offers it up to all of us as we continue on our own journeys. His insight should serve us well."

—TobyMac, Grammy-winning artist

"Mark had one of those voices that made you feel something beyond the lyric. His voice's brokenness and vulnerability gave it power, just like his testimony."

—Michael Tait, Newsboys

"Mark's story is like my story. We're both underdogs. If you're looking to be inspired, you'll find plenty of nuggets in this book to keep your head up. I frickin' guarantee it."

—Todd Hoffman, reality TV star and gold miner

"What can I say about Mark Stuart . . . my buddy. . . from the very first hour I met him back in 1986 when he asked me to join this Christian rock band he was starting, all the way to this very moment, it's without question he was marked by God to be used for His purposes, and to be an example of what it looks like to always choose God. A man after God's heart, who, in the midst of a journey with the highest highs and the lowest lows, never lost his faith or turned his back on the God he loves and serves. A gifted singer, one of the greatest performers, but moreover, an incredible person, Gods beloved!"

Will McGinniss, two-time Grammy winner, Audio Adrenaline

"From his days with Audio Adrenaline, to his tireless pursuit of orphan care and prevention in Haiti, to his deep love for his family, Mark never does anything half-throttle. He is an advocate in the truest sense of the word, an outspoken champion for those in need, and an amazing friend to so many. Mark's story of losing and finding will inspire and be used by God in incredible ways, just as it already has!"

—Leslie Jordan, All Sons & Daughters, the Fold, Nashville

"Mark's journey has always inspired me as a storyteller. It gives me hope that there is always a purpose in the struggle. His voice for the forgotten kids in Haiti is such a powerful one."

—Andrew Erwin, filmmaker, I Can Only Imagine

"Mark is a dear friend with whom I have shared a lot of life. He is a genuine soul who dreams big and loves even bigger. From tour buses to Caribbean islands, Mark has logged a lot of miles and lived a lot of life. This portrait of humanness in its adventure, candor, and grace will inspire you to live big and plunge headfirst into the love story of God."

—Jamie George, pastor and author, Journey Church, Nashville

"Audio Adrenaline played a big role in helping to grow our congregation during the formative years of the Rock Church in San Diego. As Christian music shifted and became more relevant, we leveraged bands like Audio Adrenaline to help reach our broader community. And it worked! But more importantly, the message in their songs resonated with our young church, and with so many believers around the world, to become the very hands and feet of Jesus. In *Losing My Voice to Find It*, Mark's journey inspires us. Whether our voices are broken or beautiful, we each have a glorious story to share."

—Miles McPherson, pastor and author, the Rock Church, San Diego

"Audio Adrenaline easily had one of the greatest impacts on my faith through the years. I started Jesusfreakhideout.com in 1996 as a bright-eyed Christian music–loving teen, who was heavily inspired by Audio Adrenaline's message and their pride in being labeled a 'Christian band.' Mark's ministry—and the way he has always treated me and other youth throughout the years—had a rare humility and kindness that the industry often sorely lacked. It broke my heart to see Mark lose his voice, but it's brought hope and encouragement to see that God continues to do incredible things through him. And I must say, *Losing My Voice to Find It* is an inspiring page-turner!"

—John DiBiase, creator, Jesus Freak Hideout

"I met Mark after a show in Kentucky when he was a college student. We grew up in the music business together. Little did I know how our lives would intersect in the years to follow. Audio Adrenaline was the opening act in my first headlining tour in 1992, and I was an eyewitness to the transformation of a young awkward kid into one of Christian music's greatest front men.

As much as I love Mark's music, it's his life offstage that has inspired me the most. The story of this honest, kind, broken, talented, passionate, and visionary man has inspired me to pursue the 'Good Life.' Thank you, my friend, for allowing us inside your remarkable journey."

—Geoff Moore, Grammy-nominated artist, national park tour guide

"Mark Stuart is like a member of my own family. I've known him from the very humble beginnings of Audio Adrenaline touring life to where he is now as a father, missions leader, and visionary artist. Nobody that I know personally has a more captivating story of redemption, change, and adventure. It was my honor to stand in for him as lead vocalist for Audio Adrenaline from 2011 to 2013. "Kings & Queens," the song and album, wouldn't have been generated without his passion and love for music and the people of Haiti. I'm lucky to count him as one of my closest friends."

—Kevin Max, singer, songwriter, poet

losing
my voice
to find it

losing my voice to find it

HOW A ROCK STAR DISCOVERED HIS GREATEST PURPOSE

Grammy-Winning Lead Singer of
Audio Adrenaline

MARK STUART

WITH ROGER W. THOMPSON

NELSON
BOOKS
An Imprint of Thomas Nelson

When families gather, our voices inevitably gain strength.
We come alive. We laugh. We cry. We get real. We get
loud. Somehow, together, our weaknesses are forgotten,
our selfishness is scattered, and our purpose . . . our
voice . . . becomes more clear. I thank God for my family.
My voice and this book are dedicated to them.

Aegis, my wife, for intimacy and courage.
Journey and Christela, my children, for joy and purpose.
Drex and Jo, my mom and dad, for inspiration and belief.

Contents

Foreword

As the son of missionary parents growing up in a Christian home, Christian music has always been a part of my life. My mother, one of the great influences in shaping my faith, instilled God's Word in my siblings and me through Scripture and songs. As a young kid, songs by DC Talk, the Newsboys, Audio Adrenaline, and others really encouraged me, maybe even more than the classic hymns.

I remember clearly the song "Big House" by Audio Adrenaline. The song was being sung at youth conferences, Christian camps, and kids' church everywhere. "Big House" even made it all the way to the Philippines where I was born. But honestly, I really liked the song because it talked about football. A song that connected sports and Jesus was amazing to my eight-year-old self.

After college I was blessed to be able to start a faith-based foundation and to live out God's call on my life to serve others. It was through my foundation's work to impact orphans in Haiti that I first met Mark. By this time, he was no longer the front man of Audio Adrenaline. He was instead leading an orphan-care ministry in Haiti called the Hands and Feet Project. When I asked Mark why he was no longer singing with Audio A, he simply replied that God had moved him in a different direction. He explained that he had permanently lost his singing voice due to a vocal disorder, which resulted in him losing his band, his music career, and more importantly, his platform as a rock and roll front man. While that seemed tragic, it was more than evident to me that his purpose and passion to make a difference in people's lives were being abundantly fulfilled as he fought for Haitian kids and families in dire need of help. As Mark and I spoke, I found myself once again being inspired. But, this time, in an even more meaningful way because of his new role as the front man for the Hands and Feet Project.

Mark and I were both missionary kids, and our journeys are similar in some ways. We've been blessed with platforms, and we share a passion for bringing faith, hope, and love to children around the world. We've also had career paths that God chose to take on unexpected detours. Remember this: whether you're going through life's extreme highs or lows, God can use them for his glory, because God never stops working for you and through you. Trust Him.

This is Mark's story. And I pray that it will be your story as well.

Tim Tebow

PART I

My Father's House

Come and go with me to my Father's house.
—AUDIO ADRENALINE, "BIG HOUSE"

"Do not let your hearts be troubled. You believe in God; believe also in me. My Father's house has many rooms; if that were not so, would I have told you that I am going there to prepare a place for you? And if I go and prepare a place for you, I will come back and take you to be with me that you also may be where I am."
—JOHN 14:1–3

ONE

The Arena, Part 1

My childhood church was planted in a rural Indiana town called Richland, named after the fertile soil that surrounded it. My father was the preacher and a singer, and I learned about God somewhere between the two. In the wide-open spaces of Indiana bean and cornfields, I would pray with full confidence for ways to tell of God's goodness. I had little doubt he would deliver.

The brown brick building had a sanctuary that sat two hundred people, about half the town's population. The Baptist and Methodist churches had seating for the rest. There were no stoplights or gas stations, but a hardware store specializing in farming supplies and a grocery store provided the basics.

By local standards, Richland Christian Church was a little edgy. We had no denominational ties, and we had a sound system that kept the Baptists safely away. On Sundays, we kept the organ and piano within acceptable limits for the hearing aids in the back row, but the rest of the week had no limit.

On weeknights, my father practiced in the sanctuary with his gospel group, the Mud Chapel Singers. They covered popular songs from the Cathedrals, the Stamps Quartet, and the Gaither Vocal Band. My brother and I liked to lie on the wooden pews and listen to them practice. As my dad's voice boomed through the sound system, it reverberated from the walls and filled the room like the presence of God. I sang along at times, my voice sounding small in comparison, and I wondered if one day it might sound as big as his.

David, my older brother by almost two years, learned to play the piano and became a really good musician. Since I couldn't compete with him on piano, I learned to play the drums. When he started singing onstage on Sunday mornings, I sometimes sang backup. One day, while no one else was at church and our dad was preparing a sermon in his office, my brother was playing on the sound system in the sanctuary. I rushed to finish my job of mowing the church lawn while Russ Taff and the Imperials blasted through the speakers, cranked up much higher than usual. The power was electric. My brother hooked up a couple of microphones, and we took turns singing harmonies and riffs with Russ when a high and powerful vocal came up. When it was my turn at melody again, I closed my eyes and took a deep breath—and sang from someplace new. Someplace previously hidden from me. My voice entered the microphone and came out of the speakers as something transcendent. It was as big and strong as any voice ever heard in that sanctuary. My brother stopped and stared at me. His eyes confirmed the same thing I'd heard: I could sing.

Several lifetimes later, these memories came to me as I waited in a private room at my doctor's office. The chairs in the waiting room were lined up straight and reminded me of those church pews from long ago. They faced a beige wall with enough space between them that patients could avoid looking at each other. Dark wooden arms and legs met at right angles to support seat and back cushions covered in neutral tones that contrasted only slightly with the carpet. I restacked the magazines on the coffee table and noticed the veneer had worn from the edges, revealing the wood was fake. What was supposed to be solid oak was only a composite of other materials.

Gold records of musicians who were also patients hung horizontally across the walls, including one from my band, Audio Adrenaline. Kerri, my wife, had directed the photo shoot for the album, *Bloom*, and we'd done the CD insert art together. It was the best thing we'd ever created as a couple.

Bloom had released around the same time I'd become a patient. The biggest accomplishment of my life at that time, it signified the transition from a struggling rock band to one who had made it. Several gold record plaques were given away as gifts to those who had been a part of helping us achieve it. One hung proudly in our record label's entryway. Another hung in my dad's church office. This is the one I saw most often.

I waited for a nurse to call me to the exam room. When the door opened, it was the doctor. He smiled and casually called me back. I walked down halls crammed with standing scales, medical equipment, and floor-to-ceiling files to the exam room and hopped on the exam bench, the disposable white paper crunching under my weight. The doctor grabbed his stethoscope and warmed it between his hands. He and I had met through mutual friends in the music industry, and he often came to our local shows. We shared a love of both music and the Kentucky Wildcats. During college, he'd been a radio personality, and now his soothing voice filled the room with a classic Southern baritone.

"How's your voice workin'?"

I tried to speak. Nothing came out.

He alternated the stethoscope between my neck and chest and back. I appreciated that he'd warmed it first.

I tried again. Thoughts traveled from my head to my larynx and were met with wind from my lungs. The wind passed through my vocal cords, and my lips made the shapes of consonants and vowels, but the words came out as thin as secrets whispered into a storm. Scratchy. Pale.

"I've got a show tomorrow night." I leaned in so he could hear me. "We're playing at the Arena. At the Dove Awards. We're nominated for Song and Album of the Year."

I'd started seeing him a couple of years ago after our band played a show in Nashville. That night, while onstage, my voice had completely cut out. It sounded like somebody had turned off the microphone in the middle of the song. I remember stepping back and then trying to sing again. Nothing came out. My voice was paralyzed. I couldn't finish the show. This was the first time I'd ever experienced anything like that, and I felt panicked. Two hours later, my voice came back, but I knew the problem was significant.

A specialist at the Vanderbilt Voice Center found some swelling along my vocal cords, my body's natural response to protect my voice. The specialist administered a steroid shot that bypassed my body's defense mechanisms, keeping the swelling down, and for the next album and tour, my voice was invincible. Then I learned my doctor could administer the shots and started going to him before every album and tour.

My doctor believed God was blessing people through our music and wanted to do his part to keep my voice working as long as possible so that we could reach as many people as possible. Our relationship grew beyond the borders of the usual doctor-patient confines. We became partners in ministry. His job was to medically intervene. My job was to sing about Jesus and somehow convince the audience that my voice was fine.

The problem is, our bodies are smart. They build new defenses. So as the shots became less effective, my doctor had to increase their frequency. He grew increasingly concerned, saying that if we were to continue the shots at this rate, there would be negative side effects. As he did more research, we hoped the shots would only be a bridge until another, more permanent solution was found.

"Doc," I said, my voice scratchy and distant, "give me a double."

The needle pierced my skin and muscle, and the thick liquid pushed into my bloodstream. My body initially rejected the violation, sending signals of pain and fear, but eventually, submission. I sat quietly. The tile on the floor had a pattern to it. I traced it from the wall to my feet.

"We're going to have to slow this down, Mark."

"I know."

"I don't even know for sure that this will help with your show tomorrow."

I exhaled. "I know."

When it was done, he walked out and closed the door softly behind him. I sat for a moment. The floor pattern was a maze, and I couldn't find a way out.

THE DOVE AWARDS, 2003

At the Bridgestone Arena in Nashville, a line had formed that extended down the street. Home of Nashville's hockey team, it had seating capacity for twenty thousand. The performers and event coordinators entered from the back, through doors that led underneath and into a maze of halls and cinder block rooms.

I hadn't sung at sound check. Too soon. I figured I'd do a quick voice check just before we played. I found the guys in the greenroom where the cold underground felt like the doctor's office, only with fewer posters. I looked at my longtime friend Will. He and I had started the band seventeen years earlier, while students at Kentucky Christian College. Next to him were Tyler and Ben, newer members, who felt like younger brothers. Most of the crew was there too. We had become family, and the struggles we'd faced while recording the album *Lift*, the one up for a Dove Award this evening, had given us an even stronger bond. This was our moment.

After grueling studio sessions and baring their souls onstage in city after city, the biggest names in Christian music would receive their grandest accolades and awards in front of an adoring audience. Tonight was their fairy-tale moment. For me, it was my moment of judgment.

Outside the greenroom, suits and dresses were double-checked in mirrors, makeup artists made last-minute adjustments, and artists were whisked back and forth by managers and people in black suits. I looked down the hall, hoping to spot Kerri. TobyMac stood nearby. So did CeCe Winans. They smiled at me, and I did my best preacher's kid impression and faked a smile back.

I weaved through the activity and found my dressing room. I closed the door behind me, and in the quiet, I put on a white suit and a red shirt with bold white letters that said "PREACHER," reminding me of my dad. I looked in the mirror and fixed my hair. Then I sat. Typically, I would have practiced some lines, but I was afraid to sing. I was also afraid of who I would be without a voice.

I couldn't hear anything from the show except a dim roar when the audience clapped. But the walls and the floor vibrated. Above me, through the concrete, was an arena filled with people who had paid to see the biggest show representing the height of the Christian music industry. We were the gladiators they'd paid to see. I tried to steady myself. I tried to pray. Then there was a knock on the door. It was time.

The band and crew moved to the stage during the commercial break. I looked out at the audience and saw Michael W. Smith and DC Talk on the front row. Bill Gaither was a few rows back. I scanned the seats for my wife. When I found her seat, it was empty. I felt like I was sinking under the pressure of my band. My marriage. My voice. My mind was heading toward a dark place when I locked eyes with Mac Powell of Third Day. He smiled, then gave a thumbs-up. His warmth brought me back to the moment.

The set crawled with guys in black shirts and black pants and headsets. Every movement was orchestrated for the live TV audience. The crane camera swung across the stage to focus on my face for the opening lines of the song.

There was no time to check my voice. I would find out if it worked at the same time as everybody else. My throat felt dry. The commercial break ended, and lights went up. The click track cued, and the whole arena clapped as Steven Curtis Chapman stood on the announcer's stage to introduce us. He had won more Dove Awards than anyone in history.

"Last year, this group soared to the top of the charts with a song that explored the depths of God's mercy. Performing 'Ocean Floor,' here are my old touring buddies, Audio Adrenaline!"

The clapping settled into silent anticipation. Cellos and violins soared into the intro. Then the guitar. Then the drums. The song was launched, with no way to turn it around now. Thousands of people filled the arena. Millions more watched on live TV. I stepped to the microphone. I had never felt more alone.

One more time, I thought. *Just like sharing riffs with my brother. I can do this.* Then came my opening line.

"The mistakes I've made . . ."

TWO

Richland

Belief in God was never optional in my family, or in southern Indiana. God was a casual part of every conversation. He was called on to bless meals or help pass a biology test, small requests for my small life, for which God was adequately sized. God's heaviest lifting came on Sunday, when it was time to forgive any sins that had been committed, intentionally or unintentionally, since the previous Sunday. Because the line between mistakes and sins was so thin, we were encouraged to plead forgiveness for the broadest of transgressions, though if I were to forget, I'm pretty sure my mom would pray for my sins on my behalf.

By the time I entered high school, I had experienced enough imperfections in the church to begin to question it. My mind was governed by science and math, which required consistency and accuracy. Things had to make sense. I had worked for several tobacco farmers, setting plants, cutting them down, and putting them in barns to dry. The farms were very profitable, and some of the farmers went to our church. I was perplexed. I could get a paycheck from growing tobacco, but it would be a sin to ever smoke it. I asked our youth group leaders about my moral dilemma, but the answers were largely dismissive. I ended up not having to wrestle with this dilemma, because I discovered something easier to cut down . . . grass. I started a lawn-mowing business, sitting atop a riding Snapper Comet. The job suited me well, and I could indulge in my growing love of music by listening to tapes of Bruce Springsteen and Van Halen on my Walkman while

I worked. A natural entrepreneur, I grew the business, obtaining clients with the biggest lawns in town, including the cemetery, which came with its own set of questions.

SCHOOL POLITICS

Called the South Spencer Marching Rebels, our high school marching band had made it to regionals every year since 1981. After several unsuccessful sporting attempts, I tried out for school band. My years playing music in church gave me an advantage, and I was a natural fit. My mom was my biggest fan.

One Sunday, the concert band was performing a Christmas show at the mall, where there was no need for a drum line, so I was given the humiliating task of playing the triangle. During the performance, I tried to hide behind the tuba players, but in church the following Sunday, while circled by a large group of ladies, my mom called me over.

"Mark, was that you playing the triangle in the mall?"

"Yes," I said. I had hoped the whole occasion would just slip away unnoticed.

"Honey, you are so good. It was beautiful. I couldn't see you, but I knew it was you on that instrument."

The rest of the circle nodded enthusiastically. Some asked if I would play again. They would like to come hear.

"Mom. *It was the triangle.*"

"You have a gift, honey. You should consider playing the triangle more often."

She was so sincere that if we'd had the money, I was afraid she would try to place me in the Juilliard School of percussive triangle. She brought it up again at dinner that night, much to my brother and sister's amusement. Fortunately, my dad was too preoccupied to weigh in.

As a baby boomer, my dad embodied the Protestant work ethic and fully employed it as a minister of a small, country church. There was always a problem that needed solving, either with the mechanical systems or with the faithful flock, who, though appearing perfect on Sunday, somehow managed to need his shepherding during the week. Dad was a natural problem solver, with no failure—mechanical or moral—beyond his repair. In addition to his pastoral duties, he was doing missions work in Haiti. After each trip, he told adventure-filled stories of pirate islands and waterfalls spilling into deep blue pools—and of fixing a lot of generators. He began to dream of moving there as a full-time missionary. The flip side of the Protestant work ethic is the guilt that comes with anything that brings joy, and he believed there was no way God would allow him to do something he loved so much.

I, too, was falling in love. Only my love was music. I improved rapidly in marching band and soon became the center snare, which is the lead percussionist of the whole marching band. (Some mistakenly believe the lead position belongs to the drum major, but the drum major is merely eye candy.) The band improved too, and we toured in the fall, spring, and summer. While our sports teams were good, the marching band was great, and other students took notice.

I was also an active leader in the church youth group, and with my rising popularity in band circles, I considered running for senior class president. The focus of my platform was academics and sports, nothing controversial, and I aimed at the widest demographic. I thought I had a chance until I heard my archnemesis, Garth, would also be running. He played football and drove fast cars and smoked cigarettes with popular girls and did other things beyond the redemptive powers of the praying church ladies. He didn't bother to develop a platform to run on. Instead, he passed out cigarettes to anyone who agreed to vote for him. Not surprisingly, Garth won. Handily. I'd find out much later that there was a lot more to Garth than cigarettes.

With marching band, my dad's preaching, and the busy lives of my brother and sister, it was my mom who kept the family connected. She loved fiercely and believed we could become anything God called us to be. I desperately wanted her belief.

Mom drew us together with the tool of many Midwestern preachers' wives: food. Once a week, we had family night and ordered pizza with any toppings we wanted, an expensive luxury for a family on a budget, but on this night, we ate slices of pepperoni and olive pizza with upper-class unrestraint. My dad was always first in line.

THREE

"Chevette"

In the 1980s, most teens across the country hung out at fast-food places, complaining that their hometowns were boring. However, there were no fast-food places in Richland. To get a greasy burger and fries, or to catch a movie, we crossed through farmlands and over the sleepy Ohio River into the city of Owensboro, Kentucky. It had music venues and theaters and a brick-faced downtown along a riverfront that boasted buildings above three stories, which felt like skyscrapers to farm kids.

When the movie *Top Gun* came out, I saw it with a couple of buddies at the Malco Cinema in Owensboro. I'd always had a fascination with airplanes, and the movie convinced me to become a pilot. I wanted to be Tom Cruise. I wanted to fight the Russians from the cockpit of a supersonic aircraft. I wanted comradery with guys on my team that included our own special high fives. After the movie, we dined at McDonald's. Between bites of Big Mac and fries, a plan emerged. I decided I would enroll in the Air Force Academy after high school.

In the meantime, news circulated through youth group circles that the Christian rock band Petra was playing in nearby Evansville. I had several Petra tapes, with their hard rock sound, screaming guitars, passionate vocals, and hair to match. All across our small county, students were pleading with parents to see the band live. Local youth pastors promoted the concert as an event to invite unsaved friends. A certain friend came to mind. He had never heard of Petra and would rather have gone to a Van Halen or Mötley Crüe concert, but it was unlikely those bands would play in rural Indiana anytime soon. He agreed to go.

Toward the end of the set, the band turned up the lights to give an earnest talk about the power of Jesus and the life he was calling us to. Growing up in church, I'd seen many people make decisions to turn from their sins and follow Jesus. As exciting as that always was, it somehow felt predestined as only a slight turn from the life they had been living. This friend, however, was different. He would have kept the prayer ladies busy for weeks. If he raised his hand, accepting the offer to give his life to Jesus, it would be a radical turn. He did raise his hand, and at that moment, I felt something in my own heart. It was the power of God, merging with rock and roll. Both grew in intensity and urgency, and every bent guitar note and crashing cymbal and screaming lyric sounded like the fires of Pentecost being released through the speakers. It was a new tongue, and I knew it.

Weeks went by, and I couldn't shake the concert. My friend, now a part of the youth group, was growing in his faith. Something was different in him, and he wasn't the only one. Our youth group was growing, too, with more kids than I ever expected to see. And something else was growing: a desire in my heart to do what Petra was doing, which didn't make any sense. I wasn't going to be a preacher, and there was no way a triangle-playing, rural Indiana kid could become a rock star. So, I tried to dismiss it. When that didn't work, I tried praying about it. I didn't hear an audible voice of God or see writing on any walls, but I had a strong confidence that his answer was yes. The more I prayed, the more certain I became.

The Petra experience fueled my desire for music. I sought every opportunity I could to perform, including in the school musicals *Oklahoma!* and *Camelot*, and eventually landed a place in the show choir. I got my big small-town break when the show choir decided to do a performance of "We Are the World" my senior year of high school. They needed a gravelly, rock and roll voice to belt out the Bruce Springsteen lyric. I practiced my part over and over through the church sound system. Not just the voice, but the attitude that sold it. The night of the performance, I put on my best rock and roll attire and stepped onto the stage with all the swagger of the Boss. I sang with conviction, the auditorium burst into applause, and for days after, classmates came up to congratulate me and compliment my singing. Even Garth, my onetime nemesis, gave me a thumbs-up, taking notice of my new rock and roll swagger. He even stopped calling me "band geek."

I wanted a rock band. A legitimate, in-your-face, move-your-feet, make-your-head-pulse rock and roll band. I purchased a CB 700 drum kit with money I'd saved from my lawn-mowing business. The outer drum skins were a deep blue and black, and every rim and stand was polished chrome. It was the coolest thing I'd ever seen, but it sounded terrible. My friend Timmy was a good guitar player and looked like Prince, including his yellow Gibson Flying V guitar. I asked Timmy to sing, and we recruited a tuba player from the marching band to play bass. We called our three-piece band Bassin Bleu, after a waterfall from my dad's Haiti stories. We played gigs at dances and birthday parties and even a sock hop, covering songs from Journey, Prince, Bryan Adams, and Bruce Springsteen. A dormant part of my heart came fully alive when we played. This experience confirmed everything I loved about music, and every gig and practice and writing session deepened this feeling that I was supposed to be praying for a platform.

This feeling that God was calling me to talk about him in front of groups or audiences created problems in my life planning, though. Specifically, I had no idea how music could pay for life, let alone college. Tuition at any college was beyond the reach of a small-town pastor, so I would have to pay my own way. Like my dad, I also didn't believe that God would allow me to do something that I loved so much. The Air Force made more sense. It followed a path of logic. With my grade point average at nearly 4.0, I could get a scholarship to Kentucky Christian College, where my brother already attended. I could take a year of Bible courses to ground my faith, math and science courses to prepare for my aeronautics degree, then head to the Air Force Academy. I determined this was the path I would take. I had already entered an early application to the Academy and received a preliminary green light.

When I landed a scholarship and cobbled together the rest of the tuition through financial aid, I was ready for my freshman year at Kentucky Christian. I only needed to pass some prerequisite freshman-year classes and take a physical exam. Then I'd be on my way to being a fighter pilot. It all lined up. It all made sense.

ON MY OWN

Dad was conflicted about his passion for Haiti. It seemed ludicrous to leave the stability of the US and follow his heart to a small, developing island-nation. He sought the wisdom of men he trusted in the church. They told him that

God wants to give us the desires of our hearts and assured him it was God who planted the desires in the first place. When we make the courageous first step toward the life for which he has called and prepared us, he is even prouder than a mother whose son just rocked the triangle. A switch in my dad's heart flipped from guilt to joy. He and my mom, along with my baby sister, Kelly, made plans to move to Haiti the day after I graduated from high school.

Days before graduation, my dad called me out to the driveway. He was giving me his car, a 1977 Chevette, the only new car he had ever owned. He'd always only made a few hundred dollars per week as a preacher, and with all the bells and whistles, the new Chevette cost $3,200. I had never seen my dad look as rich as he had the day he drove it home. We had lined up on the driveway and welcomed him with all the enthusiasm of a ticker-tape parade. The exterior was a refined eggshell white, and the interior had fire-red bucket seats, red carpet, and a hatch-back from which we could lean back and watch the stars zoom by on late-night drives down country roads. It had only an AM radio, but with windows down and four-on-the-floor, the highway was the only music it needed. In a few days, I would be loading everything I owned into that car. Then I'd wander bluegrass hills along my drive to begin my freshman year at Kentucky Christian College.

Standing with my dad, I thought this might be the moment he single-handedly made sense of life for me. I had enough questions about faith and what to do with my life to fill that hatchback. I thought maybe we'd take a drive together and I'd recline my seat and watch the stars and he would tell me the purpose behind them. He looked at the car, then to the front door of the house, then back to me. This was the moment. He cleared his throat.

"Son."

I leaned in. The air was still. Quiet. I held my breath.

"Here you go."

He dropped the keys in my hand.

"Good luck."

He walked back into the house. It was pizza night.

FOUR

Unforgettable Fire

The day after high school graduation, my parents and sister moved to a remote village in Haiti where communication with the rest of the world was difficult, if it happened at all. There was only one phone in the village, which was expensive to use and didn't always work, so I knew I wouldn't be able to talk with them very often. I was on my own. I spent the summer sleeping on couches or in the Chevette and lived untethered to anything except my plan to ace college and get into the Air Force Academy. I played music when I could but was ready to begin my first semester at Kentucky Christian. My brother was already a junior there, studying to become a teacher and on a path to a career, marriage, and family. More important, he had a keyboard on campus, and we thought starting a band would be a fun last hurrah together before I entered the Academy.

I crossed the Ohio River with the one-way intent of a burned bridge and pointed the Chevette east into the stilled heat of late summer. With windows down and AM radio up, warm winds filled the car with freedom and dreams and the music of wide-open roads. On the outskirts of Lexington, long, white fences outlined stately horse farms filled with thoroughbreds and hopes of triple crowns. The road swelled through rippling seas of bluegrass, and soon rolling pasturelands were replaced by the deciduous hills of eastern Kentucky.

The college sat in the town of Grayson, Kentucky, in a wide hollow of coal country, only slightly larger than Richland. A little over five hundred students lived on a campus of nicely mowed lawns and pragmatically designed buildings. Once there, I unloaded what few possessions I had and began to unpack in my dorm room.

From down the hall, I heard a blast of guitar that sounded familiar. The band Van Halen had a song called "Eruption" with a guitar solo widely considered to be among the best of all time. Rooted in Eddie Van Halen's classical guitar training, it included a series of two-handed hammer-ons and pull-offs. The song was pure energy, a pressure chamber of teenage angst that built with every note until the volcano of youth erupted and we were covered in the smoke and ash of rock and roll. In every guitar store across the country, guys with long hair tried to impress friends or girls or guitar salesmen with this guitar solo. Almost nobody could play it. To play the solo note for note, the guitarist needed a near-divine mastery of the instrument. Whoever was playing the song had great taste. I went to investigate.

Standing in the room, guitar in hand, was a studious-looking kid with glasses and a professor's haircut. He was too absorbed in his guitar playing to notice me. I tried to determine where the song was coming from. My jaw dropped when I realized this guy was actually playing it, note for note. When he finished, he looked up. I spoke first.

"Hey, bro. What's your name?"

"Barry. Barry Blair."

He already had a cool stage name.

"What classes are you taking?"

When he responded, he spoke with the introspective seriousness of all accomplished guitar players.

"I'm here to start a band," he answered.

"Well, that's great," I said. "I play drums, and my brother plays keyboards. Let's do this!"

He gave it some consideration. We were at a small Bible college in eastern Kentucky. I was doubtful there would be many other options.

Finally, he said, "Okay." Then he added, "Who's going to play bass?"

WILL MCGINNISS

As with most Bible colleges, Kentucky Christian was a religiously conservative, blue-collar college where students at that time didn't have the theological leanings, or financial resources, to have serious musical instruments. My brother and I had already hit the jackpot with Barry. What were the chances that lightning would strike again and we would also find a bass player? The next day, before parent orientation, we met in front of the Lusby Center to again discuss our need for a bass player, when a nearby parent overheard our conversation.

"Hey, boys. Boys," she said. "If you need a bass player, my son is really good." I stared at her for a moment, unsure of how to respond.

"He's in Waters Hall. Room 217. You should go talk to him. Go." It sounded more like a command than a suggestion. She gave us a look that confirmed it was. So, we went to Waters Hall.

I didn't believe there would be a bass player in room 217. My only thought was that whoever was in that room must be the dorkiest guy on campus if he needed his mom to help him find friends.

When we reached the room, I saw posters of bands I'd never heard of on the walls. Lounging on a bunk was a guy who looked nothing like any other kid on campus. Or anywhere. He wore a Tour de France–style biking hat and had a tail of long hair that clearly broke the personal appearance rule in the student handbook. He wore holey jeans, another rule broken, and pegged them above his L.L.Bean moccasins. He rose nonchalantly, gracefully extended his hand, and spoke in a pleasing, unstartled voice, as if he had been waiting for us to show up.

"Hey, guys. I'm Will."

I knew right away there was something special about him. We jumped right into talking about music. When we mentioned a band like Van Halen, Will would bring up a band like U2, pointing to an *Unforgettable Fire* poster on the wall. I didn't know what an unforgettable fire was, but Will had it. He was connected to something different. Deeper. And not just with music. Though he was seeking, like the rest of us, he was seeking from some different place that gave him an advantaged angle in the search. On a campus looking for truth, he was looking for grace. In a doctrine that praised certainty, he was open to questions. Will was a walking poem. I'd spend the rest of my life trying to be more like him.

Barry finally asked Will about playing bass. Will did in fact have a bass, and like everything else about him, it was cooler than anything we had. The only problem was, he didn't know how to play it. He had purchased it a couple of months prior to the start of school. Over the years I've wondered about that.

It didn't make sense to go to college with a bass. It's an instrument that requires others to play with. Guitar, keyboard, even drums, they can all be played by themselves. A certain amount of glory comes with those instruments, usually with their own solos. The bass is not an individualized or glory instrument. It's more of a bridge. It connects the rhythmic to the melodic. The bass by nature is about others. Techniques for playing the bass could be taught. Barry could teach those. The unforgettable fire within Will could not be taught. The fact that he would purchase a bass in anticipation of college should have told me everything I needed to know.

QUESTIONS ABOUT GOD

As at any institutionally religious college, classes at Kentucky Christian began with an indoctrination into what you were supposed to believe. Every student took a full course load of Bible classes. Most professors toed the prescribed doctrinal line, teaching it with a dogmatic certainty. I'd grown up with this teaching, so it was familiar and comfortable, but I always assumed there was a place for other Christian beliefs, like we were all at an eternal party together in one huge mansion. Some of my professors didn't share this view. They lived in small houses by themselves, and it wasn't a party.

I had friends who were Methodists and Baptists and Catholics. When professors taught ecclesiastical absolutes in my classes, my hand went up with these people in mind. Were they all going to hell? Answers usually included a succinct biblical reference and a dissuasion from follow-up questions, or they were given with a wink, suggesting that though they had to give those answers, they were unsure of the answers themselves.

One Bible teacher taught from a different perspective. He usually answered difficult questions with a simple question back. He asked what we believed. And why. After examining every belief I had about religion and faith, I wasn't sure of my own. Or if I believed anything at all. The more certain everybody else was, the less certain I became. My uncertainty and questioning led, years later, to an understanding about the big tent that Jesus invites us all into, and I would write songs that cut across the restrictive beliefs of denominations.

DESTINY

Our first band practice sounded like a throng of pawnshop instruments wailing in their last throes of death. Since we hadn't found a singer, I reluctantly took on the role. Then we found a drummer to take my place on sticks. Practices were held in the second floor of the choir room in the campus chapel. We practiced more than we studied, and our music improved quickly.

We named the band A-180, as in, do a 180-degree turn and follow Jesus. Our early lyrics weren't any more literary. The music we played was straight-forward rock, and our first song, "He's Coming Back," sounded like a hybrid of Poison, Bon Jovi, and Bill Gaither. One song would have been at home on a U2 album, another on Van Halen. We were fascinated by some Christian music coming from Los Angeles and quickly took notice of bands like the Altar Boys and the 77's. Every new sound we heard was a new possibility, and we tried them all. Like a painter studies the masters, we studied the sounds of every rock band and discussed them deep into the wee hours of the morning at all-night diners.

My entrepreneurial instincts kicked in. We played anywhere and every-where we could. We charged a modest fee and made T-shirts, and a little bit of money started coming in. I cut a deal with the school: we would promote Kentucky Christian at youth group shows in exchange for the school paying for our transportation. As a result, the band became a regional success. We even got scholarships for playing in a school-organized recruiting band called Destiny, for which we wore matching turquoise suits.

My bandmates and I saved our money, found a local studio, and cut a record. We hustled our A-180 album at our shows and on campus and quickly sold all the copies. But despite our success, I didn't think it would last or that God would allow us to do this full time, so I never strayed too far from my original plan.

FIVE

Top Gun

I relished the laws of math and science in my classes at Kentucky Christian. I enjoyed the logic that governed them. As a result, I was one of only three students from the entire state nominated to become an Air Force Academy cadet. All that was required was to keep my grades up and take a physical test that included push-ups, sit-ups, and a timed one-mile run, along with a blood test to make sure I wasn't smoking anything illegal. The blood test was a nonissue. But the run could be a challenge. The only exercise I got was playing on an intramural basketball team with Will, named the Barking Pumpkins.

I also worked as a librarian. It helped pay my college tuition. One day, a headline in *Runner's World* caught my attention. A champion marathoner said his secret to success was eating a bit of chocolate before each race. I thought that was a handy bit of information for my upcoming physical test.

I did several things to prepare for it. First, I bought some aviator glasses. They were knockoffs, but from a distance, they looked just like the ones Tom Cruise wore in *Top Gun*. I reread the *Runner's World* article and figured if a little chocolate helped to win a long race, then *a lot* of chocolate would surely win a short one. I started eating the night before the fitness test. I ate a whole bag of Reese's Peanut Butter Cups, believing that the added protein in the peanut butter would only add to my success. Then, on the way to the run, I stopped at a convenience store and purchased an off-brand bag of chocolate donuts. I wasn't sure if I'd be able to eat the whole bag, but then I thought about what Maverick and Goose would do and downed them like our country's national security depended on it.

The three nominees from the state of Kentucky stood in the middle of the University of Kentucky's memorial gym. My competition was the quarterback of the state champions and a nationally ranked gymnast. They told me about their heroic accomplishments, single-handedly beating the competition in a big game and pulling off physical feats nobody else their age could do. I told them about show choir. I felt a little like my knockoff sunglasses. I still managed to pass the fitness requirements. Barely. I crawled off into the grass to take a nap.

The blood test was next. I'd never taken drugs or even smoked a cigarette, so I figured it was in the bag. After having my blood taken, they asked me if I needed a little treat to get my blood sugar levels back up. I assured them that I didn't.

When I returned back to Kentucky Christian, I already felt like a hero. The library periodical section that had introduced me to the secret power of chocolate also introduced me to an organization called Mission Aviation Fellowship, which was a group of pilots serving Jesus as missionaries. They typically started in the military, and when they completed their service, they began serving the whole world. They flew in places like the African Serengeti and the Amazon jungle and between jeweled islands of the Caribbean Sea. They even wore the same sunglasses. They were rock stars. Light bulbs came on. This combined Bible school and the Air Force Academy. It was my platform. I anxiously waited for the letter, and when it finally came, I opened it slowly with the excitement of Christmas.

> Dear Mr. Stuart,
>
> Thank you for your interest in the Air Force Academy.
>
> We regret to inform you . . .

What?! Regret?!

My heart sank as I read the letter. I'd failed the blood test. My glucose levels were off the chart. They suggested I see a doctor.

My excitement turned to anger, then confusion, then a strange relief, and that relief turned to more confusion.

SEEKING THE SUPERNATURAL

As a math and science guy, I had no trouble believing there was a supernatural being. There had to be a creator because every other option went against the laws of physics. The law of conservation of matter suggests that matter cannot be created or destroyed; it can only change. So, all the matter that currently exists had to come from someplace different. It couldn't have created itself. There had to be a supernatural beginning, and thus, a creator. That any science would say at one point there was nothing, and then there became something, is the ultimate hypocrisy. I understood this. It made sense to me. But I couldn't make the jump from believing in a God who is the Creator, to the Jesus of my childhood faith, the One who lived in our hearts, helping guide our decisions toward the will of God. I just couldn't get there anymore. That was a leap of faith I wasn't ready for.

I got in touch with the Academy to discuss my blood test. I explained to them what I had done, and they said I could retake the blood test. I told myself, all I had to do was refrain from eating a bag of donuts and I was in. But now I was plagued with doubt. Not just from the initial failure but also from the subsequent relief. Was there something else for me? Everything pointed back to the band, but there were some real problems there too. Yes, doors were opening. We'd played tons of shows, traveling as far south as Texas, and momentum was building. The music was tight. Our live shows were packed with energy, and we could hype any crowd. But the lyrics lacked the depth of purpose we needed. I took some English classes, and my teacher saw promise. Eventually I figured I would become a good lyricist, but we needed something to happen sooner than that if we had any chance of making it out of our hollow.

I knew I was made for something big, and deep down, I knew it was music. I desired to be in a big rock and roll band. I even believed that God had put that desire in my heart. I wanted to live the biggest life I could, but believing that I could be successful in a band required more faith than I had at the time. I could pursue the Academy, but I knew it wasn't the life I was supposed to live. I knew that entering the Air Force would be running from the platform I'd been praying for since I was a young kid. The biggest and best lives we can live are the ones that scare us to death. And there's no way we can live them on our own.

Music opened more doors than I ever thought it could, including paying for my education. Still, I couldn't believe that God would give me the desires of my heart. I was driving back from a show in the Chevette, thinking of my dad and remembering him saying the same thing about serving in Haiti. My heart pounded, my eyes blurred, and the air went thin. I was having a panic attack.

I pulled over to get out of the car and catch my breath. The heavy Southern humidity silenced all sound except the distant chirping of cicadas. I breathed. In and out. Slowly. I regained my heart, then my mind. I gave a long exhale and wiped the night sweat from my brow. It became clear to me what I needed to do. I needed to go see my dad.

I told the band I was going to Haiti and wasn't sure when or if I was coming back. I needed some time to figure out my life. I knew I was letting them down, and I felt terrible about it. If I left, it would likely be the end of the band. The pain was visible in their eyes. There was a collective feeling that something big was happening, but I couldn't see it or believe it. And I couldn't move forward until I had eyes that could. I needed to know if Jesus was a real and active participant in my life. If he was real, and he wanted to live in my heart, he'd first have to rearrange it and throw some junk out to make room for his furniture. If he wasn't real, I needed to put this whole sham behind me.

From my window seat on the flight to Haiti, I watched wooded hills disappear behind clouds and studied the movements of the flaps on the aircraft's wings. It was the science that defeated gravity. A couple of hours later, we descended below the clouds to an endless blue horizon and landed on a tiny island of green. As I departed the plane, in my front pocket were my passport, my questions about God, my desires for music, and a hope that my father could make sense of it all. In my back pocket was a ticket to the Air Force Academy.

SIX

Haiti: The Pirate Coast

I stepped off the airplane into a hot and damp world filled with music. An international language of hospitality, the music was a welcome balm in the terminal after the disorientation of flight. A local folk band was playing compas, a wildly popular national folk-style music, on guitar, accordion, maracas, and tanbou, a type of barrel drum. Their tight sound suggested years of practice and mastery of their instruments, and their joy was nearly palpable. I imagined Haiti was a hard place to make it as a musician. I knew what it was like to haul instruments around and set up in the hot sun and play to a crowd of disinterested strangers. I threw what spare cash I had into the guitar case.

It was good to see my family. My dad looked as happy as he had sounded on the phone. He was at peace with his purpose in Haiti. Under French rule, Haiti had once been the wealthiest colony in the New World, supplying half of the world's coffee and three-quarters of the world's sugar. The French, however, had created their export business on the backs of slaves imported from Africa, and the terrible conditions led to the Haitian Revolution and the world's only nation ever established from a slave revolt. Sovereignty came at a crushing cost. France blockaded the island with warships, demanding a payment for lost slaves and property equivalent to $21 billion. The infant nation of Haiti was forced to finance this payment from France. It took 122 years, but the debt was paid. Just in time for the devastating totalitarian regimes of François "Papa Doc" Duvalier and his son Jean-Claude "Baby Doc" Duvalier, which led to more debt and a wrecked economy that made Haiti the poorest country in the hemisphere. Communities are now held together by a patchwork of social services, including the children's hospital my dad was building.

Dad directed me to a Daihatsu dump truck. It had a small bench seat in the front that barely fit my mom, dad, and sister. I wondered where I would sit. Dad pointed to the back, where a wooden bench was attached to the side of the bed and on the bottom was a layer of whatever had previously been dumped. A cloud of dust rose when I tossed in my bags. The 142-mile drive from Port-au-Prince to Saint-Louis-du-Nord on the north coast took eight hours on a good day. My sister, Kelly, joined me to keep me company, and since the box of the dump truck blocked the back window of the cab, I had to stand on top of the bench, lean forward, and bang on the top of the cab if either of us got hungry or had to use the bathroom.

The village of Saint-Louis-du-Nord is poor, like the rest of Haiti, but also isolated. It sits on a thin strip of land between mountains and the Caribbean Sea. Across a channel is the legendary pirate island of Tortuga.

In many places, the main road connecting the town back to the country's capital and any services it supplied wasn't a road at all. It was a slight directional suggestion through a rocky river bottom or a fading hint of asphalt between washes. There were a lot of rivers to cross and not many bridges. Many sections weren't passable during the wet season. Power and phone lines were scarce, and where they did exist, were intermittent. Whatever social services once served the area had evaporated during the Duvalier years, crumbled remnants of a lost hope. The village was on its own.

My family lived and served on the campus of Northwest Christian Mission, a stone's throw from the sea. Dad brought his work ethic to Haiti and was building the children's hospital with a sense of urgency. Every day the hospital wasn't built was a day kids went without the services it would provide.

Before coming, I'd written Dad a letter and told him about the issues I was having. The doubt. The angst. Not knowing what direction to take. He said he had some ideas that might help me when I got here. I was looking forward to sitting with him and having him tell me how to pull my life together. He said to meet him in the morning.

I got up before dawn and walked over to the worksite where Dad was already working. He gave instructions to the local construction crew, then called me over. I wondered if he would suggest the safe path through the Air

Force, or if he'd urge me to follow the unknown with music. I started talking, giving him a little more context to my problems. He handed me a shovel. I looked at the shovel. He pointed to the jobsite.

"Fred will show you where to dig."

I watched Dad walk off, then turned to find Fred.

Fred was Haitian and a couple years younger than I was, though his body appeared older and his smile more childlike. He pointed to a place in line with other men using pickaxes and shovels. We dug footers for the first floor of the clinic. The work was hard with our rudimentary tools. Once footings were dug, we filled the base with rocks, laid steel rebar, hand-mixed concrete, then poured it using old buckets and concrete floats made with scrap two-by-fours. Every day was the same. Up before the sun, work a couple hours, eat breakfast, then work until three. I was outworked by everyone.

Fred worked with me before and after he went to school, and at night we'd climb onto a roof at the edge of the campus and watch stars fall behind the pirate coast of Tortuga. Each falling star felt like something once certain in my life, now vanished. I wondered with each disappearing star if God still knew their numbers, or if some had slipped beyond his sight. I wondered if I'd slipped beyond his sight too. Haiti seemed even more distant with the night sounds of crickets and barking dogs and far-off voices that I strained to hear but could not understand. The land felt no more near in the light. Dirt roads, cut through tropical trees, led to villages with half-built buildings, steel rebar reaching in every direction from cracked concrete roofs. In the morning, kids traveled the roads barefoot or on bicycles or donkeys. By afternoon, the roads carried a steady din of whining motorcycle engines. Every motorcycle was overloaded with people or water or construction supplies, even livestock. The country was in a constant state of motion without ever getting anywhere.

Fred and I became friends. He spoke better English than some of my classmates in Kentucky. He was also a good soccer player, and once, he invited me to play in a local game, then quickly came to the conclusion it was better for me to just watch. We explored along the sea and in the mountains and played pranks on other workers, but our favorite time was when the day's heavy air was laid to rest and we had the cool night breeze on the roof to ourselves. He taught me Creole. In exchange, I taught him to play guitar. There was something pure about Fred. He was as poor as the rest of the country, never knowing where the next meal would come from or even if it would come, but hungry or not, he smiled. Each time he did, I understood the gospel a little more.

◀×

I soon realized that there was no room for my unbelief in Haiti. The supernatural was at work everywhere. Voodoo drums played in the darkest hours of night. A demon-possessed woman agitated a church service down the street. Other times, it was a peace anchored deeply into the making of the world. Not the swaying palm trees and umbrella drinks version of peace we've bought into, but a peace with urgency, something of great strength that required action.

I saw that peace in my mom. She ran a pharmacy, filling prescriptions and meeting with mothers in the community every day. In an isolated corner of one of the world's most difficult countries, she loved fiercely and fought against tides of hopelessness for the lives of sick and dying children. Sometimes she lost. More often, she won. In all cases, peace glowed angelically from her. Mother Teresa–like. Her peace came from an endless supply of borrowed strength enabling a tenuous body to wake up the next day and do it again. In all cases, the supernatural felt physical in Haiti. Present. Personal. And I learned to avoid the dark places.

We lived in a low-slung concrete-block house with intermittent electricity. There wasn't much to do in the way of family entertainment, so some nights, we'd light candles and play board games and cards, or create impromptu musical performances. My only connection to the outside world was my Walkman. I listened to it while digging ditches or while on the roof, watching the same stars that drifted past the hatchback of Dad's Chevette as he drove the broken roads of another world. I found comfort in Amy Grant's album *Unguarded*. Her lyrics were rooted in a great hope, and her music moved my heart to believe them. After dinner, my parents pulled dining room chairs into the living room, where Kelly and I sang songs from that album. We sectioned off a stage in a corner of the concrete living room and performed as if in an arena. My dad clapped his hands and my mom smiled at me as if she held a joyous secret she couldn't share.

By all accounts, we were now poorer than ever, but we never felt poor. Our needs were met daily. Our family was closer than ever.

My dad had heard of a church in the mountains that needed Bibles and someone to teach one Sunday morning. The road was too steep and washed out for the dump truck, so he sent me on our dirt bike. It was a half day's ride to the village. Partway up the hill, a little boy waved at me to stop. He lived far up the hill and wanted a ride. I told him to get on the back. He was surprised that I spoke some Creole and flashed a smile to show me his gratitude.

The boy said he thought he was nine, but didn't know for sure. He had no shoes and no shirt, and his shorts were frayed at the edges. It was a school day, but he wasn't in school. Schools in Haiti are private and require tuition to attend. If you don't have the money, you don't go. Kids who didn't go to school spent the day doing family chores or were left to fend for themselves. The poorest were sold to other families and carried water for their new owners in exchange for food. The road was lined with barefoot children carrying five-gallon buckets of water up a hill my motorcycle struggled to climb. Three miles up the road, the boy tugged on my shirt and before I could slow down, he had jumped off the back. He tumbled and bounced and dusted himself off like it was no big deal, then disappeared through a thicket and into a trash-filled clearing where wild chickens scratched at dirt with no seeds.

I continued up the mountain through villages so remote the children had never seen a white person. Boys and girls gathered, gesturing to one another as I rode by. The farther I ascended the mountain, the more primitive the world existed. I arrived at a village made up of a collection of small structures constructed of found materials. The typical home had thatched walls and roofs over dirt floors that turned to mud in the rainy season. There were no windows. The front door was a sheet hung on a rod. There was no plumbing or electricity. Despite the jarring lack of Western comforts, I felt more comfortable among the villagers than I had anywhere in years. I was sent to teach them about Jesus, but I was the one who learned the biggest lesson. They were not only content living with next to nothing, they were joyful. I was confused, humbled, and amazed.

SEVEN

The Forgotten Edge of Earth

Fred and I continued our nightly rooftop "club." Two others joined. Sonny was the son of the campus security guard, and John Joseph lived nearby. My Creole was getting better, but it was the universal language of music that knitted us together. Fred and I played guitar and sang, and Sonny and John Joseph played high and low beat boxes while also singing, providing a modern Haitian folk rhythm steeped in African roots. Our music was a blend of the regional compas style and my American rock influences. My friends taught me Haitian gospel and folk music, and I taught them "Born in the USA." They loved Bruce Springsteen. Over the next six months our music got tight. We even wrote some original songs, some of which made it on a future album. Our rooftop group could have given that airport band some serious competition.

I climbed the rustic wooden ladder early one night to spend some time alone on the roof. Stars were soupy, reflected on the ocean's mirrored night glass. A breeze blew from the starry channel, sweet with smells of the tropics and heavy with salted Caribbean Sea. In the distance children sang in unison. It was a children's song, with a children's cadence, but it carried the joy of one who has suffered. The music came from an area considered poor even by the standards of an already poor nation. Still, the children's voices rose. Their song gathered with the stars and knocked on the doors of heaven.

When Fred arrived, I asked him what the song was. He said it was a popular song with a catchy melody that was sung in local churches.

"The song is called '*Lakay Papa Mwen*' . . . 'My Father's House.'"

He sang the lyrics. As he did, an already wide smile bridged all the way to a hollow in eastern Kentucky.

> *Come and go with me,*
> *To my Father's house.*
> *There is joy, joy, joy,*
> *In my Father's house.*

The last line hung between the stars. After some silence, I asked Fred why he sang.

"God hears me when I sing. And when I sing, others hear God."

Fred's unlikely friendship would shape my life. In the gap between our ethnicities and economic status and language was the music. And in the music was something that could not be explained. Only felt. It was the tingling in the spine and the feeling of rebirth. On that roof, through friendships bonded in a poverty ignored by the rest of the world, I found a key to the backdoor to heaven. It was a song sung by those who still believed that in a fallen world there was a good Father who had a house big enough to hold their joy. The door was sized for children. I could only get in on my knees.

Spiritual doubts are a first-world luxury. In Haiti, faith infused the air, thick as humidity. There's a desperation for Jesus. In the US, there's an option to not need God. To reject dependence and rely on oneself. Haitians called upon the supernatural for every aspect of life. Their worship was brighter, stronger, more powerful. Prayers were more fervent, sermons more urgent. Faith was completely untamed. There were Christians. There were Catholics. There were religions traced to tribal African beliefs. All of it was infused with differing amounts of voodoo, and none of it fit within any lines of denominational belief in the US. Based on the hard-lined beliefs of many American denominations, the whole of Haiti was going to hell. This mélange of beliefs only further confused my path to faith.

My Haitian friends believed in miracles, so I asked for one. Some tangible proof for faith. Some sign that Jesus was real. But it never came. I *could* get to God. I knew that there was order in the universe and thought that the idea of matter coming from nothing via the big bang defied the very science of the scientists who believed it. But I couldn't get all the way to the cross. I couldn't get to Jesus.

We were picking up building supplies in the dump truck when I asked my dad if he'd ever seen a miracle. If he had any proof of Jesus. My dad had been a science teacher before he became a preacher-turned-missionary. He had an intellectual capacity as great as any man I've met. I knew he was intellectually honest enough to say he couldn't scientifically prove Jesus existed. But he must have seen or experienced a miracle.

"Nope. I've never seen a miracle."

"Then how do you know Jesus is real?"

"Listen, Mark. You're not going to come to an intellectual point of acceptance about this. If God gave each of us a miracle, there wouldn't be any need for faith. At some point, you have to just make a decision about what you believe. Everybody does."

I was hoping he'd seen a miracle.

"The atheist who believes the world started from nothing has no more proof than the Christian who believes the world started from something. They choose to believe one thing. I choose to believe another. I felt something in my heart, and I chose that. That choice led me down a path, and that path led me to Haiti. I've seen this world at its worst, and in spite of that, I've seen people at their best. This is the greatest joy I've ever known."

I stared out the window. There was a group of kids playing soccer on a dirt-and-gravel field with no shoes. They were laughing. My dad pointed to the kids full of joy.

"There's your proof."

THE SECRET

I'd fallen in love with Haiti. The culture. The people. The music. Haiti occupied a different time in the world. It was a land of adventure as big as you wanted it to be. There was a clear contrast of beauty and depravity. On the same day, I could see a beautiful ocean, as clear and blue and vast as the sky, and along it, starving children carrying buckets of water half their size to primitive homes barely bigger than an outhouse. It's in the contrasts that life is most honest. There were no illusions about having any control. Greater forces governed. Global politics. History. God. To survive, you had to let go. It was in the letting go that I finally found freedom, and that freedom was Haiti's gift to me. In return, I wanted to stay and help. I could dig ditches with Fred and erect a building with my dad and pass out medicine with my mom. I wanted to do more, but this could be a start.

I told my mom I wanted to be a missionary. She listened intently and asked some thoughtful questions. Then she asked about the songs I sang on the roof. When I talked about the music, her secretive smile returned.

"Mark, honey, you are made for music."

"But what about missions? What about Haiti, or the Air Force and becoming a missionary pilot?"

I gave her my list of reasons why missions made more sense than music. There was no guarantee with the music. It would likely be a huge failure, and I'd end up doing something else anyway. But the real reason I didn't pursue it was that I felt guilty about it. Mom and Dad found a deep joy in serving, and through it, I could see the evidence of Jesus in their lives. Even though I felt the same kind of joy in music, being in a band didn't feel as important as what they were doing. I believed there was no way God would want me to do something as insignificant as play music instead of the gritty, life-changing work of being a missionary. I felt guilty about even desiring it.

"Don't you start limiting what God can do with your life. We didn't believe we could be missionaries in Haiti, and look what God's done. Just as sure as God gave us a love for Haiti, he gave you a love for music. He wants you to be filled with joy. Music is every bit a mission field as this is."

I looked to the sea. We stood on a forgotten edge of earth. Christopher Columbus had first landed a few miles to the west of here after crossing the Atlantic in search of a shortcut to India. After years of my heart being adrift, it felt like I, too, had discovered land. Music was my new world, full of the same promise and fear and hope. Since I'd arrived, I'd been immersed in music. Sounds of Haiti and compas and Amy Grant washed over me. I'd written half a record on a rooftop with people who did not speak the same tongue but whom I understood through the language of music. My eyes could finally see it: I had been baptized in the music around me in Haiti.

My mom's secret was that she could see my path where I couldn't. It led through a band being formed at a small college in similarly forgotten foothills of Appalachia. Music was my mission. I never saw a miracle. There wasn't a dramatic moment where I could throw a list of sins into a fire or plant a new flag of faith. I only felt something in my heart, a soft voice from behind saying, "Take the next step." Though I couldn't touch or hold or see that voice, I chose to follow it 100 percent. I tore up the Air Force letter and flew back to Kentucky. In my front pocket was a passport, along with a new understanding of faith and a commitment to chase its mysteries down whatever roads it led. In my back pocket was the beginning of a song that would change everything.

PART II

"We're a Band"

For the Son of Man, we will take a stand.
—AUDIO ADRENALINE, "WE'RE A BAND"

*"Greater love has no one than this: to lay
down one's life for one's friends."*
—JOHN 15:13

EIGHT

A-180

After missing the fall semester, I returned from Haiti for the spring with born-again enthusiasm for music and our band, A-180. Luckily, the guys were still around, and while I was gone, had just continued on their paths. I showed them the songs from my Haiti rooftop sessions, and we dusted off the instruments and got to work.

With this new material and energy, we were singularly focused. There is no more intense or satisfying comradery than playing music with guys you love and respect. It's better than *Top Gun*. It's better than sports. In sports, you work in unison to execute plays that a coach has worked up. Derivatives of a thousand plays before. You win or lose and give high fives, and everybody goes home to wash mud from their knees. In a band, everyone brings an instrument that on its own is just raw noise. Everyone is incomplete. Flawed. Every gift, every note, every beat, every drop of sweat, every childhood ridiculing taken for the sake of being different—it's all given as a sacrifice, and a hope that God will show up and redeem the soul of each sinful note of music and turn it into something holy. Music is an idea. A whisper and a promise that things will be better. That you are not alone.

The appetite for Christian music among students was skyrocketing, and the administration tried to keep up with the demand with a steady stream of concerts. As student ambassadors, we were commissioned to liaison with traveling bands, attend to their needs, keep them entertained, and often warm up the concerts by opening for them. This mostly went well. When White Heart challenged us to a basketball game, we recruited our Barking Pumpkins ringer, a six-foot-eight ministry student who had played Division I football for Bowling Green University. I'm pretty sure that was White Heart's last show at Kentucky Christian College.

When DeGarmo & Key played at the campus, we sat mesmerized at the feet of our musical heroes. Christians have a dangerous tendency to make heroes into something they are not. We turn musicians and pastors into celebrities and regard them as little gods. The danger is, we believe it. And sometimes they do too. The '80s were a bad time for celebrity pastors, with their kingdoms crumbling on national TV before audiences of eroding faith.

In modern history, nearly every movement out of national and moral quagmires was led by music. Vietnam. Civil rights. Apartheid. Music is the moral compass we return to because it's the language of our hearts. Musicians are the prophets who point the way. When we turn them into gods, the whole thing crumbles.

Eddie DeGarmo wanted to ensure this wouldn't happen on his watch, so he was as authentic about his frustrations and failures as his music was brilliant. His stage show was a judo move, redirecting our adoration of him to where it belonged: to the God of music and the hearts it was created for. I studied Eddie's every move, looking for the trick, the sleight of hand. There wasn't one. There was only a pure heart to lead an auditorium connected through a collective joy of music into a transcendent moment, where we rose above the limitations of this world and ourselves and touched something eternal. This is the kingdom on earth. A sneak peek into promised glories. Often, it comes through music.

As much as I loved the music of the church, I knew it needed to change. The music of the world had shifted. It was full of raw angst, questioning, and uncertainty. The absolutes that the previous generation had tried to pass down were holding up with the same certainty of the *Titanic*. Our generation saw the iceberg and ran for the life rafts. Every student alive in the '80s felt this tension and wanted to hear it in the music. This was the new sound.

The West Coast ushered in a new era of punk, with bands like Green Day and the Red Hot Chili Peppers. Violent Femmes, the Replacements, and Hüsker Dü led the alternative way out of the upper Midwest. In the South, R.E.M. combined punk and pop sensibilities into a new folk-rock movement. Anthem rock filled stadiums throughout the Midwest. Everywhere hip-hop was on the rise. Soon, the Northwest would hit the mainline of American youth angst through a band named Pearl Jam, and the whole thing would blow with the explosive uprising of Nirvana, along with their poetically authentic and tragic fall.

By the mid-'90s there would be no nirvana. The hope of a transcendent state with no suffering and no desire and no sense of self would die with the band. That was our generation's music. It would be our generation's path if we couldn't find another. I wanted to write music that led to a different hope. The same hope found in the souls of the suffering in Haiti. The same hope I'd found on the rooftop with one of that country's musical prophets. I wanted to sing so God would hear me. I wanted to sing so others would hear God.

Demand for Christian music was growing. As an answer, Christian music niches developed, supported through regional music labels and festivals. But nothing answered on a mass level. Christian bands like DeGarmo & Key filled the adult, contemporary Christian need, but not for this volcanic pressure building below the surface of the church. We didn't want to be a niche band. My prayers for a platform took on the fervency of my Haitian friends. I was developing a vision to bridge the divide between music and theological infighting of the American church through the one language we could all agree on: rock and roll. The platform I prayed for was a mass one.

Through our ambassadorship, we heard the rumblings of a band launching from another Christian college. At Liberty University in Lynchburg, Virginia, Toby McKeehan, Michael Tait, and Kevin Max Smith formed a band called DC Talk. Toby rapped. Tait sang pop. Kevin sang rock. Their blend of rock, rap, and pop music, infused with gospel-themed lyrics, opened a new door in Christian music and would soon change it forever. The combination of their youth group–safe lyrics and energetic stage performance gained a widely popular following from the outset. A lot of great Christian music was being recorded, but only DC Talk was going mass. Quickly. They opened the door for a new generation of music. It was the doorway we needed.

A NEW WAY TO WORSHIP

That summer we were ready to expand our musical wings. But the wings we could afford were small, taking us only as far as Lexington, Kentucky. We rented a house and got jobs bussing tables at Daryl's Grill and a regional

Mexican food chain, Chi-Chi's. Then we got to work playing music. Though Lexington wasn't known as a haven for local bands, it did have large churches that allowed us to play to much bigger crowds. We began planning for a new album featuring several of the songs I'd written in Haiti. The songs combined hair-metal anthem rock with the traditions of Southern rock and roll. They were a mess. But it gave us something to sell so we could supplement our steady diet of chicken chimichangas and breadsticks. With the help of a college buddy, we built a screen-printing machine to print our own T-shirts embellished with the short-lived fad of puff paint. Our following grew. Merchandise sold like crazy. We learned to survive as a band.

The previous semester we were able to retire our turquoise suits and hang up the Destiny side gig for good. Still, we played to promote the school in exchange for tuition, providing much-needed summer shows at regional conferences.

Every summer our college hosted the Summer in the Son conference, a weeklong event of worship music, teaching, and fun games for high school students. On one of those days, I wandered into the campus chapel, where the house band was about to lead the visiting students in worship. The chapel, with its padded pews and matching carpet, was nothing special. The stage was stacked with antiquated gear, the fog machine spit out just enough haze to reflect the minimal light show, and the projector was cued to shoot the worship lyrics onto the screen just behind the band. I knew a couple of the band members, including Rob Harris. He was a couple years older than me and carried a deeper awareness of God with him. They weren't rock stars, just dudes with instruments.

As the band played their set, the crowd of students moved closer to the stage, filling the spaces between the pews. They weren't moving in because of the hype. They were drawn to something bigger than themselves. From the back of the room, I could see the silhouettes of arms lifted as the band delivered reverent, powerful melodies and ushered an invisible presence into the room. My arms tingled. I pushed through the crowd to the very center of the room, where I was surrounded by hundreds of bodies and voices and grace and beauty. Rob began to sing.

"Behold the Lamb of God, who takes away our sins . . ." I'd never felt so loved. For the first time in my life, music connected me in a profound and intimate

way to the Father. To the Lamb. In that moment, the veil between the here and hereafter thinned, and I could see through to the other side. It was majestic. I cried tears of joy from a place in my heart I didn't know existed.

We played every opportunity we got. Though we rarely got paid, the education in live performance would return thousandfold. I knew from the beginning my voice couldn't hold a crowd. As much as my mom would say otherwise, it just wasn't that good. I didn't have the tone or the range required of a front man for a successful band. At first, this bothered me. Then I found something more important: conviction. All of that praying and angst and doubt and triumph gave me a sacrosanct conviction that God would show up in the music. We just had to believe it until it poured from every drop of sweat sacrificed on the holy ground of a rock and roll stage. I believed it 100 percent.

Summer camps and youth groups became our stock-in-trade. The ten thousand hours of perfecting our craft came in youth group basements and ark-themed summer camps. We learned to command any awkwardly sized flannelgraph and poster-lined youth room filled with reluctant teenagers forced to attend by parents and volunteer youth leaders. Our stage show commanded their attention. All of their attention. They'd never seen a band come completely uncorked the way we did. They didn't know whether to open the doors and let the sound out or call in the pastor to pray for deliverance. By the time the school year rolled around, we were a bona fide regional rock and roll success. The only problem was, our region was in the remote hills of eastern Kentucky.

NINE

Audio Adrenaline

DC Talk started their career by playing the Christian college circuit. When they showed up at Kentucky Christian, we were eager to meet them. They were a band clearly on the rise, doing it the way we wanted to do it.

We played on a different stage, and they came to watch our set. Compared to DC Talk, our music was amateurish. But our live performance was strong and got the audience hyped and ready for the professionals. Afterward, we hung out together, and the beginning of a genuine friendship formed between us.

A-180 was also the campus worship band, and we led a worship service the next morning. Toby slipped in the back to hear us. My experience worshiping with my friend Rob at the Summer in the Son conference birthed in me a desire to provide life-changing vertical moments for our audiences. We infused lyrics desperate for deliverance from the screwed-up messes we've made for ourselves with a rock and roll confidence that we would in fact be delivered. If the lyrics didn't move someone toward the throne of God, the music forced them out of their chairs and kicked their butts in that direction. Toby loved what we were doing. We spoke afterward, and he suggested we infuse some of whatever was happening with our worship into our A-180 live sets.

A-180's first major headline was at an Illinois youth convention. It came shortly after we played a large, regional youth group lock-in. The lock-in was our first experience with a big crowd of our own fans. Kids absolutely freaked out. They knew the lyrics and sang them as if they were their own. They danced all night, and anytime we stopped playing, they screamed. So, we didn't stop playing. At the end, I gave an impassioned talk about what Jesus was doing in my life and asked if anybody else in the room wanted to know the Jesus I was getting to know. Kids walked forward. At the end, the room wasn't filled with angst or doubt or confusion. It was filled with joy. We played the Illinois youth convention with the same conviction and impact. The result was our first real paycheck: $4,500. More money than any of us had ever seen. Instead of putting the money in our pockets, we thanked God for it and spent it on pyrotechnics.

Despite our growing regional success, we couldn't get any breaks into the music industry. Eastern Kentucky and the rural South weren't on the industry's radar. DC Talk was signed to ForeFront Records, and Toby said he'd go to bat for us with the Artist and Repertoire (A&R) division of the label. It was a much-needed shot of hope, but to get a real break, we needed a miracle.

THE ARMY RANGER

Our miracle came packaged in Bob Herdman. Bob was a new student transferred from the army. He had served as an army ranger and somewhere had lost his way. He hoped attending a small Christian college would help him find it again.

Bob arrived on campus in a jeep with the top off. He had the muscles of an army ranger with a thick Magnum, P.I., mustache and the matching short shorts. Girls swooned. He took them for rides in his jeep, and they always came back wide-eyed and giggling. The campus never saw anything like him. He was the perfect addition to our circus. Bob offered to run sound for the band. We thought he loved the music, but when feedback started in the speakers halfway through the set, we realized it wasn't the music he loved. The soundboard was deserted. And way in the back was Bob, leaning casually against the gymnasium wall, surrounded by a throng of college girls.

Bob and I shared responsibilities as resident assistants on the third floor of Waters Hall. There were strict rules about girls in the rooms and loud music. Specifically, there shall not be any. One day, when returning from the cafeteria, I could tell before I even stepped on the lawn that someone was breaking the loud-music rule. The situation worsened when I got to the third floor. The music was Judas Priest. Not the music that should be blaring across the campus of a conservative Christian college. Worse yet, it was coming from Bob's room.

Walking in to see what the heck was going on, I was attacked by a phalanx of angry guitars coming from a stack of speakers. Bob was jumping up and down erratically on the bed as if it were a trampoline, with muscles bulging from his tank top and short shorts. I tried to get his attention, but the music was too loud for him to hear me. When he finally saw me, he kept jumping and extended his arms out, pointing to the speakers. His mouth moved excitedly. I couldn't hear anything he was saying.

"What did you say?" I yelled.

More crazed mouth moving. No sound.

"What did you say?!"

"This music is like audio adrenaline!!!"

Mysterious poems appeared on campus. There was no rhyme or reason to them. Nor did they contain either rhyme or reason. They just randomly appeared in the night. They were always neatly typed and carefully taped anywhere students might find them. Near mailboxes. Outside of classrooms. In bathrooms. They would be torn down only to be replaced a couple nights later with an even more bizarre poem. Soon they included the pseudonym "C. B. Hobenogen." This mystery poet became a celebrity on campus, with everyone wondering what his or her real identity was.

Band practices continued to go well. We were growing fast in our individual skills and as a band. Yet, two challenges continued to hang as a dark cloud over the choir room. The first was that we were struggling with exciting lyrics. The other was the sinking feeling that we may never be discovered. As the front man, I assumed the job of band cheerleader and encouraged the guys that we were on the right track. God had this. It was only a matter of time.

Bob came to practices with me and became friends with the others in the band as well. After a particularly depressing practice, on the way back to the dorm, I confided in Bob my growing unease. We'd be graduating soon. I had torn up my backup plan of becoming a missionary in Haiti. I'm not sure if Will ever had a plan. I desperately wanted something to happen with our music but feared we were running out of time. Bob put his hand on my shoulder.

"Mark."

"Yeah.

"I have a confession too."

The way he said it made me nervous.

"What is it?"

"I'm C. B. Hobenogen."

After Bob's confession, we wrote lyrics together. He had a knack for creating broad lyrical concepts. We'd slip away in his jeep to pen them, then take them to rehearsals, where Barry would work up some magic and Will would add some artistry, and soon a set of new songs appeared. With these new lyrics, our songs were getting stronger, answering the first of our two problems.

At one of our practices, Bob brought in lyrics for a song called "DC-10." The only catch was, we had to play the song in his favorite, aggressive rap-metal style. The lyrics were ridiculous but entertaining: *If a DC-10 fell on your head and you're lying on the ground all messy and dead . . .*" It was a fun distraction and made it on our A-180 album, but it wasn't the music or lyrical style we were going for. Bob tried to get us to do more songs like "DC-10," but we weren't interested.

In what was becoming a regular routine, I walked into Bob's room to tell him to turn down the music. With a quick turn of the knob, he subdued his army of sound and flashed the type of grin that typically preceded a preeminent, deviant scheme.

"I have some great news!"

I cautiously indulged.

"What is it?"

"My aunt died!"

I wasn't sure how to respond. He grabbed a piece of paper from his desk and shoved it in my face.

"Look! She left me $1,500." He smiled. "I have an idea."

His idea was to record a couple of the rap-metal songs under the name Audio Adrenaline. He'd pay for the recording and even promote them. Though this wasn't a musical direction we were interested in, at our core we were prank-sters and always up for a good time. Maybe something fun would come of it. We did the recording, and as promised, Bob hired a local radio promoter to promote the song. For the rest of us, the fun was over. Time to get back to real music.

Our senior year of college was winding down, and though we continued to pack regional shows, we never got the break we were looking for. The band was running out of steam. Our drummer was losing interest and was more committed to his career in finance. My brother was now married and couldn't continue to attach his future to a rock and roll pipe dream. Our practices got fewer and farther between. Though none of us would say it, A-180 was coming to an end. There were a few more shows on the books, but after that, it was looking like the dream was over.

LITTLE SISTER

My brother and I received an urgent message from our dad. We needed to talk ASAP. It was difficult and expensive to line up phone calls, so we knew it was important. My dad said my sister was sick and needed to come home for testing. She was very weak, and her blood counts were way off. Dad's voice was heavy and defeated.

When we finally got the diagnosis of cancer, it seemed unreal. It was too heavy to even comprehend. My fifteen-year-old baby sister had leukemia. My brother and I left school immediately to join the family at a hospital in Evansville, Indiana. Dad and Mom pulled us aside to tell us the situation. Kelly could live, but she had a long fight ahead of her. My mom was the source of strength during this moment and many more to come. She had a forceful reminder for me, my dad, and my brother: "This family has been preaching and singing about the power of Jesus for years. We have two choices. We can move forward in fear, anger, or feeling sorry for ourselves, or we can face this knowing God has only good things in store for us." She added, "We either believe this or we don't."

We chose to believe. Not that we had much of a choice. Mom's heart and mind were set.

My parents had no way to pay for the treatment. They left Haiti and moved to Memphis, Tennessee, to live near Kelly while she received experimental cancer treatments at St. Jude's Children's Research Hospital. My dad's heart was divided. He was needed and fully present with my sister, but part of his heart was still in Haiti. That was his dream. He knew God wanted him there and questioned why God would take him and my mom off course like this. He made short-term trips back to Haiti when he could, but it would be a long while before they could move back full time.

At St. Jude's, Kelly received the best treatment possible at zero cost to my family. St. Jude's even paid for temporary housing for my family during the two-year treatment period, and when it was over, Kelly was cancer-free. This was a true miracle, and to this day we are so thankful for St. Jude and what they did to cure my sister and save our family. In the heart of Memphis, with all of its struggle and striving, St. Jude's is a beacon of hope for families all the world over.

"MY GOD"

At one of our practices, Bob bounded in with his usual can't-be-contained energy. He had a Christian music magazine with him and began to excitedly flip the pages until he found what he was looking for. He pointed to a page with the radio charts. The song "My God," recorded under the Audio Adrenaline name, had landed on the Christian hard rock charts. It was at the very bottom, but still, none of us could believe the rap-metal prank had succeeded. We high-fived each other and enjoyed a good laugh. Except for Bob. He was serious.

Bob brought the magazine again the next week. The song was now at number 28. The following week it advanced to number 13. Friends told us they'd heard our song on the radio. The week after, "My God" moved to number 8.

Bob found us again the following week with magazine in hand. I had no idea where he was getting these magazines. I hadn't even known they existed until Bob showed them to us. This time, though, his face was expressionless. I assumed the whole thing was over. Bob pointed to the charts. "My God" was at number 4. It was playing on radios from coast to coast. People everywhere were trying to figure out who Audio Adrenaline was.

I told Toby what was going on and he talked to his record label again, giving them our A-180 recording once more. They still weren't interested in A-180 and asked him if he knew who this Audio Adrenaline was, the band in the top 10 on

Christian hard rock radio. Toby told them it was the same band, and soon we got a call from a very confused A&R music label executive who had watched the Audio Adrenaline song quickly climb the charts. He wanted to meet with us.

I knew enough to be cautious about the music industry's revolving doors. For A-180 a door was closing, but for this weirdly unlikely idea of Audio Adrenaline, a door was opening. There wasn't time to figure it all out, or to build a plan. It was hurry-the-heck-up-and-move then see what happens or watch-the-doors-close and wonder what happened. The party was on the inside, and it was happening now. I'd stood outside long enough and wasn't going to wait for that door to open up again. These breaks don't happen often, and I knew deep down if that door ever opened again, the party would be over. So, without a second thought, we jumped into the Christian music industry, and our world began to spin.

We sat in the lobby of the Opryland Hotel in Nashville, waiting for the record exec to meet us. As A-180, we'd put in thousands of hours of practice and thousands of miles on the road playing to thousands and thousands of fans, yet we couldn't get a serious look from any record label. This Audio Adrenaline band the record exec was coming to meet had never played a live show. It never had band rehearsals or sold demo tapes or made merchandise or talked late into the night about the virtues of four-on-the-floor rock anthems. It was a song on the radio, penned by C. B. Hobenogen, that had been recorded by college pranksters. Audio Adrenaline was a hat trick. An ace up our sleeve for a game we didn't know we were playing.

We couldn't even find the right lobby. After two hours, we realized we were in the wrong lobby. We arrived at the correct one to find the A&R executive from ForeFront Records getting ready to leave. When he saw four clearly out-of-place kids, he unbuttoned the middle button of his suit and walked over to us.

"Are you Audio Adrenaline?"

"Yes, we are."

"We've been hearing your song on the radio. We'd like to offer you a record deal."

We got a record deal for a single rap-metal song from a band that didn't exist. Our card had been played, so we got out of there before he realized it was the only card we had.

TEN

The Dog House

I had turned twenty-two and graduated from Kentucky Christian College. Then in an eerily familiar déjà vu, the day after graduation, my band and I packed everything we owned in the Chevette and moved to Nashville. On our first day in town, we met at our record label's office. The building was shaped like a two-story flying saucer, with a medical office on the first floor and ForeFront Records taking up the entire second. The entryway, although small, was lined with gold records and larger-than-life stand-up cutouts of our Christian music heroes. The space transported us from the pedestrian nobody-from-nowhere life found "out there" into an illusory, the-other-side-is-greener life of "in here." We'd become insiders. We'd made it. I imagined our album hanging next to the others and approached the receptionist with borrowed rock star swagger.

"You boys are Audio who?"

I dropped the swagger.

In a conference room with no windows and a long table, we met with our marketing and A&R team. Our main A&R rep had contemporary Christian music hair, slightly tousled on top but not too much, and held in place with a large amount of hair product so as to not risk crossing any musical genre lines. He looked like California. He excitedly launched into the style of music the label envisioned us playing. With wide eyes and movie-star good looks, he and others in the room described this music in great detail to us—the kids, the grand experiment, the one-song radio wonders, the disposables.

"Are you ready for this? Are you excited? We see you guys as being the edgier version of DC Talk!"

"We want you to be pop accessible, but with big anthem hooks. Edgy, but also youth group safe. You should appeal to youth groups, but with the hard rock and rap sound they love."

I looked at my bandmates, wondering who was going to be the rapper.

"We've seen some studies of what music church kids are listening to, and we've come up with the sound that will work to reach them."

"It should sound like Red Hot Chili Peppers mixed with EMF—"

"Combine that with the hard rock of Metallica and the alt rock of Depeche Mode—"

"Mix that with some pop sounds of Michael Jackson and new wave like INXS—"

"And add some of the U2 sound—"

"But with rapping."

"You got it?"

I wondered where the video camera was hidden and when a guy would jump out to say we'd been punked. These guys had no idea what they wanted other than that whatever it was, it should sell records, like DC Talk. They sent us on our way and told us to come back with a grip of new songs combining every element from every group currently on MTV.

Soon after landing the contract, my brother and our drummer quit, preferring to move on with their lives instead of undertaking the album. The rest of us set out to find part-time jobs and a place to live. We ended up in a place in a sketchy part of the city, where we took turns sleeping on the floor. With me on vocals, Barry on guitar, Will on bass, and Bob helping with lyrics, we began creating the songs we thought fit the description the label execs told us would work.

Barry and I worked on music composition and melodies for the lyrics Bob was writing, while Will worked on finding us some transportation. We were used to playing with keyboards and drums, so Barry programmed electric drumbeats for us to practice with until we found a drummer.

When it came time to record the self-titled album, *Audio Adrenaline*, we met the producers at Amy Grant's Salt Mine Studio. It was a small but tidy studio, with hung carpets and foam mats on the wall to deaden sound. I fell to the floor and extended my arms like I was paused mid–snow angel. This was hallowed ground. Amy's music had been profound in my life. Christian music history was made in those rooms, and now we were a part of it.

Confused about the sound the label was looking for, and still without a drummer, we began by experimenting with different drum programs. The small budget put us under a tight deadline, so songs were rushed and unorganized. One was called "The Circuit Riding Preacher," which was a mix of bluegrass and heavy metal because . . . why not? The songs seemed pretty good to us, so we took them to the label executives, who said, "These are terrible . . . but we love the drum machine!"

I'm pretty sure they loved it because it meant we wouldn't need to pay a drummer. Though they sold it to us differently.

"That's the sound of the future!"

A few more rounds of this and I began to feel like I'd just made the biggest mistake of my life.

Nighttime in our neighborhood was filled with a mix of honking horns, yelling, and sirens, which ultimately didn't matter much. Between working and writing an impossible set of songs, we hardly slept anyway. If not for leftovers brought home from our restaurant jobs, we would have starved to death. But somehow we managed to turn in a handful of acceptable songs.

The album led with our best Beastie Boys impersonation in a song called "One Step Hyper," followed by our best Red Hot Chili Peppers impersonation, "PDA." None of the songs felt true to our band's heart. Barry was a legitimate rock and roll guitar player, perhaps the best in the industry, but he was reduced to simple pop rhythms to support songs that were merely a shadow of those the label wanted us to emulate. I reminded myself that this was our one lucky shot. I had prayed for a platform since childhood, and God was delivering it. If I had to become a rapper, then that's what I would do. We finished the record and gave it to the label, hoping the execs knew what they were doing. We sure didn't.

"PDA" was based on a college rule about public displays of affection, of which we were all offenders, but it led to the idea that Jesus dying on the cross was the biggest display of PDA for the world. This, unfortunately, was our best lyrical concept on the album. And the execs loved it. The label made a music video for "PDA" and arranged for us to tour with DeGarmo & Key. We met at the office for details about the tour. At least we'd be able to fulfill our dream of touring in a real rock and roll tour bus. We asked if we could check out the bus we would be riding in.

"Bus?"

Apparently, we had misunderstood something.

"You have to provide your own transportation. Also, you will not be getting paid."

It took a moment for that to register.

"Where's the tour?"

"Canada."

Our frustrations temporarily receded behind our imaginations. We were international superstars! We'd only too soon find out why we were the ones going on tour in Canada in the winter. Nobody else wanted to. It was freezing.

Fortunately, Will's search for transportation turned up a vehicle that, by combining our tip money, we were able to afford. It was a small Chevy Econoline van with a V-6 engine and no windows. It looked like the Scooby-Doo van. Which was appropriate. It was parked in a backyard, being used as a dog house, and it had two front seats, partially consumed by its current occupants. The back was large enough to put in a mattress and some pillows. We vacuumed for two days, then headed to Canada, taking turns driving, navigating, or lying down in the back. Eddie DeGarmo offered to ride with us for a stretch to help build comradery between the groups, but he didn't last long. The heater didn't do much to stave off the frigid arctic air coming through unsealed windows. Also, watching snow and ice pass by underneath through the rusted-out holes in the floorboard creeped him out a bit.

ELEVEN

The Naked Truth

DeGarmo & Key's audience was more of a sit-down, legacy rock and roll crowd. They'd never seen anyone like us. Based on the record label's insistence, we used a preprogrammed drum machine, which meant the only instruments onstage were Barry's guitar and Will's bass.

Bob wanted to be onstage but didn't know how to play any instruments. We gave him a keytar, or a keyboard shaped like a guitar and worn with a guitar strap. We plugged it into an amp but never turned it on, figuring nobody would realize he wasn't really playing. Bob didn't like the restrictions of the cord, so he crafted a "wireless" kit—a small box made out of cardboard—and attached it to his belt. Unencumbered by a cord, or any musical reality, Bob went crazy-eyed wild with his keytar; I rapped and yelled and jumped; Barry's fingers flew all over his guitar; and Will's hair whipped in wide arcs. At the end of a song there were stunned stares and nervous clapping from a few folks sitting in the back.

Our tour with DeGarmo & Key only lasted six shows. The crowd responses were the only thing colder than the air flowing through the floorboard of the dog house cruising down Alberta highways. Luckily, we had a few other youth group and camp shows scheduled. With our dog-house van proving reliable, we were excited to headline our own shows again, even if they were in smaller church basements. With the mediocre response to our new music on the DeGarmo & Key tour, we needed to jazz up the show a bit. We needed something special. Bob had an idea.

Bob spent a week and several hundred dollars building a swing set for his keytar. As the keytar swung back and forth in front of Bob, he'd pretend to play for a part of the song, then dramatically push the keys away from him, sending the keytar on an arced swing toward the audience. This gave him time to give a defiant rock and roll fist-to-the-air pump before the keytar swung back to him. The A-frame swing, built with two-by-fours and construction-grade hardware, took up more room onstage than me, Will, and Barry combined. It may or may not have had lights on it. I can't remember now because I've tried to erase what I'm about to tell you from memory.

At the next show in Elizabethtown, Kentucky, we unveiled the A-frame keytar swing set. It was placed center stage, where a normal rock band would have put their drummer. With its unpainted wood, quarter-inch steel cables, and U-bolts sticking out everywhere, it was a true architectural marvel onstage. About five songs into the set, Bob got bored. He began swinging the keys farther and farther away from him. By this time, the rest of the band had forgotten there was an audience. Our eyes were fixed on Bob's crazed face. Surely he wouldn't attempt a full rotation? *Oh, Lord, please tell me he isn't doing this.*

With a grin that looked like the Joker's from *Batman*, Bob wound up to shove the keytar as hard as he could. This, of course, broke any illusion of actually playing. It didn't matter. Bob was committed. When the keytar reached the zenith of its arc, fifteen feet in the air, cables buckled and wood cracked and U-bolts broke. The entire structure collapsed onto Bob and knocked him backward over the choir loft knee wall. Above a pile of rubble, and beyond the knee wall, the only proof Bob was still alive was his combat boots and hairy legs moving to the beat of the music.

GEOFF MOORE AND THE DISTANCE

We needed new transportation. Fortunately for us, Geoff Moore and the Distance was heading out on a long West Coast tour and needed an opening act. We were already big fans and even covered some of his songs with A-180. Geoff was a Christian radio superstar with a decidedly younger audience than we'd encountered in Canada.

We met with the label to discuss details and were astounded to learn that this time, we would get paid. We still weren't making enough to support ourselves as musicians, but getting paid to go on tour was a dream.

"Amazing! How much?"

"Fifty dollars per night."

"So, we each get fifty dollars each night we play?"

"No."

I was relieved. There was no way fifty dollars a night would be enough to feed ourselves, pay for gas, and occasionally get a cheap hotel room so we could take showers. Then he added, "The fifty dollars is for the whole band."

I stared at the manager.

"There's four of us," I said. "So, we each will get paid $12.50 per night?"

"Yes. But there's a catch. You also have to be the sound crew, the lighting crew, and help load gear in and take them down."

"Anything else?"

"Yes. You have to drive the bus for Geoff Moore and the Distance. Can you guys drive a bus?"

Bob and I looked at each other. The bus would also be towing a twenty-thousand-pound trailer full of gear.

"Totally," Bob said.

"No problem," I said.

We'd never even been on a tour bus. We could barely drive our cars. The lives of ten guys on Geoff Moore's bus were seriously at stake.

We walked outside to look at the tour bus but didn't see one. With Christian music hair and used-car-salesman smiles, the label team pointed to an airport shuttle bus with a massive trailer. It was a converted passenger bus with bunk beds built in the back and a couch crammed in between the bunkhouse and the driver's seat. Bob and I would have to sleep spooning on the couch.

At least we were getting paid. We sold the dog house and loaded up the shuttle.

After the A-frame fiasco, we looked for a new instrument for Bob. We needed his incendiary stage presence, but we didn't want to endanger the first row. We reached a creative compromise. Bob rigged a used drum machine so he could play sampled drum sounds during the show. We also found an old snare-drum harness from a marching band and attached the electric drum machine to the harness. A feathered marching-band hat would have perfectly completed the ensemble. Even with the restrictions of a cord plugging into his drum machine, C. B. Hobenogen's showmanship electrified the audience. He was a genius.

On our first night, we connected with Geoff's younger audience right away. Our time honing live shows in countless church basements and school gyms returned dividends. Youth groups went wild over the Audio Adrenaline songs and sound. We brought the energy kids felt, asked the questions they asked, and played the music they identified with. It was a passionate expression that we were collectively going to follow God in a different way. We gave audiences permission to strip away the inhibiting rules of faith forced upon them. Faith was freedom. Unabashed. Unashamed. Uncontained. We popped the cork and generations of religious constraint found freedom and freedom fueled the party and the party would not stop. Kids danced and moshed and raised their hands and fell to their knees. We worshipped God together.

Promoters took notice, requesting Audio Adrenaline to return, and word started spreading about an explosive new band. We had little radio success. There was no Spotify or YouTube. It was complete word of mouth. Kids went into mom-and-pop music stores to ask for our albums, but mom and pop had no idea who we were. Albums flew from our back tables, along with every band T-shirt we made. But the very few times we checked in with the label, it was as if we were on different planets. They were somber on the phone. Radio wasn't picking up the songs. Distribution was slow. What we saw was completely different. We were leaving everything onstage, every night. After the sixty-city tour, I was so exhausted I ended up in the hospital with walking pneumonia. But on the road, in the moment, I had been alive. Maybe for the first time in my life.

Geoff provided the big brother education on the music industry we needed, giving us the version nobody talked about. The behind-the-scenes situations. Who to watch out for. Who to partner with. How to pay the bills. How to survive. We wouldn't have made it very far without him. Geoff also taught us how to enjoy the ride. On days off between shows, we visited places like Yellowstone and the Grand Tetons. Geoff was an avid outdoorsman, and it became clear that music was only one dimension of his life. He found a way to weave them all together to create an amazing touring life for himself and the guys around him. Geoff's tour was the model we would build every subsequent tour on.

On that first tour, we learned not to take the music life, or ourselves, too seriously. A great touring tradition Geoff shared with us was the tour-ending prank, where on the last show, each group pulled a prank on the other. Since it was our first real tour, Geoff told us not to worry about it, just be aware. The Christian music industry is a small town where everybody knows everything about you. One of the ways bands would decide who to tour with is by how much fun they would be to live with on the road for months at a time. The end-of-tour prank was a part of that equation.

EARLY EDUCATION

We had played a show in Kalispell, Montana, and were headed to Spokane, Washington. It was my turn to drive Geoff's bus. The first part of the drive followed the western border of Flathead Lake. The lake is the largest by surface area west of the Mississippi, and its ink-black surface perfectly mirrored a vast sky stretched so thin it could not hold back the light of heaven. Millions of stars broke through. The lake collected their light and returned it to a perimeter of evergreens silhouetted against the distant snow-peaked mountains of Glacier National Park. The scene was peace descended, as warm and welcoming as a heavy woolen blanket on a northern winter's night.

The road turned west onto Interstate 90, and I slipped into a driving trance. My thoughts turned to my father. In many ways, I was continuing his path in music and preaching, and I had questions for him. Life was happening fast, and I felt unprepared. For the first time I was trying to completely trust a God who the world told me I was a freak for believing in. I wondered if Dad had ever felt the same.

A feeling of loneliness hit heavy as the Cummins diesel engine shifted into low gear and slowly churned up a steep mountain grade. The mountains closed in with snow piled high along the edge of the highway. Soon the edge could not be distinguished for all the snow on the road. I leaned forward and gripped the wheel tightly. I regretted lying about being able to drive a motor coach, and the desperation behind the lie. Snores and the heavy breathing of deep sleep came from the back.

In the first hours of morning, the bus approached a 4,700-foot pass through the Bitterroot Mountains, along the mountainous Montana–Idaho border. A tour bus full of men who had careers and families and a future rested in the hands of the Audio Adrenaline experiment, for which I was responsible. I felt a slight tap on my shoulder.

"Hey bud."

Geoff and I had often talked in these late-night hours. He was patient and kind with me, and on that tour we formed a friendship that still lasts today. Geoff was showing me how to enjoy life with the men I was traveling with. The music was a gift from God, not a job.

Lowering his voice so he would not disturb the guys sleeping, he said, "I just woke up and felt like I needed to come talk with you. How are you doing?"

The sound of his voice brought an immediate calm to my spirit, and his question eased my nerves. I turned my head to him, and facing the middle of his waist, I learned something new about Geoff. He liked to sleep naked.

The last show of the tour arrived. Geoff called us backstage for a time of prayer and encouragement before we all went our separate ways. His stage crew didn't join us, but that was normal. They were probably setting up the show.

In the locker room backstage, Geoff gave each of us an impassioned hug and told us we had a great future ahead. He repeated some of his most important lessons to ensure we returned to Nashville properly educated. He thanked us for being such great touring mates and led us into a time of prayer. From there we walked straight onstage for our last set of the tour. Our show started in the dark, with us lined up, our backs to the audience. Since we didn't have a drummer, we stood in a straight line below an oversized Audio Adrenaline banner. The banner was also in the dark. When the lights came on, the crowd would first see the banner, and then us standing there. It was our dramatic introduction to our new audience.

While we were praying backstage with Geoff, his stage guys had used gaffing tape to alter our banner. They replicated the font perfectly, removing some letters and adding new ones. They turned the beginning *A* into a 4 and worked their way through the rest of the banner. It was the end-of-tour prank. When the lights came on, we were lined up in our positions, and we read the altered banner at the same time as the audience.

"4idiots all-in-a-line."

Education complete.

After the tour, the label called us in. We went to the same office, where months before we were the best thing to happen to Christian music since DC Talk. This time, they informed us that our record sales were disappointing. Our songs weren't radio friendly, so the album wasn't getting the air support it needed. When we told them about the energy in our live shows, they just stared blankly. There wasn't any table dumping or chair throwing, but we all knew what was happening. One record. One tour. One chance.

TWELVE

"We're a Band"

Something in us wouldn't quit. We went back to our restaurant jobs and brought home to-go box leftovers and started writing the songs we'd wanted to write all along. No more mainstream hit replicas. It was time to be ourselves. Time to ignite the unforgettable fire burning in each of us. Our hearts had found their way on tour. It was time for art to follow suit. Barry led the way with pent-up guitar licks, and Will smoothed them out with a timeless cool. Fueled by the anger and embarrassment and confusion we'd felt in the relationship with our label, Bob and I dug deeper. We needed songs to prove our place as a band. For the label. And for ourselves.

I was troubled by our first record. It wasn't who we were. We needed to return to our roots and start over. At our core, we were a rock band. An amber-waves-of-grain, sea-to-shining-sea, music-up-and-windows-down, back-road-to-nowhere, freedom-searching, Jesus-loving rock and roll band. If we were to be judged, we would be judged by that. The industry had turned us into a musical experiment, and we needed to become a band again.

In our writing sessions, Barry's guitar detonated with wave after wave of distortion-filled, blow-you-to-the-back-of-the-arena explosions. We felt a righteous anger about what had happened to us and channeled it all into a song of declaration called, "We're a Band." We wrote the lyrics to remind us of who we were and where God was taking us. It came from something Geoff had taught me on the road. A band is an us-against-the-world brotherhood. We were a legitimate rock and roll band that created meaningful, emotional, even guttural music. We needed to plant a flag on the plot of earth God gave us. For the world to know it. And for us to know it too.

"We're a Band" was the line in the sand that we dared the world to cross. It opened with the simple lyric, *"FREAK! is what the world calls me."* I was okay with that. Being a freak was countercultural. Being in a rock band was, and always will be, about going against the flow. If the flow was going to call us freaks, and say we couldn't pray on our campuses, and call God's Word "hate speech," then fine. We'd be freaks. And we'd write the music to put the world on notice that we were no longer ashamed of it. "We're a Band" was straight, gut-level rock. And it was about Jesus. It was four minutes onstage to tell the world that we were upping the ante. To say, "We're all in, and it's not a bluff." There was so much power behind the lyric about Jesus dying and coming back to life that the song felt explicit. Our audience felt it too.

In live shows, you could feel the energy of the crowd. It was anger and joy and happiness. It was the liberation of saying it was okay to believe in this man called Jesus. Our song held in tension the opposing feelings and the qualities that make up belief. Courage. Doubt. Declaration. Taking a stand. It raised the flag of the core of our faith. Jesus died, rose again, and is coming back. It put it on full display, then asked the question, Where will you be when he returns?

The world called for manners. Some cultural truce was made between the church and the world that gave us Sunday mornings and said we should be satisfied with that. Some of the church had bought into this. The attitude was that you can believe in God, but don't take it too far. Singing "We're a Band" onstage was about taking it too far. We were so fed up with trying to be who we weren't, sick of anything remotely reconstructed. We needed an anthem that screamed who we were as a band, and who we all were in Christ, with absolutely no shame. The glazed-eyed religious and the secular did not see it and did not want to. I'd seen babies in Haiti crying through pains of bloated bellies while they slowly starved to death in the arms of mothers desperately asking the church to stand up. To fight. I couldn't have cared less about manners. I sang that song with the deepest conviction of my belief, and in my doubt, I sang it even harder.

That song turned Audio Adrenaline into a band. It gave us permission, and the goal, to rock harder than any other music that was out there. When Jesus did come, it would be to a triumphal soundtrack that sounded more like rock and roll than like harps and hymns. We recorded a video for "We're a Band" with the youth group of Louisville's Southeast Christian Church and played it every night for our entire touring career. Something was happening with Christian youth during the '90s. We felt it on the road, in every venue and town we played. "We're a Band" collectively represented all of it. It was music uniting a group of kids who had no voice, giving them a new voice, and telling them we were all in it together. They were in the band too.

THE END GAME

Our record deal had been based on a single song that made it to number 4 on the charts. Our plan had been to make it as A-180, but now we were seeing God's trick play. If we had made it into the music industry by the strength of our own plans, our future would only have been as big as we could have imagined it. God is in the business of *more than you can imagine*. It came as no surprise that none of the songs on that first, self-titled album had received any radio success. It also came as no surprise that in spite of the poor radio performance, we were able to sell more than seventy-five thousand records. These albums sold mostly on the enthusiasm of our live shows. However, the success metric of the day was radio. Only radio could drive people into record stores across the country. We couldn't play enough live shows for that. The record label thought they knew what the audience wanted and how to give it to them. We hadn't become the new, edgier version of DC Talk. Why wasn't it working with us? The experiment failed. The solution was to drop us and throw something else against the wall and hope it stuck.

I didn't know it at the time, but Toby went to bat for us with the label again. He argued with them not to drop us. He told them there was something special happening in our live shows; our music and performance were impacting a new generation of youth in ways other bands of the day were not. We deserved another chance. Thankfully, Toby prevailed, and we were given the chance to write our own songs and record one more album. But it would be our last chance. Before we got started, Toby pulled me aside to give me more advice. He said to be ourselves. The magic that made Toby believe in us was what he saw back on campus when we were leading worship. It was a combination of songs desperately reaching for God and music sturdy enough to keep us standing until he answered.

Pressure built for our next album from all sides. We were young men in a world of grown-ups who wanted to control every aspect of our lives. Our school told us how we should believe. The record label told us how we should sound. The world told us that we were freaks for believing in a God who was bigger than their ambitions. We were through with all of it.

Audio Adrenaline would no longer be censored. From now on, we were going to only record songs we believed in, power them with a conviction that God had owned rock and roll from the outset and was calling the Devil's bluff, and deliver those songs with the explosiveness of a pyro-infused band who had nothing to lose. If we were going to go out, it would be by going all in. With the band. With our songs. With God. He responded by taking our belief that something big could happen and multiplying it by a factor we couldn't imagine. Faith is the entry point to a meaningful life. The key comes before the unlocked door.

With this new conviction, we went into the studio to record Audio Adrenaline's second album, *Don't Censor Me*. It wasn't the best album we ever made, but it was a great first step toward becoming the band we wanted to be. When I gave our first copy to my dad, he told me we had a massive hit song on our hands with "Big House." I didn't believe him.

PART III

"Never Gonna Be As Big As Jesus"

I could be about as good as any human could. But that won't get me by.
—AUDIO ADRENALINE, "NEVER GONNA BE AS BIG AS JESUS"

"He must become greater; I must become less."
—JOHN 3:30

THIRTEEN

"Big House"

When I was young, I didn't want to go to heaven because Sunday school descriptions made it seem isolated, lonely, and cold. Infinity sounded like a place where if you made a wrong turn, you'd be lost forever. Streets of gold sounded frigid and unforgiving. Falling on them would certainly result in a broken arm or concussion—or, best case, damaging the gold and making all the adults mad. The choices for my soul's eternal resting were bleak. It was either Death Valley or the South Pole. I had nightmares about both.

Our live audience was growing, and I talked nightly to kids about the things they struggled with or were struggling through. There were lots of broken families. Many kids were lonely, with no meaningful friendships. They didn't know where they belonged, or if they belonged anywhere at all. The church was supposed to be an answer to this, but sometimes youth groups had the same cliques as school, and the outsiders felt rejected even there. I wanted to write a song to give hope to these kids and call us all to something bigger. If heaven was the Christian's calling card, there had to be a better version of it than what was sold to me. I also felt heaven that we experience a small part of here on earth needed to be explained with tangible descriptions. If some part of us is eternal, then surely that part can recognize home when it sees it.

I couldn't wrap my head around the idea of infinity. The only known comparison was the dark night sky extending beyond the solar system and the black holes and the dying stars to someplace always a little farther than our telescopes could see. Who knew what was out there? The best answer was *nothing*.

Empty space. Dark and cold. The whole thing freaked me out. It wasn't until a night watching those same stars from a rooftop in Haiti that I warmed up to the idea of heaven. As Jesus pointed out, it's children who often lead the way.

Two things often absent for children in Haiti are fathers and houses. Cultural forces rob them of one; the economy robs them of the other. Even so, when Haitian children sang about a place of eternal joy, it was their Father's house they sang of. From my own childhood misgivings, I immediately understood why. A house worth singing of is a place of ultimate belonging, where pantries are stocked with food and a lush green lawn is always freshly mowed. It's real, with an address that can be found, and big enough that we can all fit. This was an idea of heaven I could wrap my head around. More important, I could communicate it to others, and I could invite them there.

As we were creating the songs for *Don't Censor Me*, I titled one "Big House" after a Bill Gaither influence. He had a children's song called "Jesus, I Heard You Had a Big House." My dad's band used to cover it, and we'd do a puppet show for the church using that song when I was very small. The lyrics were always comforting. As I wrote out ideas that would describe heaven to an audience grappling with its tangibility in a life of struggle, if they believed in it at all, the voices of Bill Gaither and the children of Haiti harmonized in my head.

In my career, the best songs we ever wrote were the ones that seemed like they were always there. They were birthed in creation as songs for the angels, and when it came time for the saints on earth to sing those songs, God gave us the ears to hear them. All we had to do was write them down. This is how "Big House" came to be. It was a gift. I knew it upon penning the first line on paper. I could feel the rest of the lines crammed behind, waiting to escape their gravity and float through radio airwaves and land in the hearts of believers and seekers around the world. I brought the idea to Barry to see if we could give it some shape. His guitar produced some needed structure. We quickly corralled the idea and gave it a home before it went someplace else.

THE RIFF

Barry was a student of classic guitar riffs, everything from Cream and Led Zeppelin to the anthem rock of the '80s. He could play any of them and, by doing so, figure out how they worked and why. The guitar riff is the foundation on which rock and roll builds its house. It anchors a song's concept into a rich canon of music, ensuring the rest of the song knows where to return home. In the early '90s, the rock guitar riff came back around to include the timeless yet contemporary sound of soul's funk-guitar traditions. Bands like the Spin Doctors were making magic with it. I could hear the magic seeping into Barry's late-night guitar ruminations.

When I told Barry the idea behind "Big House," he played a guitar riff he was working on. He thought it would complement and provide a broad enough scope for the song. We felt our first album had lacked gravity, so it drifted needlessly into the indulgences of momentary pop. We were anxious to anchor the music of our second album in the virtues of rock and roll, our native musical language. The message God had put on my heart didn't require a new sound; it needed an old one, a sound that had been proven and had endured almost as long as the message itself. With it, we could place the message of "Big House" in the culture's universal language. No translation needed.

I sang the pre-chorus and chorus to Barry the way it sounded in my head, which is always a scary proposition. Barry fretted his fingers up and down the guitar neck to find the key closest to what I was singing. He landed on simple A over E chording for the chorus with a high-fretted verse that included a slight chromatic slide, giving it a melodic twist. The sound was vintage, with hints of soul. We settled into the rhythm and picked up speed. With a fast flicking of his wrist and on-and-off chord dampening, Barry added a sense of urgency, but managed to keep it all upbeat. We were onto something. We just needed to find our groove.

Starting in A-180 and continuing through the long run of Audio Adrenaline, I observed correlated patterns between song tempo, measured in beats per minute, and audience reaction. There's an emotional connection between tempo and what anybody's going through at any given time. Entry, tension, and release. My mathematical mind loved the concept of this, and my scientific mind loved to experiment with different BPMs and measure the impact. I obsessed about beats per minute in our live shows until finally achieving a level of mastery with it. Our live shows were designed over a BPM timing arc. It was a pulse we could raise and lower, giving the heart a workout. "We're a Band" was pegged at one hundred BPM. There was an ephemeral moment between beats, amplifying the strong rise and fall of the rhythm. It gave time to leave the earth and still return on the downbeat. It was perfect for jumping and moshing, embodying the intensity of living a life for Christ in a world that often stands against you.

In concerts, we always started our shows with shock and awe. Jumping and moshing ensued, communicating: *this is going to be a party.* Once everybody had come in and found their places, we'd dial it down a bit, creating a moment of honesty, a space to let go of whatever was keeping the audience from joining. We'd settle into a rhythm of tension, reflecting on our own sins and what Jesus did to wash them away for us. There would be an emotional release, and then, kicking it up a notch, acknowledgment of the beauty of God and our gratefulness for what he had done in our lives. Finally, it was full-blown worship and celebration, allowing anyone who was on the outside a chance to enter the party before it ended. Singing about heaven should always be a quick-footed, hand-clapping affair. With "Big House," we turned the BPMs up, landing on 112. "Big House" would be a song to dance to.

Barry's intro guitar riff followed the less-is-more path of the most iconic riffs in rock and roll history. It started with a quick strike and slight hold of a two-string, throaty A chord, followed by a crunchy three-noted rise, and a soft landing on a warm E. There was slight sustain to get lost, a quick light-flipping strum to remind you where you were, a repeat of the riff, a classic Wurlitzer organ sliding intro, then comes the band. There were no indulgences. Just a quick announcement that the party was about to begin. By the time the second riff started, the audience would be up and ready to dance.

I imagined "Big House" as a life rope long enough to reach even the farthest castaway. In a series of vignettes progressing through the American youth landscape, each line of the first two verses begins with an authentic statement of empathy: *"I don't know where you lay your head . . . I don't know if you got a family."* On our first tour, I had realized just how different kids' experiences were. Rich. Poor. Mansions. Shacks. Moms and dads. Moms, no dads. I couldn't pretend to know their lives, so I didn't. I did what I felt the previous generations did not. I admitted that I did not know. I didn't have the answers for this generation's questions, and I didn't want to pretend that I did. But there was one thing we all have in common. I felt it as much as everyone else. We were searching for something. So next, a line before the hook, I aimed at the deepest, darkest, loneliest corners of our hearts, where the sun struggles to shine: *"I don't know if you feel love at all. But I bet you wish you had."* Then came the invitation we are all waiting for. The invitation to belong to something bigger than this world and our troubles in it: *"Come and go with me to my Father's house."*

It was the yearning of Haitian children. It was the yearning of all children. After the invitation came a series of images of the heaven I wished I'd fully known as a child: *"It's a big big house . . ."* Then we get to explore the house together, room by room, and collectively experience a holy and everlasting joy. I imagined a lawn large enough for me and my friends to play football or where I could play catch with my dad, or even my own kids. An infinite, emerald green lawn, rising into a rainbow of light; warm sun and cool grass, soft and forgiving, and always leading back to the Father's house.

We recorded "Big House" in the winter of 1993. It essentially has its roots in a kid's song sung in great hope by some of the world's poorest children. It's had its many critics. It's been made fun of for being musically simplistic and theologically light. Yet, in the ironic truth lens of history, the song has outlasted its critics. "Big House" endured because it's a childlike take on the biggest question there is: What comes after this life? This question has been asked by every people group since the dawn of time. We ask it because a signature of heaven has been imprinted on our hearts. With "Big House," I was letting go of trying to understand all the complexities of religion. Others could debate them for as long as they wanted, but I was through. I was ready to jump past a seemingly infinite number of irrelevancies between believers and experience the joy promised to all of us. In heaven and on earth. I'd soon find that millions of others wanted to join me.

FOURTEEN

We Have a Hit

In the days before the internet, radio was everything. It was the ultimate curator of music, where people went to discover new bands. The DJ was a big brother who had the goods and would let you in on the secrets of what was really happening in the world. The radio was also where you went when hope was gone. It was where, in one last desperate attempt, you turned the dials, praying the very voice of God would tune in through some distant DJ telling you it would be okay and giving you a song to get through the night.

Audio Adrenaline had already been hailed as an up-and-coming live band, and we had the goods to put on a great show, but we hadn't created the kind of song that sticks to your soul and that you find yourself humming hours later. A band that hoped for any success needed a radio hit. It could make a band.

There was a DJ at KOKF in Oklahoma City named Ken Farley who started paying attention to what we were doing. Like me, his life was altered at a DeGarmo & Key concert where he first heard authentic music that tapped into hope and redemption and healing. While other stations weren't able to get past the mess of music on our first album, Ken thought Audio Adrenaline was doing something progressive and supported us on air. When "Big House" released, he was among the first to play it.

The goal with any potential radio single is to first get placed onto the listening format of whatever radio stations are willing to play it. From there you watched the weekly "adds"—how many new stations were being added every week. These statistics were closely tracked, then published in weekly industry magazines. Music stores decided which albums to stock on shelves based on what the magazines reported. Once the stores made their orders, the big wheels of the music-distribution machine turned. Forward motion was impossible with live shows or record labels or word of mouth. Only the power of radio could make those wheels turn. Once they did, multiplication magic began to happen.

"Big House" started playing on only a few radio stations, maybe a dozen. The opening guitar riff grabbed listeners by the collar, shook them, and said, "Listen: something new your way comes." The first verse told them, "Someone understands you." Then the pre-chorus said, "Come with me; there's something I want to show you." The chorus set the hook with the promises of heaven. By the time the song was over, listeners were calling the radio station and asking them to play it again. They *needed* to hear it. Stations listened. It got more plays on the format. First, light rotation. Then medium. Then heavy. More stations added. Then more stations. And more. Listener requests kept coming, and the radio adds kept growing. Within a few months, every radio station in the country was playing "Big House." Then came the stores. Then distribution. "Big House" became the Most Requested Song of the Year, and later, it was named Song of the Decade. Radio got the big wheels turning. Four kids from Kentucky could have never anticipated what came next.

"Big House" hit number one on the radio. It was rock enough that it first hit number one on the Christian rock charts. But parents also loved it, and "Big House" also hit number one on the Christian pop charts. Behind that, "We're a Band" also climbed to number one on the hard rock charts. Every format, in every corner of the country, was playing Audio Adrenaline every hour. What made "Big House" fresh was that it was built on a guitar riff. Until then, there wasn't much pop music based on riffs. Bands like DC Talk and the Newsboys were getting on radio with more beat-driven music. The opening of "Big House" was a dirty, distorted, funky, groovy riff that let you know something interesting was coming. It was vintage enough to remind the adult contemporary crowd of their favorite rock bands, and fresh enough to keep the kids on the rock formats happy. It all hit in one pivotal moment, and the rest of the industry did what it was made to do.

People no longer wanted to wait to hear "Big House" on the radio. They wanted it *when* they wanted it. Fans went into the stores and picked up copies of our second album off freshly stocked shelves. Sales information was slow getting back to the label. We just continued doing what we were doing, not knowing any of this was going on. Sure, we heard it on the radio, and even called in to request it, but we had no idea about the sales that followed it.

Our label called us in, and we met with Greg Ham, a rising star at ForeFront, who would eventually become president of the label and instrumental to our success. But at that time, he was one of the chief label executives, and we were nervous. It was like going to the principal's office. He got right to the business at hand.

"Do you know what's happening?"

We were clueless.

"'Big House' is number one on multiple formats. Your album is selling twenty-five thousand units a month." He pointed to the album for emphasis. "You have a hit record . . . a massive hit record."

A few months earlier, we were about to be dropped by the label. We were so busy trying to make it, we didn't know what was going on. Suddenly, next to DC Talk, we were the best-selling artist they had. It turned out that what I felt were weaknesses in "Big House" were actually its strengths. People loved the predictability of it. Just as we felt the song had always been around when we wrote it, our fans felt the same way the first time they heard it. By the second chorus they were singing along, and it stuck in their heads for the rest of the day. Its theological simplicity wasn't intellectual suicide. It was intellectual surrender. People were tired of religious debates. They wanted to know if heaven was real and if we could experience some of it now. The wide smiles and the joy and the dancing with friends to a simple song answered that question.

For me, "Big House" was the answer to a different question. It showed me how the platform I'd been praying for since I was a child was going to work. It tied everything together. My early fears of heaven. Haiti. The winding road through college and the Air Force and missions. For the first time, things made sense.

We filmed a big-budget music video where I awkwardly lip-synched to a film camera a few inches from my face. Parallel to radio, music videos were the biggest influence of the day. Kids wanted to put music to a face and see the band for themselves, deciding if they could relate. The video was nothing more than a filmed version of our live stage antics. In an unscripted moment, Will climbed atop a church balcony and stage dived into a crowd. It may have injured several of the kids on set, but it made every kid who saw the video want to see us live. The video was sent to youth groups through Interlink, a curated subscription box that youth pastors relied on to find the best music of the day, and allowed every youth group in America to play it. The label began selling hundreds of thousands of records. We had found our voice. The next step was to take the album live on tour. A lot of things were about to change.

FIFTEEN

Free at Last

When our second album, *Don't Censor Me,* hit the street with our biggest hits to date, "We're a Band" and "Big House," DC Talk had completed their dramatic takeover of Christian pop music with their album *Free at Last.* That album was certified platinum, a rare accomplishment in the music business regardless of musical genre, and DC Talk became one of the first contemporary Christian artists to perform on late-night television. Their cover song, "Jesus Is Just Alright," originally made popular by the Doobie Brothers, stayed at the number one spot on the Billboard CCM sales chart for thirty-four weeks.

At this point, our live show was solid, radio was in our back pocket, and we had a hit song. Still, I was plagued by doubts about my ability to be an effective front man for a rock and roll band at this level. I was both thrilled and terrified when Audio Adrenaline was asked to open for the Free at Last tour. We'd again have to prove ourselves on the road. But this time, the stakes would be much higher.

We used money from our album sales to buy a box truck for the tour. Our label suggested we purchase a tour bus instead, but I still wasn't convinced this game of musical chairs was going to last. A box truck would be useful in whatever blue-collar job I acquired when the music stopped and I didn't have a chair. It was at least a step up from the Scooby-Doo van. Our illustrious touring truck was a used moving truck with a small cab and a large cargo space. Only a couple guys fit up front, so we built in bunk beds and threw a couch in the cargo area. Since we needed the far back area with the roll-up door for our growing collection of musical gear, we divided it off with a two-by-four and plywood wall and created our home between the cab and the mobile storage area. We cut a door in the side and a window directly behind the back of the cab. This was before cell phones, and we weren't smart enough to buy walkie talkies, so the box window behind the cab was our only form of communication with the driver. Someone in the back would bang on the window and wave into the rearview mirror to get the driver to stop for car sickness or urgent bathroom breaks. For less urgent bathroom needs, there were empty Gatorade bottles. The crowning glory was an RV air-conditioning unit we mounted on top of the box truck and rigged to a portable generator mounted to the frame behind our rear right wheel. Our rig was an Americana mansion on wheels, about three steps below cousin Eddie's in the movie *Christmas Vacation*. When we pulled into a venue with our names on the marquee, people assumed we were the road crew.

DC Talk's live show was a finely tuned machine. This was serious business for them, and they were focused and artistically proficient at a level we were not accustomed to. Toby was a relentless perfectionist. He got the best performance out of everything and everybody every night. Their show was on par with any touring act of the day. This professionalism was new to an industry known more for cheapness and cheesiness than for innovation. Toby set a new bar for popular Christian music, and it would never be the same. When they got onstage, it was a tightly choreographed performance of dancers and hype and rock-rap-soul vocals timed perfectly to massive drum loops and a killer live band. Every detail was examined thoroughly and executed perfectly. There was no deviation.

They would have been an impossible band to match, but for all their success, we had an ace they didn't: a hit rock song with indie-rock angst. We were a rock band dominating the Christian rock charts. Nobody realized yet the shifting musical preferences in the church. Contemporary Christian music was still considered "safe" by the church's gatekeepers. Church leaders still viewed rock and roll with suspicion, worried that worldly influences would penetrate the hearts of Christian youth through strong beats and loud guitars. However, contemporary Christian music was endearing itself to the adult crowd, and rock music was rapidly rising in popularity. A generational movement was afoot that embraced Jesus *and* rock and roll. Fans rejected outright the prevailing fundamentalist view that rock and roll was the Devil's music. Instead, they agreed with Larry Norman: "Why should the Devil have all the good music?"

If rock and roll was a tool for the Devil, couldn't it also be a tool for God? For this new generation, the question was merely hypothetical. They'd already answered with their hearts and for the next decade would also answer with record-breaking album and ticket sales.

Until now, Audio Adrenaline's touring career had been an all-out battle. We'd roll into a new location every night with a plan to turn up the volume and rock the stage with a disciple's conviction that what we sang about was worth staking your life on. The crowds would stand erect with arms crossed and a show-me attitude. They wanted to know if we had something worth saying and the rock and roll gravitas to back it up. We'd had to prove night after night that we deserved the audience's time and hard-earned ticket money. We had rocked from a nothing-to-lose place of desperation and a fear that we'd be discovered as the imposters we often felt we were. We'd fought too hard for too long to be turned back now. We lacked the polish and made plenty of mistakes, but the sweat was real, and ultimately, the fans respected that.

On the Free at Last tour, things were different. A hit song covered a multitude of sins. Now, all we had to do was let the opening riff of "Big House" rip through the arena and tear the roof off, and the crowd screamed so loud we couldn't hear the next few bars of music.

This perfect combination of Audio Adrenaline's rock singles dominating radio and DC Talk's massive pop record created something entirely new for us: huge audiences. DC Talk was the modern hero of Christian pop music lovers and bridged the musical divide between adults and youth in the church. We appealed to the more alternative crowd. Together, we drew buses of youth group kids ready to dance, sing, and mosh. Throngs of sweaty kids showed up hoping Will would stage dive into their pit. He usually did, even if he had to clear a four-foot security gap in front of the stage to do it. Where it was hard to quantify our growing popularity on radio, it was easy to see from the stage. Where there used to be eight hundred people in an audience, there were now eight thousand. Then ten thousand. Then fifteen thousand. With the stage lights on, I couldn't see the back of the arena. All I saw was an ocean of bodies swaying to a tidal wave of music blasting from a two-story stack of speakers on either side of the stage. We took turns talking Will out of stage diving from those speakers.

The defining moment of success for a band is when the audience takes a song that you've bled onto a recording, spent a lifetime trying to live and understand, and sings it back to you ten thousand voices strong. In that moment, the song goes from *mine* to *ours*. It's one . . . two . . . three . . . four . . . and . . . lightning strikes from steel-wound guitar strings, and thunder rolls from toms and a kick drum, and the crowd makes the microphone irrelevant. The gathered call upon our *King*, and this collective "us" transcends the moment and enters the throne room of heaven. This is the *kingdom*, and it's *happening now*. We've lit the match, and the place is about to burn with holy fire. There's dancing and singing, raising hands and falling to knees. There's repentance and restoration. There's joy. It's heaven on earth, and for one glorious moment the world is unveiled and we get to see it, the bride of Christ, beautiful and radiant, doing what we were made to do. *This is the party*. And the best part is we're all invited.

WHAT IS HAPPENING?

At the end of the night, after watching Toby and crew pick up where we left off, after hours of signing autographs, after loading our gear, and after late-night talks with the band, I crawled back into a crappy bunk bed screwed into the side of a used box truck and wondered what in the world had just happened. It was undeniable. I'd seen it with my own eyes. Felt it in my own soul. Still, I struggled to believe it. It was a math I didn't understand, where one plus one equaled three. I recounted the facts. Yes, we'd put on a great show. Yes, our musical chops had grown. Yet, the facts didn't add up. The night was too big. Too good. I concluded it was a fluke. It would take years and a lot of heartache before I finally understood this was the basic equation of grace. We aren't meant to understand it. Just accept it as the gift it is. Then return it to others.

God cannot direct the steps of those who refuse to be in motion. We each have a path in front of us that leads to our biggest, best, and highest purpose. It's the dream we've been given but are not yet prepared for. We stare at the path knowing not what's required, only that it's more than we're capable of. It's designed that way. We need only the faith to begin, to put one foot in front of the other and to trust the called-upon wisdom at each fork we face. Fear is a slow quicksand at the foot of the trail. The longer we stand in place, the deeper we sink. God is patient. He'll throw as many ropes as we need to keep pulling us out, but until we're willing to take the uncharted path toward our destiny we will just keep sinking. God wants us in motion. He wants us traveling the path through the dark woods and fire swamps in preparation for the dream. The bigger the dream, the more difficult the path. For if we're not prepared, the dream will destroy us.

It took seven years to land our first hit. In that time, we had recorded two albums as A-180 and two albums as Audio Adrenaline. We'd played more than a thousand shows and used a Chevette, a dog-house van, and a box truck to get us there. I'd quit many times. It was too hard. I had watched other bands we played with get signed. I'd second-guessed and doubted myself and God. If I'd known at the beginning how hard gaining a platform in music would be, I would not have done it. However, I had put my head down and allowed God to direct my path, never knowing if this music thing would ever work. Looking back, there was no secret to success. There was only doing the hard work and trusting God enough to take the next step. It's along the way to a dream that the important stuff happens. And it was at the end of myself where I found a new strength.

THE OPENING ACT

Our job as an opening act was to warm up the audience. Every night we under-promised and over-delivered. In so doing, we won the respect of the audience and DC Talk. The industry took notice. We got calls for more tours and even some festivals. In those days, festivals were where bands made their names as headliners, and subsequently, enough money to quit their jobs at Red Lobster. To succeed at the festivals, I could no longer act as a front man for an opening band. It was time for me to step up.

Toward the end of the tour we played a show in Colorado, and we decided to spend the day before the show snowboarding at Arapahoe Basin. Michael Tait and Toby joined our crew, and we had a great day on the mountain. The sun was bright and hot, and I didn't need a jacket. I also didn't wear goggles. By midday my eyes stung, and my vision got blurry. Thirty minutes later, as we were driving down the hill, I was crying because my eyes hurt so bad. Then the world went dark. I couldn't see a thing. I started freaking out first, followed by the rest of the band. The show was the next day and couldn't be canceled.

The doctor said I suffered from snow blindness. I would be completely blind for the following day, including the show, but then would see again. He put something on my eyes to ease the pain. When showtime arrived, Will led me to my spot onstage. I wore dark glasses and kept one hand on the mic stand all night so I wouldn't fall off the stage. I never saw the audience but could feel it in their response: we were ready.

DC Talk arranged for a pastor, Michael Guido, to come on tour to keep everybody spiritually grounded and encouraged. We needed it. We were an unprepared posse of boys suspended in an untethered world between adolescence and manhood. Add to that money and fame and arenas full of fans, half of them female, and it could have been a recipe for imminent disaster. It was Guido's steady presence and Toby's resolute focus that kept it all together. On tour, you live on top of one another, and eventually everybody gets on everybody else's nerves. DC Talk acted like brothers and fought like brothers. Then they worked it out like brothers. I watched how they operated and realized that part of their success was the brotherhood created around their music and their deep love for one another. This extended beyond the three of them. The DC Talk brotherhood included road crew and management, sound and lighting guys, promotional teams, and trusted advisers. Toby was clearly the visionary, but he needed a large team to make the vision happen.

Toby slowly brought me into the brotherhood. He mentored me in spiritual growth, songwriting, and showmanship. He saw a lot of potential in me. Like him, I was a top-down writer, more of a producer and packager than a musician. With every song and show and album, I started with a vision of something I wanted fans to feel, then worked through sounds, sights, and live experience to produce a space for that feeling to take hold and transport them to a place they wanted to go but couldn't reach on their own. Toby watched me do this with my little band and little box truck and told me that if I wanted to take this thing as far as it could go, I would need to build my own brotherhood to help me get it there. Toby introduced Audio Adrenaline to his management company, and they gave us the blueprint to becoming an A-level artist. Then he introduced me to a couple of people who would shape the rest of my life.

SIXTEEN

Cowboy Music

Rock and roll is a fickle business. A hit song or a successful tour doesn't mean you'll be around the next year. So far, we'd been operating on a youthful combination of gut instinct, raw talent, and a willingness to work harder than the next guy, even if that meant working myself right into a hospital room. This is a good recipe for a star that burns brightly for a moment, then crashes through the atmosphere, scorching the earth and everything around where it lands. To build the platform I envisioned, we needed to stay on top of the music game for the long haul. There's much to worry about with a band, and we'd reached the limit of our capacity beyond writing and playing music. We signed with True Artist Management, and in turn, they assigned us our first road manager. His name was Scott Brickell.

When I first met Brickell, I thought he was a football player. He was built like a tight end: six foot five and shaped like a brick. His imposing figure was softened with blond hair and a deep Southern drawl that could calm a storm and bring reason to a wild bunch of red-necked rock stars. He was a numbers guy by trade, and that would be needed. But I wanted to build something bigger than the band, with an impact even bigger than that. I needed someone outside of the band who would share this vision and who could implement it in the areas we could not. That would require a strong mental and physical stature.

I immediately hit it off with Brickell. He had an intuition about where we were headed, not just musically, but our direction in a fast-growing and ever-shifting marketplace. The music business requires constant action and quick movement. The labels care about who's selling records now. It's easier for them to find a new boat to jump into than to turn the ship of a band who's near the top. Every band is only as good as their last record, and you never quite know who's really on your team. We'd already been through a cycle of being the best up-and-coming band our label had ever seen, to nearly getting dropped, only for enthusiasm to rise again with a hit song. To build a music career for the long haul, I needed a steady hand to endure the relentless roller-coaster ride of the business. I could sense in Brickell an equal teammate. I could handle the vision; he could handle the implementation.

Brickell and I became close friends, quick. Like me, he was a fan of music and had experienced its transcendental power. We also shared a youthful clarity and need-to-prove-yourself drive that young visionaries face on their road to becoming men. We talked deep into midnight highways between shows, dreaming about the future of the band. He was the first to catch my vision of how far we could go. I saw a musical platform developing on the culturally shared foundations of rock and roll. I knew we could write songs for the masses and communicate through the lyrics and performances God's desire for us to face our fears and jump into the river. This vision included intimate albums with brave, vulnerable songs and a live show spectacle that competed with any tour on the road at that time. We had enough raw talent and energy to get our ship out of the harbor and into the ocean. That alone is never enough for any form of art to endure. You can't be the engine and the rudder. Brickell could take our big ideas and steer the ship to get us there.

Having a road manager also solved some practical issues. We were still not getting paid enough from royalties or as the opening act to put gas in the box truck and food in our bellies. Record labels got paid with record sales, so they focused on radio, stores, and record promotions through tours. Concert promoters got paid through ticket sales, so they were motivated by how many seats a band could fill. In order to eat and drive to the next show, we relied mostly on merchandise sales. Our merchandise table was routinely buried in the worst location in the venue. Sales reflected that. Brickell fought for a decent location to sell T-shirts and hats and the nail crosses we assembled in the back of our truck. He was the first person to come along who made sure we could eat.

THAT BAKERSFIELD SOUND

The road is a high-wire circus filled with curiosities and dangers that stack the odds against building a successful romantic relationship. Every night is a new city and a new stage and a chance to remake yourself into whatever you want to be. On any given night, I could be a pensive front man or a preacher's kid or an outgoing rock and roll star or some combination of all of it. Whatever part I didn't like I could cast off and remake myself for the next night. A successful touring act's engagement with the world is a daily routine of professionals, ranging from road crew to publicists to marketing agencies, all focused on making you seem larger-than-life, followed by an enraptured audience confirming that you are. In the Christian music world, we try our best to deflect this praise toward a worthier recipient, but in our flesh we all desire recognition. An arena stage is an overdose of this. The stage made us *different*. We were treated *differently*. I began to think the rules of the real world didn't apply to the worlds made possible by sold-out arenas.

Romantic relationships developed on the road had to straddle two worlds. One was a world of adoration and no responsibility, with limitless opportunities for fun or entertainment or distraction. Your only obligation for the day is to show up onstage for an hour to deliver the party the audience has paid for. There's dancing and singing, and afterward, a line of people wanting a picture and an autograph. This is the world of the circus. To us, the other world was the normal world. Diapers and groceries and working in a cubicle for a boss whose idea of a party is switching up his coffee mug for the day. Meshing these two worlds was very, very difficult. Primarily because our whole aspiration of becoming a rock star was formed around a new world without the restrictive rules of the one we'd been trying to leave behind. But to live by our own rules is fallible at best. To invite someone else into that is a disaster.

Despite these odds, the other guys in the band were figuring out how to merge the two. Some were married and some were dating and all were finding meaning outside of the musical life. The music itself was finally starting to take on a life of its own. We were making a living, and there was a clear path forward to becoming professional musicians who could support a real life. I'd put off even thinking about a relationship until my career was stable. Now that it was, I looked at my bandmates with some envy. The rock and roll life is untethered.

It isn't anchored to anything real. My heart was adrift and tired and looking for safe harbor. One night after a show, Toby overheard me talking about wanting to meet someone. A couple days later, he casually mentioned that I should meet his sister. She lived in Southern California and would be at the Santa Monica show. I appreciated his concern, but I wasn't interested. It would be too weird. The tour went on, and I poured my soul out onstage every night.

During sound check in Santa Monica, a girl walked in and out of the arena as if she were trying to find someone or something. She had a casual Southern California beach style, with ocean-blue eyes and long blonde hair gracefully flowing from beneath a cowboy hat. Everybody stopped what they were doing to look at her. Even with her just-off-the-beach look, she had star power.

DC Talk always had girls following them around, so I assumed she was another groupie. I awkwardly waved to try and get her attention. It didn't work. One of the sound guys piped up.

"Dude. You're a lead singer. You should go talk to her."

"No way. She's out of my league."

The crew was clearly disappointed in my cowardice, so I asked them, "Do any of you know who she is?"

"That's Toby's sister."

I suddenly got a new burst of confidence.

"Never mind. I do want to meet Toby's sister."

I looked up and she was gone. Only a diffused glow remained in the doorway where she left. I wasn't sure if it was from the sun or from her. We finished our sound check, but I was so taken by what I'd seen that I couldn't concentrate. I left the stage and headed to the greenroom to pull myself together. A few moments later Toby walked in. California dream girl stood next to him with the glow of the sun still upon her.

"Mark, I want to introduce you to my sister, Kerri."

I'm not sure what I said next. The three of us chatted for a bit about things I have no recollection of and they left. Before she walked out, she turned and smiled.

"I'm coming back for the show."

The door closed. I sat in hopeful silence.

With a new inspiration, I rocked harder that night than I had the whole tour. Almost every song ever written is in some way about love. The making of.

The longing for. The ecstasy. The heartbreak. Christian rock is no different. It's love we search for, the love found through God. And it's his love that makes all love possible. This is what we write about. It's what we all long to experience. Love is the fuel of rock and roll. I was energized by the source of music.

I found Kerri after the show. We snuck into a quiet corner of the arena to talk. We shared a love of the Bakersfield sound and West Coast country singers, like Dwight Yoakam and Buck Owens. I could see the influence in her style. She hit the best crossover notes of country without being cliché. I'd long admired the sound, first introduced to me by my father, but had yet to find a way to incorporate it into my music. She had some ideas—not only for the music but also for a cohesive visual style we had yet to achieve onstage or with our album artwork. Kerri was a stylist and photographer by trade and talked of broad narrative aesthetics in which our music might fit. I was enraptured by her ease and style, but mostly by her beauty.

It was the middle of March, and the beach was only a few blocks from the arena. The air was crisp, and the sun was setting behind the Santa Monica pier as the lights of the Ferris wheel reflected on the Pacific. We were the newest characters to walk into California's golden promise. Soon the beach would be covered in fog, but now it was spring, and everything felt possible. Kerri was moving to Nashville to launch a photography and styling business. I was becoming a bona fide lead singer.

We had almost everything in common, except she was a Washington Redskins fan, while I was a die-hard Dallas Cowboys fan. In the football world, this is an irreconcilable difference, but in romance, not so much. She was following the tour up the West Coast, taking photos and spending time with her brother. We made plans to see each other at the next stop, and when I left the arena, I felt whole again.

Our love grew as the tour went on. At night I performed in packed arenas, and during the day we lingered in sun-filled cafés, dreaming of a life we could create. We shopped in stores I never knew existed, and Kerri helped me craft a personal style I'd always wanted but was too dopey to achieve on my own. I could trust her with a part of the rock and roll business I was never comfortable with: the rock-star part.

I had always been on the dorky side of style, but as the band's popularity grew, so did the demand for photo shoots and posters and album covers. There was an expectation by labels and promoters, even fans, that in being in a band, you had to look the part. If I could trust Brickell to partner with in the business and vision of Audio Adrenaline, I could trust Kerri to partner with in art direction and branding. In the days before digital, photography took real talent. She had it. She was gifted in knowing where we needed to go and was comfortable and competent with photographers and stylists. (They were like dentists to me.) A great working partnership quickly formed between us. There was no doubt we could make great art together. I hoped we could make more. By the time the tour reached Seattle, I was in love.

In Seattle, the effects of hit songs on the radio reached their climactic peak. The audience was all in. So were we. There's a beautiful exchange between the audience and artist when we collectively open up our hopes and vulnerabilities. Because of what my heart was experiencing *offstage*, I was able to leave more of it *onstage*. The audience gave it back multiplied. I walked off after a great set to where Kerri was waiting for me. I told her what I was feeling. All of it.

We talked so intently for so long that I didn't notice the arena fading from ten thousand souls searching for God to only two searching for each other. The crew did its work to erase all evidence of what had transpired, and we were alone in the easy twilight of a rock and roll show. Bright lights were replaced by an ambient glow, and the ceiling darkened like a moonless sky. Through the soft light I could see rows upon rows of chairs circling and rising and disappearing beyond the light. They didn't feel empty. I felt the gathered presence of lingering angels. They took their seats in grand circles where all the hope and restoration and eternal love that earlier was celebrated hung in the rafters and echoed into two young hearts on the arena floor. I found a small radio, inserted a tape, hesitated for a moment, then pressed play. Cowboy music warmed the space. I grabbed Kerri's hands and felt their warmth. First in her palms. Then her back. Then her neck. I reminded myself to breathe. Slowly. Softly. There was only the sound of music's longing and the rhythm of her soft breath. Until the early hours of morning, we danced in the company of angels.

SEVENTEEN

The Shed

Like all things in rock and roll, my relationship with Kerri moved fast. I finished the tour, she moved to Nashville, and on January 1 we were married in Las Vegas. I asked Brickell to be my best man, and our lighting director, Drew Baca, walked her down the aisle. We honeymooned in Maui, but something didn't feel quite right. Kerri seemed distant, as if she were uncomfortable with me. I thought maybe it was honeymoon jitters. We had dated quickly and from a distance, so I could understand that. But I saw something else in her eyes: doubt and fear and regret. I had imagined this moment as the time when all my loneliness finally disappeared. Instead, it increased. On the beach, as the sun shed its last colors of day, we sat detachedly. She went back to the room, and I watched the sun sink beyond the Pacific. Remnants of light bravely made their last stand in clouds of pink and orange, reflecting on stilled waters. Soon, I sat alone in the dark.

We returned from our honeymoon, and before my wife and I could talk about what happened in Hawaii, I left for our next tour. I'd be gone for months, which is why wives of touring musicians are often referred to as band widows. I regret it now, but at the time, it felt like a relief. For all the mysteries and uncertainties of marriage, the road was familiar and comfortable. The guys asked how things were. I told them things were great, and as long as I was on the road, they were. I slipped into my music life. My wife got started with her business.

THE SHED

There was a lot of anticipation for what Audio Adrenaline would do after the massive pop success of "Big House" and the rock success of "We're a Band." Pressure built. We felt it from our growing fan base, the label, even ourselves. We were still kids, growing up onstage, with our musical and personal flaws in plain sight. No one ever said it out loud, but the underlying question was, *Are we capable of making a true rock album?* We'd declared in a massive anthem that we were a band; it was time to show our cards. The Christian music world watched to see if we really had a hand to play or if we were bluffing all along. I knew what was at stake. In those days, hits alone didn't make you a band. Albums did. If we didn't deliver a titanic album, we'd be seen as imposters, and the whole gig would be up. We found a cheap storage shed with no air conditioning in a little town called Antioch, just outside of Nashville. In that shed we began sweating out an album.

For the first time in our career, we were musically unshackled. It took us four albums and almost ten years of playing together to get there. The label set us free to write the songs we wanted, and their confidence gave us a much-needed boost. After the experimentation of the last two albums, Barry was ready to get back to his musical roots. Pent-up guitar riffs exploded in the shed. His inspiration came from vintage hard rock bands, with guitars that jammed every corner of arenas. This was evident in the riffs he was producing. But there was also a groove and a hint of funk mixed in with the hard rock that made the sound modern. This retro rock foundation with a modern groove gave the underlying sound a mass appeal, making it perfect for the themes emerging in the lyrical storytelling elements of the album.

As a band, we were wary of the celebrity status being placed on us. In addition to the pressures of competing with other bands and producing a hit album, we also felt pressure to deliver a spiritual message that connected with people and moved them toward Jesus. I was essentially becoming the pastor I'd never wanted to be, with all the unfortunate public scrutiny that comes with that role. We were judged for what we said onstage. For what we wore. For how we conducted our lives. We were musicians and unprepared for any of this. But ready or not, it was now part of our life and job. Immediately I sensed the

Devil attacking me with thoughts that I wasn't worthy of the platform we'd been given. My response was to agree.

The album thematically took shape around the idea of how small we really are in comparison to Jesus. While on tour, I watched a replay of the famous Beatles interview where John Lennon said that they had become more popular than Jesus. There's been a lot of debate about what he really meant with that comment, but it gave me the concept for our lead track. I disagreed with the Beatles singer and thought it was a cool idea that no matter how popular anybody got, nobody is ever going to be as big as Jesus. Not only was it a cool idea, but this revelation also relieved the pressure we felt about what we had to become. We didn't have to become as big as Jesus. Or the Beatles.

I brought the idea to Barry, and he showed me a riff that matched the lyric to a tee. It was built on an alternate drop-D tuning where the lowest E string was tuned a whole step down to D. This gave the guitar a lower range in open, throaty power chords common in Barry's heavy rock influences. But instead of playing it heavy, he gave it a Lenny Kravitz–style groove, with quick, syncopated strumming that made you want to stand up and dance. The song wasn't necessarily a response to the Lennon quote, just a natural admission that whether we wanted to be musicians or business moguls or movie stars, even at the peak of any worldly success, we are infinitely insignificant compared to the immensity of our Creator. The song celebrated the freedom found in this. In an ironic musical twist, the chorus reflected this idea perfectly. In all hit songs, the chorus is the biggest musical moment, when all the instruments and vocals come together to emphasize the bigness of the song and the artist's capabilities. In the chorus of this song, the music drops out and is entirely submitted to the lyric and song's title, "Never Gonna Be As Big As Jesus." The biggest life we can ever hope for comes from submitting it all to Jesus.

I felt so emboldened by this idea I wanted to write another song where we could flex the full power of a submitted life. Barry, finally able to display the authority of his guitar, wrote a monster riff that I had to scream over to be heard. The song was a lightning bolt live, electrifying the audience and drawing them into the truth—whether they wanted to acknowledge it or not. For the lyric, we kicked around the idea of all the kings, with all their power, who've come and gone throughout history. Yet, only one King remains and is still alive and at work in hearts around the world. This led us to the line *"I'm not the King / I just sing."* Our lives are limited. But I felt so much power in the limitlessness of Jesus that every time we played this song, it blew the roof off so there would be no separation between us and the love of God. I loved singing that lyric. I felt its power every time.

After writing two massive, declarative songs, we needed some songs to ground the album in our common experiences. "Walk on Water" was a reminder that when we're cast about in the sea of our fear, keeping our eyes on Jesus is the only thing that will keep us from sinking or from being afraid of the crashing waves. "Man of God" was about the tension of being onstage, talking about faith and Jesus, while knowing that we struggle with the same things as everybody else. We felt a hypocrisy in the fame, along with the guilt and shame of walking onstage as sinners trying to point people to God. Though it wasn't one of our most popular songs, "Bag Lady" was another big guitar contribution from Barry, and "Good People" was a fun song about the friends we were making all over the country. We weren't finished writing, but there were enough songs to test the sound and concepts of the album, and we were blown away. It was the album we'd always wanted to make. Something special happened in that shed. Ideas flowed, and we felt we had something important to say and the time to say it right. It was through sweating out these songs that we finally felt like the band we were capable of being. It was time to head to the studio.

EIGHTEEN

"Bloom"

Our first touring partner and longtime hero Eddie DeGarmo was now our executive producer at the label. When we told him we wanted to make a straight rock and roll album, he said he had a friend who could help. He introduced us to John Hampton of Ardent Studios in Memphis, Tennessee.

John had recently produced the Gin Blossoms's massive hit record and was responsible for the sound of other guitar-driven artists we admired, like the Replacements, Stevie Ray Vaughan, and ZZ Top. All of rock and roll history can be traced through a single thread that runs through Memphis. Ardent was filled with producers steeped in that history. At the time, Christian producers in Nashville focused on making pop-oriented, formula hits that fit the requirements of Christian radio. These Memphis producers didn't care about Christian radio. They didn't even know what it was. Rock and roll was their religion, and they passionately protected it. We'd been invited to their church. We came with supplication.

Memphis had a historic and weathered grit that gave the streets a distorted tone. The darkest undercurrents of our country culminated in the shooting of Dr. King on Mulberry Street. Those rising tensions seeped into the records recorded at Sun Studios on the corner of Union and Marshall streets. Just around the corner on Beale Street, aging neon signs glowed upon bricks molded from the blues that became the foundation of rock and roll. A few blocks from it all is the slow and wide and muddy Mississippi River, the ancient water highway that brought the blues from the delta and carried downriver the ugliest moments of our nation's history and the music that tries to reconcile and make sense of it all.

For me, Memphis was even more personal. As I walked its streets, I couldn't help but be reminded of my little sister's cancer fight. This is where God showed up in a big way for my family. In Memphis, I felt the struggle and the hope. It was right in front of me. Raw. Real. Undeniable. Though the songs we had were good, this was the filter we needed to run them through.

John Hampton taught us how to make a rock album. At the direction of our label, our previous records relied on drum loops and synthesized tracks. We crammed something into every available space of a song to create a wall of sound. John didn't believe in any of that. If we couldn't play it live, it wasn't going on the record. Though Ardent didn't follow the Christian music industry, they respected our music. "You guys are making rock and roll" was the language of our common ground. Authenticity was the key ingredient for a great album. We had to believe every note we played and every lyric we sang. If we didn't believe it in the studio, nobody would believe it on the album. There would be no tricks or programming, only the organic sounds created through our instruments. It was through John that we also learned about the spiritual spaces in the songs. These were the spaces that had room for the hopes and longings of the listeners. Without space on a record, its meaning is limited to its noise. It's through the space that listeners can bring their own stories and the songs become theirs.

This was before the digital recording era when drumbeats could be fixed, vocals could be tuned, and every recorded sound could be isolated and adjusted. Today, bands don't even have to play on their records; it can all be done through computer-generated sounds and samplers. For this album, we recorded old-school, like our musical heroes, on two-inch analog tape. This meant we had to perform every moment of every song because there was no way to "fix" anything after it was recorded. Our imperfect human-ness drove the authenticity of the sound. Even the tape itself had a say in the character. When sounds hit the tape, they melted a little, becoming warmer and rounder. To get the vintage tones we wanted, we had to rely on vintage gear and all its idiosyncrasies. While recording drums, they would mic the room so even the qualities of the room itself bled into the recording.

This was controlled through angled walls covered with carpet and foam and other wall hangings infused with the smells of cigarettes and whiskey from preceding musicians. This was how the great records of old were made, and like a believer who finds heaven, our producers had found their promised land and never left.

Everything was finally starting to click with our music. It felt good. We were challenged by limiting the recording to what could be played live, but the greatest power is found in restraint. The music was better because of the limitations. It forced us to rely on our storytelling and conviction. We also learned to have more patience with the music. Every song didn't start with a symphonic onslaught. It could start simply, and each time the music circled back to the verse, more story could be added. In this way, the song could grow along the way. Become more involved. More interesting. It could be as simple as adding a background organ or a second guitar. We also learned to lean into the lyric and melody along with a good beat. If those weren't good enough, then the song shouldn't be on the record. Eddie DeGarmo joined us and played Wurlitzer and B3 Hammond organ on a few tracks. When the day was done, we went down to Beale Street to enjoy legendary blues and Memphis barbecue as we relished in finally making the album we'd always wanted to make.

The album found its sound and soul in Memphis, but it still needed a few more tracks to complete the storytelling and to provide some fresh moments onstage. Bob's wife suggested a song called "Free Ride," written by Dan Hartman and originally performed by the Edgar Winter Group. It had been a top 20 hit in the early '70s. Lyrically it fit the album perfectly. It described the challenge of finding your way alone through the mountains and valleys. Only by taking someone else's hand can you be led where you don't know how to get to. The song symbolized the grace I needed to navigate the foreign lands in which I found myself. We interpreted the music through our childhood lenses of corn-fed rock and roll, and though the sound was vintage, by stripping it down to the studs of guitar, bass, and drums, it was also timeless and became a long-standing piece of our set. Todd Collins produced it in downtown Franklin. "Free Ride" was a way to tip our hats and pay tribute to the sound we grew up with, and also provided closure for the album. The music was ready.

BUSINESS PARTNERS

To capture the feeling of what happened in Memphis and our growth as musicians and as men, we decided to call the album *Bloom*. My wife and I talked on the phone a couple times a week to share with each other the passions we had for our separate artistic endeavors. Her photography and styling business was also taking off, so we brought her in to help develop the album artwork. She wanted complete creative control. She had a clear, innovative vision and a trustworthy eye, but I didn't want to force her on the band. That can break bands apart. So, we worked on it together.

I wanted the artwork to reflect where we were going with the music, stripped down and timeless. Kerri was a student of classic rock and roll photography and knew how to accomplish this. She brought in a New York City photographer and styled the band in vintage clothing that wasn't in-the-moment fashionable but was timeless and better showed our personalities. I wore a cowboy hat and buttoned-up shirt that felt rooted in the small towns I grew up in, and Kerri used more dramatic and intentional lighting for the photos. The imagery for *Bloom* bucked the whole system and went back to our roots. The look was symbolically rebellious toward what we were previously forced to look and sound like. For the cover concept, we landed on a cold background with a beautiful flower growing out of it, then simplified the type font to call less attention to the band and symbolize the humility in discovering the bigness of Jesus. The album's story was ultimately one of hope. That you could bloom even from the hardest of circumstances.

Since our honeymoon, our marriage had been frozen in time. When we'd returned from Hawaii, I'd immediately gone on tour, and Kerri had dived into her business. I hoped that working together on this album might thaw things out so we could find our own groove. Though we worked well together on the album artwork and the stylistic direction of the band, our interactions felt more businesslike than intimate. Something was clearly wrong, but I wasn't equipped to handle it and didn't have anyone to talk to about it. I had seen musical heroes of mine expose their marital troubles and then be skewered by the public and the industry. This left me too afraid to show my own flaws. The tension felt strangely familiar. Like preachers' kids, Christian artists were expected to be perfect. At least publicly.

Kerri and I were young, though. I thought it would just take time, that we'd figure it out eventually. She seemed satisfied with how things were, so I decided it was okay to just focus on our careers. After all, there was no doubt we'd produced something beautiful and enduring with the artwork of *Bloom*. Perhaps we could produce a great life one day as well. Though our marriage felt cold, I was hopeful. Maybe, like the album cover, a flower could grow from it.

Our band became adults while recording *Bloom*. Recording in Memphis had been a risky move that paid off massively for us. We had finally made the record I knew we could, with everybody performing at their highest levels. Barry's guitar rattled the soul through monster riffs, then drew you deeper with quiet melodic moments. My voice performed at arena rock levels. There seemed to be no vocal limit, and I felt a great excitement in the power of my voice. This was the level of singing I'd always dreamed of. Though I'd soon find the dream to be short-lived, I reveled in it at the time. Additionally, my wife and I had created an enduring piece of art together, and the whole world felt perfect and right. The band was growing in popularity. As the title suggested, life was in bloom. The album took flight, becoming our first certified gold record. It was hard to believe all that God was doing. Alone in prayer, I gave my voice to God and asked him to do his will with it. I had no idea what all this would bring.

PART IV

"Get Down"

You can't live your life to please yourself.
—AUDIO ADRENALINE, "GET DOWN"

"Now that I, your Lord and Teacher, have washed your feet, you also should wash one another's feet."
—JOHN 13:14

NINETEEN

Duct-Taped Rock and Roll

In 1995, around the time we were finishing up the recording of *Bloom*, our friends from DC Talk released a song called "Jesus Freak" that went ballistic, and they asked us to come back on tour with them. The tour began the following spring and was billed by promoters as a Super Tour. DC Talk was at the pinnacle of their success, and with the release of *Bloom*, we were the rising stars in the industry. We played nightly in A-level arenas to crowds sometimes surpassing twenty thousand people. One notable absentee from the audience was my wife. Without the tools to work on our marriage, I just put it on hold and went out and did the only thing I knew how to do: put on a rock show. My plan was to double down on the band and figure everything else out later. There was only one thing missing from this plan. A drummer.

It's easy to find a drummer for the studio. Requirements are mainly the ability to show up on time and play a precise beat. A live drummer needed this and more. A touring drummer anchors a rock show with a steady beat and needs the professionalism and gravitas to rein in other bandmates who drift into their own timing. Our shows were designed to be a hurricane of energy and sound whipping through the audience on one song, leaving a wreckage to be tended to through the subtle work of the Holy Spirit on the very next. This required a near-telepathic connection between band members. The problem is, rock stars by nature are fiercely individualistic and play to their own beat. Onstage, we had to be one and play to one beat. That beat is established and protected by the drummer. Any band member who gets lost needs only to look back to the drummer. If the drummer gets lost, the whole band is lost.

One kid selling T-shirts for us was also a drummer. I didn't know much about him or his drumming other than that he was just out of high school, where he played in a band called Donut. Ergo, he was young. He watched as drummer after drummer failed our auditions. Many were twice his age, and all had significantly more experience. Some overplayed. Some underplayed. Some hit too hard, some too soft. Some attributes were definable, but many weren't. In addition to the technical aspects of drumming, we also needed a great showman who could add to our live performance in that great rock and roll equation where the whole is greater than the sum of the parts. We were looking for that "it" factor, and you either had it or you didn't. Because of the importance a drummer has in a band, finding one is a Goldilocks effort. When the kid got his turn in the audition, it was just a courtesy to keep him happy with his T-shirt job. He stunned us all. He paid attention to our notes and played with an animated intensity that belied the metronomic precision of his beats. The quality of his drumming was matched only by his personality. The kid's name was Ben Cissell. He was only nineteen, and his first touring experience was about to be in big arenas with historic crowds. It would be a test to see if he was the right fit for our band. Trial by fire is a colossal understatement.

The Jesus Freak tour lived up to all the hype surrounding it, breaking all previous Christian rock tour records. Though we were playing to sold-out audiences, we still felt like we'd snuck into the party. With our first royalty checks from *Bloom*, we upgraded our touring rig, but it was still a converted box truck with no restroom. At a festival leading up to the tour, Barry woke up with a massive headache and stumbled out of the truck throwing up. Something was wrong, but we didn't know what. It turned out that our box truck was giving us carbon monoxide poisoning. But since we only got paid when we played, Barry did the show sitting on a stool with a fifty-five-gallon trash can next to him. He'd throw up in the middle of the song and just keep playing. For us, every show and every audience was important, so there was no way a little carbon monoxide poisoning would get in the way.

From the very beginning, DC Talk was a highly polished pop group with an entire executive team focused on keeping them on top of shifting music trends. With "Jesus Freak," they shifted from a pop-and-rap mix to more of a rock-and-rap mix, solidifying them as bona fide superstars. The band was led by three world-class singers. On top of that, another six or seven incredible backing band members were onstage at any given point. These included two guitarists, a bass player, a keyboardist, a drummer, a percussionist, a DJ, and a team of lighting and sound guys, and practically everyone on stage could sing. In every category, they had the best talent to be found. We were a few dorm-room buddies; a teenage T-shirt-seller-turned-drummer; and Bob, who, bored with his marching-band electric drum machine, had just picked up rhythm guitar. DC Talk had two state-of-the-art tour buses and two semis carrying the most sophisticated musical equipment of the day. We peed into Gatorade bottles.

Audio Adrenaline was the sole opening act. We had forty-five minutes to fill with our version of hard-pounding, runaway-train rock and roll, and nobody else in the band could sing that well, so I carried most of the vocals, the preaching, and the talking. I felt like it was all on me, and my anxiety grew. Then one night, my voice disappeared. The lyric in my mind traveled through my larynx and vocal cords, but no sound came from my mouth. I tried again, and still nothing. Terrified, I turned around, and Ben caught my look. He pounded the drums harder and took the music up to fill the gap where my vocals were meant to be. For several heart-stopping moments, no sounds came from my mouth. Then as quickly as the switch flipped off, it flipped back on, and I was able to resume singing and finish the show. Compared to DC Talk and other popular Christian bands, it felt like we were barely held together with duct tape and superglue.

It's hard to see God while he's at work in our lives. Sometimes we notice him later when we look back or when we find that we're struggling less the next time an issue comes around. Sometimes we never notice him at all. I certainly didn't see him at the time. I wanted the best of everything, like DC Talk had. Barry was a great guitar player but didn't like to be on tour. Will put on a great show with a ton of energy but would sometimes lose his way during songs. Ben was a kid. Bob was just learning how to play. I was not a great singer, and to make up for it, I sang louder and harder than I should have. I ended each show exhausted and sweaty and surprised that the audience had responded so passionately. God gave us just enough every night to accomplish the task he set before us. Nothing more.

Somehow it worked. What we couldn't accomplish with talent alone, we did through grit and sweat and complete dependence on God to carry us through. The audience connected with us because they felt like us. There was no way the average Joe could make it with a supergroup like DC Talk. But the average Joe could make it with our band for sure. Like our fans, we felt like the underdogs, with all the odds stacked against us, but we believed just enough that God would somehow make music with our mess that it gave us the courage to show up and try. We showed up every night expecting God would too. If he didn't, we were all in trouble.

Our friendship with DC Talk grew even stronger on this tour. We could tell they loved each other, but as tight as they were onstage, we could see cracks developing backstage. They were each heading in a different direction artistically, and we wondered how much longer it could last. We didn't dig into it much, though, because we were experiencing our own cracks. Barry grew increasingly uncomfortable with the touring life and how big things were getting. Audio Adrenaline was no longer the hat-trick band that got signed on a fluke. We were playing at the highest levels in the industry and were experiencing all the stakes that came with it. Things would not be slowing down anytime soon. This was tough for Barry, who missed his family deeply while on tour. Seeing how hard it was for him made me question why my marriage worked better while I was on the road. I had assumed that was normal. Barry told me privately that his touring days were numbered. I tried to talk him out of it, but he was in a different orbit. I put this all out of mind as we headed into our last show and the inevitable end-of-tour pranks that come with it.

DC Talk's stage was built with a section that jutted into the crowd. This was their most significant set piece of the night. It was set up like a hipster living room, with artisan rugs and lava-style lamps and a couch with vibe. The scene was similar to *MTV Unplugged*. At the key moment of every night, Toby, Michael, and Kevin would dramatically walk out to this section for an acoustic set. They played their slower, more intimate songs, like "Hard Way" and their cover of Charlie Peacock's "In the Light." It was a special moment highlighting the vocal prowess of Kevin and Michael and the preaching of Toby. When the acoustic songs ended, the three of them sat on the couch for a heart-to-heart talk with the audience. This was the most important part of the night, and they took it very seriously. Under no circumstances were we allowed to go near this section of the stage. It wasn't even lit until the hallowed moment arrived.

On the last night of the tour, in the darkness of the DC Talk set change and their giant band moving to the acoustic living room set, Ben walked out with them. He just sat down next to Michael and started reading the paper. Then the lights came up. At that moment, everything stopped. There was a crack in the Christian rock continuum. Toby looked confused. Michael and Kevin began laughing. The rest of us were offstage, half laughing and half-mortified. Ben simply crossed his legs and turned the page of his newspaper. As the musicians initiated the intimate acoustic set, Ben read the comic section sitting next to Michael, Kevin, and Toby on the couch. He never broke character. For the rest of DC Talk's biggest moment, on their biggest tour, on their last night, in an arena full of zealous DC Talk fans, a nineteen-year-old kid commanded the stage by reading a newspaper with his legs crossed. We had found our drummer.

TWENTY

Changes

The rock and roll clock is twenty-three hours of pure tedium—driving, sound checks, truck stops, terrible diners, public restrooms, sleeping in parking lots, waiting backstage, shouting "Hello!" to fans from a town we've only barely seen through the bus windows—followed by one hour of pure magic when our songs are echoed in our fans' voices and together we ascend to a space that is neither heaven nor earth but a holy bridge connecting the two. Yet, it's not for everyone. We got off the Jesus Freak tour and were immediately asked to go back on tour for seventy cities with Steven Curtis Chapman. It would be another season passing without noticing the colors in the leaves. A lot of life gets missed while on the road. This was too much for Barry. He wanted to live with family in a house with a yard to play catch in, not just write songs about it. Halfway through the Chapman tour, Barry called it quits.

Our friend Brian McSweeney from Seven Day Jesus learned the songs from Barry and temporarily stepped in to finish the tour. Brian was a great guitar player and showman but had an additional, much-needed talent. He could sing. Since my voice incident on the last tour, I'd grown increasingly nervous about carrying 100 percent of the vocals. Brian could help carry the show with his voice and his showmanship. He came as sweet relief. I tried talking him into playing with us permanently, but he was no longer interested in being in Christian music.

Steven Curtis Chapman opened us up to a huge new audience, and our fan base doubled. His boys were enthusiastic about Audio Adrenaline, and he understood what we were trying to accomplish with our music. He became a mentor and friend, and as I studied him, I learned more of what it took to become an A-level artist. Mainly, that it required an incredible amount of work that nobody ever sees. He handled it with a level of integrity and graciousness that was amazing to watch. The lessons I learned from him would prove important in challenges faced throughout my career. Starting with finding a new guitar player.

THE WONDER KID

Since we were on tour, we auditioned through video. Guitarists from all over the country sent recordings of themselves playing our songs. At first it was entertaining to watch balding, middle-aged men relive their glory days for one brief moment on VHS tape. Then it became discouraging. Barry's talent was in a class all its own. I feared it might be impossible to find a player as good as him. Finally, a video caught our attention. First it was because of the backdrop. The video was filmed in a bedroom with a kid's unmade bed and *Star Wars* posters taped to the wall. Then a very young-looking kid appeared and played Barry's guitar riffs lick for lick, rocking through our entire set. The whole time, we expected the kid's mom to step in and tell him to turn down the music and make his bed.

We watched the video several more times, then sent it to Barry. He called back with a surprising response: "This is your guy."

The kid's name was Tyler Burkum, and he was the real deal, matching Barry note for note between his homework and chores. We invited Tyler to audition live by sitting in with us before our show in the Minneapolis arena. He played perfectly. Between songs he dabbled casually with complicated riffs I'd never heard of, almost as if he was bored. He could also sing as well as he played. This was the first time I'd ever met a prodigy. God had given Tyler talents he didn't even realize he had. We invited him to join the band for our next run, which was a two-week stint in Australia. He said yes, but there was a catch: he was only seventeen, and his parents had to make me a legal guardian so he could leave the country.

IN A CLASS ALL HIS OWN

Barry Blair's contribution to Audio Adrenaline, and to Christian music, cannot be overstated. Through an exceptional level of skill, Barry brought guitar-driven innovation to the industry. His monster guitar riffs tore the roofs off arenas and ushered in a massive era of Christian rock that is likely to never be repeated. He patiently suffered through Audio Adrenaline's awkward early albums to finally produce his best work on *Bloom*. With that album, Barry helped create an enduring piece of art that continues to reach and inspire people today. In a BREATHEcast interview, he summed up his view of music:

> Music speaks to people straight to their heart beyond language and then when you tie that emotional impact of the music with words, you're just able to make an incredibly powerful impact on people. . . . It's a gift that God has given us that there is nothing else quite like it. There are other art forms that are all beautiful, but music has a legacy with the church and the Bible all the way back to the beginnings. God uses music to speak to us and for us to worship him. There's a deep history of faith in music. I think that's an important history that needs to stay.[1]

We'd been on the road for nearly eighteen months, and in that time we'd lost and found half of our band. We were exhausted. I thought I'd have a moment to rest and reengage with my marriage. The label had other plans. It was time to make another album. We'd left everything onstage on the two biggest tours there could possibly be; there wasn't anything left in the tank to put into an album. On this, the contracts were clear. A new album was due, and it didn't matter what we had or didn't. This was the business.

TWENTY-ONE

"Some Kind of Zombie"

Our fourth Audio Adrenaline album, *Some Kind of Zombie,* was written from the back of our tour bus. There was no garage. No sweating. No deep collaboration or debate or grit or making it happen. There wasn't even a full band. Barry was gone. Tyler was finishing high school. We pieced together borrowed music from transitional musicians and worked toward fulfilling our contractual obligations. We were burned out. Our spiritual and creative well was running dry, and we needed some time for the well to refill. But there was no time. This is the downside of the music business. It's still, above all else, a business. Music labels have a business objective that requires albums to be sold. If we couldn't record one, there were plenty of other bands who could. The label suggested we cover other people's songs, but we'd fought hard to become our own band and didn't want to reach outside for music. We started writing from an empty well.

A strange thing can sometimes happen when you're worn all the way through. Instead of asking for God's strength, it seems easier to rely on your own. Leaning on God's strength also requires waiting on his timing. We know his timing is perfect, but for pressing obligations and contracts, it doesn't feel that way. We'd honed our recording chops and strengthened as musicians. We leaned into that strength and ended up cutting a collection of songs that pure music critics would cite as some of our best work, but that our fans felt was lacking. With the exception of a couple tracks, what was missing was the proven formula of us desperately asking God to help us write his songs. They were still good songs, and nothing was wrong with them musically or spiritually. They were just exactly as big as us, and not nearly as big as God.

The zombie concept came from scriptures about how we have to die to ourselves to be born again. In this way, when we are the most dead, we are the most alive. Get it? The idea was a stretch, and looking back now, I would have done it differently, but at the time we thought it was cool and tried our best to make it work. The title track benefited greatly from a guitar riff that Barry contributed as his last gift to the band. Other than that, the big moments of the album strayed from guitar-driven anthems and leaned into modern euro-club sounds made popular at the time by U2's *Zooropa* and *Pop* albums. Still, the music was a lot of fun to create, and the album resonated with those among our fans who were attuned to the musical trends of the day. The others were left scratching their heads. I asked Kerri for art direction, but we couldn't agree on anything. I'd been touring nonstop, and she was busy building her business, so I tried to believe we were just missing each other. However, it was hard not to feel that the business aspect of our marriage was now at risk too.

KANSAS

Before the touring cycle of *Some Kind of Zombie* began, I was asked to produce a breakout album for an up-and-coming artist. The artist's name was Jennifer Knapp. As I got to know her, it was hard to escape her passionate love for Jesus. It bordered on complete desperation, and she was unashamed in her vulnerability. She begged Jesus into her lyrics and chords and melodies. Jennifer was one of the few people I've met whom I wasn't sure I was worthy to work with. There was a palatable sense that she knew something about grace that I didn't. Her very breathing seemed connected to it. Her songs were beautiful and intense and desperate. They ripped me apart.

We asked Jennifer to come on tour as the opening act. Nobody knew who she was. To win over an audience, her music had to go up against the all-out sonic assault of the O. C. Supertones and the hard-driving anthems of Audio Adrenaline. On the first night of the tour, Ben and I watched her from behind the curtain. Jennifer was a tiny, five-foot girl from Kansas, alone onstage with nothing but her guitar and her voice and her desperation for Jesus. She looked so small, with the massive audience extending far in front of her. Then she started. Her voice built like a storm across the plains, as a long-suffered grace washed over the crowd. The audience sat in stunned silence. She connected to the deepest place within people, deeper than anything we ever did. I can't explain what happened when Jennifer sang. Her voice floated above the crowd and flooded hearts with love and understanding and forgiveness. I was nominated for a Grammy as the producer on her first album, *Kansas*. The album went on to become gold. Her heart already was.

THE O. C. SUPERTONES

Our favorite song from the *Zombie* album to play live was "Blitz." We wrote and recorded it with a band called the O. C. Supertones, and then we asked them to open for us on tour. Ben is a savant when it comes to music, with encyclopedic knowledge of rock and roll history and a better pulse than anyone on what was happening in every genre of modern music. He'd been listening to the Supertones since they first came out and thought they'd be a great fit with us. He was right. As we matured, we needed a band to do for us what we'd started out doing for others: bring the hype. And nobody brought it like the O. C. Supertones. They were blowing up as a ska band, complete with a horn section that took their already powerful songs to a whole new level. Their set was forty-five minutes of pure energy that brought the Southern California sunshine everywhere we played in the US.

With the Supertones, we'd found our touring soul mates. Ben initiated them through his love language: fun. One day I saw him sitting casually in the corner of catering with his camera pointed nonchalantly at the ice chests filled with drinks. One of the Supertone's horn players lifted the cooler, screamed like a middle school girl, jumped back, and dumped his lunch all over himself. Ben had rigged the cooler by tying a snake to the bottom of the lid so when someone opened it, a snake jumped straight at them. Worse, sometimes he'd unscrew the water lines of the sink closest to the stage and leave the lines pointed to your crotch. Everybody in a band learned quickly to use the restroom before going onstage. The only thing more embarrassing than running offstage in the middle of the show to use the bathroom is walking onstage looking like you peed your pants.

Either Ben or the Supertones had something fun lined up every day. We surfed, snowboarded, rode scooters through small towns, played pranks on each other, and had epic kickball tournaments. We even played concerts. When we did, we reminded the crowd that heaven was going to be the best time ever and that it was okay to experience some of it here. I needed the message more than anyone. Our album wasn't selling well. There were issues at home. And I couldn't shake what had happened to my voice on the last tour. Things were heavy everywhere else in my life, and when I thought about it, depression set in. But onstage, with my closest friends, with our fans, I was able to rise above all of it and for a moment just enjoy being a child of God.

CRACKS

Something was happening with my voice. It was subtle at first, but grew over the course of the tour. It came and went unexplainably. I was able to rationalize it publicly, but secretly I was losing control in some octaves and couldn't hit the higher ranges. I also couldn't make it as full as some of the songs called for. To help hide it and fill in the gaps of the bigger songs, I had Tyler help with the singing. I also had my cousin Mike Owsley join us. He was an all-around good musician and singer. Mike played keys and sang background vocals. Between his and Tyler's voices, I could back down my vocals a bit and make it work without anybody noticing. Or so I thought.

Drew, our lighting director who'd previously sung in a metal band called Angelica, told me I was damaging my voice. He recognized it during rehearsals, and said I needed to sing differently to protect it. I'd already seen a voice specialist, after my voice dropped out on the Bloom tour. The specialist couldn't tell what was happening with my voice and suggested that I get a steroid shot. So I did, and it worked. The shot took down the swelling and inflammation along my vocal cords, and for a while my voice was invincible. When the shot wore off, I took another. The shots were administered through a doctor, and at first I only took them before recording an album or starting a tour. The doctor recommended only two shots a year, so I had to be careful about the timing.

Now I was needing them more frequently. The cracks were widening, and I didn't know what to do. It scared me. I took another shot and sang harder. The tour ended. I went home.

At home, my marriage felt a lot like my voice. Kerri and I were drifting apart. I wanted to fix the cracks before they became chasms. After the tour, we took a vacation. I was hoping it would be the quick marriage shot that would heal our relationship. But when we got away from the distractions of my band and her business, the brokenness felt insurmountable. In my marriage and in my voice. I was coming to realize that there were no shots to fix either. My only hope was that maybe I could keep them going long enough for God to perform a miracle.

Sales reports from the *Zombie* album came in. They weren't good. Less than half of what *Bloom* had sold. We were again called into the label to talk about our "options," which, with record labels, means a passive-aggressive one-way conversation often started by someone who has never been in the studio or been on tour for months on end. And in the music business, there's really only one option anyway: make a hit album with hit songs. In addition to my voice and marriage, I felt the weight of our careers. Just when I thought we had "bloomed," we were knocked down again.

TWENTY-TWO

"Underdog"

Growing up, we never had much money. We had less when my parents moved to Haiti, and even less than that when they moved back to the US for my sister's cancer treatments. After Kelly was released from full-time care at St. Jude's, my dad took a preaching gig back in Kentucky. His missionary career in Haiti had been cut short, but he did what he needed to do for my sister and her ongoing treatment. Every few months, Kelly was required to travel back to Memphis for testing. On one of those loops, my parents stopped in Nashville and requested some time for a "conversation." My dad seemed discontent. He looked around my place.

"You're doing really well."

I felt an underlying tension in the compliment.

He moved on to talk about Haiti, but I was stuck. Even though he hadn't said it, I thought maybe he needed some money. I was starting to have some financial success and had been meeting with financial advisers. I attempted to parlay this into some financial advice for my dad.

"Dad, have you planned at all for retirement?"

"What are you talking about?" he said, curtly.

"Retirement? Money? Do you have a plan?" I asked.

He pushed the rim of his glasses farther up the bridge of his nose, his large hand bearing visible signs of toil, then leaned forward as if to emphasize a point.

"Mark, I don't need money. Why in the world would I be worried about money?"

There was no irony in his question. When he said that I'd done well, he'd meant that I was making a kingdom impact. He was proud of that. His discontentment was not about money or lack thereof. His retirement plan, along with every other plan, was the Lord. Kelly was in remission and doing great. His discontentment was about not being able to serve in Haiti. He genuinely could not have cared less about money, and the idea of going into retirement was borderline offensive. He had come to talk about the mission field. He wanted back in the game. I was embarrassed and felt small for asking such a ridiculous question. On the contrary, my dad and his faith were larger than life. He was a rich, poor man.

After some self-examination about the *Zombie* record, I realized we went more alternative than anthemic partially because of my increasing discomfort with being the front man for a successful rock group. I didn't believe I was a good enough singer, or husband, or anything, to be given such a platform. I was happy being the opening act. There's no pressure. A headliner needed to bring something worth saying to the world. I lacked the faith for that. My way out was to make an artsy record. It's equally as ridiculous to shy away from the platform God's called you to out of false humility as it is to seek it out of pride. We are all called to be the headliners of our lives.

Audio Adrenaline had felt like the underdog from our beginnings at a tiny, rural college to now, when I feared I had ruined our careers and it was all coming to an end. There are two perspectives of being an underdog. The first is victimhood, which I dangerously slipped into after *Zombie*. The other is complete empowerment. When the world is stacked against you, and things are harder than you could ever imagine, there's no way to take it on in your own strength. But God is strongest in our weakness. It's the underdog that most needs God. And that combination makes us unstoppable. This is how our fans felt. They were blue-collar moms and dads trying to raise kids with an enemy opposed at every opportunity. They were students standing up for their faith on campuses that claimed prayer "offensive" and truth "hate speech." Life is hard. Faith doesn't make it easier. A hit record isn't born out of convenience. It's born from toil and pain and suffering and perseverance. Our fans understood this because it was their life too. We were all underdogs. Together, through good ol' rock and roll, it was time to call on our Father to tip the scales back in our favor.

HUME LAKE

At the end of the summer festival season, a friend set us up with cabins and a space to write our fifth album at Hume Lake Christian Camp in the mountains of central California. After *Zombie* and the festivals, we were tired. Uninspired. Defeated. We needed a reset. The camp sits on the meadowed western edge of an intimate alpine lake. The clear water is surrounded by ponderosa pines, and the view from the meadow to the east is of two small mountains softly descending to a shallow, V-shaped point. Between the V of evergreen trees is a view framed into the granite heart of the Sierra Nevada Mountains and the deep divide of Kings Canyon National Park. The camp was established in 1946, and the presence of angels rejoicing over souls redeemed in this high place hovers over the water. We felt the restorative work in our own souls as we were reminded how to be kids once again, dancing and singing before the Lord. It was suggested to us to write our next album in a famous studio at a five-star location. Sleeping in wooden bunks at a kids' camp in the still-wild mountains of California was a better fit.

We set up our instruments in a wooded mountain chapel and expectantly prayed through the timbre of drums and open chords. The first song to come was "Get Down," a tune about humbling oneself. This is one of the great truths about our faith, that when we are humble, purposefully choosing to "get down," it is God who will lift us up. And he lifts us higher than we can lift ourselves. People often misunderstood "Get Down" as a party song. Maybe it was. But if so, it was because of what God does. Not because of anything we can do ourselves.

Next came "Mighty Good Leader." Tyler was coming into his own. He dropped guitar riffs like breathing. His fingers did stuff his brain didn't even understand, and if he played something you liked, you had to stop him before he went on to the next brilliant riff. We looked through old hymnals for concepts. Looking forward is always exciting, but sometimes we need to look back for anchoring. Hymnals dig into the deep roots of our faith music. My cousin Mike came across an old hymn called "Mighty Good Leader." We liked the concept of that, and with our top-down writing method, we started putting together a story of someone needing to be rescued from a busted life and the triumphal hope of knowing *a mighty good leader is on his way.* This song went back to our proven formula of big lyrical concept plus monster guitar riff equaling a hit song. "Mighty Good Leader" became an even bigger song than "We're a Band." The whole song was crying out to God that we needed to be saved. We sang it with the conviction of sinners in need of rescue.

These were mountaintop songs. Huge anthems to be sung with the mighty gathered. We came down the mountain as men who'd experienced God. There were more songs to write, but the Hume sessions set the tone for the album. Hume sparked something within us. We felt like kids again, enjoying the gifts of music and friendship and sharing it with others. We tested the new songs at the remaining festivals with great success. Crowds went wild. For the first time in a long time, we were excited to record again. To finish the album, we booked Tejas studio on a farm belonging to Gary Chapman and Amy Grant. We gained back our confidence at Hume Lake, from the One who called the mountains into place.

"GOOD LIFE"

The Tejas studio was a couple of big rooms built at the end of a barn that looked over Gary and Amy's farm. The rooms were decorated with leather chairs, vintage rugs, and steer horns on the walls. Gary also had a huge collection of vintage guitars and amplifiers that we were welcome to use on the recordings. Tyler was in heaven. We'd be recording, and Gary would show up with ATVs and tell us to take a break to go muddin' on the farm. Then at night, we'd have bonfires with Gary and his celebrity friends and talk about music and the stars and our purpose in life. Gary's purpose was to make sure we felt welcome and squeezed as much out of life as we could.

Gary and Amy were both funny, warm, and incredibly gracious. Gary gave us the keys to everything they had and told us we could use the studio as long as we had fun doing it. Amy was one of my musical heroes, and it meant a lot to be recording on her property. This all showed on the album.

I wrote one song on the album for a friend going through a terrible time. Luis was a professional photographer living in Dallas who took pictures of our concerts whenever we came through town and spent time with us after the show. On our most recent stop, I barely recognized him. He had dyed his hair and lost an unhealthy amount of weight. He told me his wife had left him. I invited him to Nashville so my wife and I could spend some time loving on him. He told me the rest of the story.

He had spent months trying to save the marriage. The devastation on his life was complete. Now, he couldn't eat. He couldn't sleep. He was a shell of the man he used to be. He explained how his every breath was now a complete dependence on Jesus. There was a point where he didn't know how he could move forward. We were in tears. Then, he looked up and smiled.

"As hard as this is, I've never been as close to Jesus in my life."

His broken marriage was a conduit to the most intimacy he had ever experienced. Jesus held him through the darkest nights. Everything he once clung to was gone, except for Jesus.

"I have everything I need."

I was already kicking around the concept for a song called "Good Life." I wanted to know what it really meant. I had succeeded professionally, but didn't feel like I was living the "good life," or even knew what it was. After talking to Luis, the song came to me.

This is the good life.
I've lost everything.

Charlie Peacock, another musical hero of mine, helped us finish the song. He'd been writing and producing Amy's biggest pop songs. "Good Life" became one of my favorite songs we ever created. It wasn't a massive arena rock song, so we didn't play it in concerts often, but it still became a radio hit. It was an intimate, personal song, meant for a private moment between the listener and Jesus. As a songwriter, you never know how a song is going to connect. It's tempting to try to force a quiet song onstage, but sometimes it's best to just let a song be. As much as I loved "Good Life," I had to let it go onstage. I gave it to Jesus and asked him to use it in his own perfect way and in his time.

The biggest hit of the album was "Hands and Feet." I was watching the news in my living room when a story came on about a mudslide in Central America that left thousands either dead or homeless. Immediately I wrote out the lyrics: *"An image flashed across my TV screen."* The song became a hit on the radio, but more than that, I sensed it becoming a movement. We wrote the song "Underdog" about the hope that comes when you've *"been beat up, been broken down"* because there is *"nowhere but up when you're facedown."* This was our anthem. We wrote a few album tracks to round out the themes of the record and rerecorded "DC-10" as a throwback to our A-180 days, where the audio underdogs began, then came up with a fresh take for the cover song "Let My Love Open the Door."

Underdog was our first self-produced album. After making Jennifer Knapp's gold album, I had a lot of confidence in my producing capabilities. It was unusual at the time not to have a big-name producer on the album, but it felt right to us. The whole process brought us back to who we were capable of being, and our time at Gary and Amy's farm brought back our joy.

Underdog was a fresh start for us. The songs became iconic anthems that we played for the next eight years. With the album complete, it was time to remind our fans of who we were, and to bring the much-needed message to underdogs like us that God does his best work in our greatest weakness.

TWENTY-THREE

Billy Graham

The expectations for the Underdog tour weren't as big as for the Zombie tour. Since *Zombie*'s sales had dropped off, so had the excitement and touring support from our label. Even after a number of hit songs and a gold record, we still felt like underdogs at our record label. Labels chase momentum. We were on a downward trend, so our label hedged their bets. The Christian music genre was exploding (largely thanks to DC Talk, the Newsboys, and us), and like their secular counterparts, Christian music labels preoccupied themselves with the next big thing. This left marketing resources for tour support thin, including smaller budgets for radio promotion. The label placed one of their new bands on our tour as an opening act and seemed more interested in them than us. That band's career unfortunately didn't last long. It didn't matter. We knew what we had.

Our new songs felt like a sweet reunion with our fans. The secret sauce for an epic Audio Adrenaline live concert consisted of three things. The first was gut-level, rebellious anthems that showed we were unapologetic about our Christian faith. Second were massive guitar riffs, rooted in a vintage sound, ripping through arenas. And the third was something particularly unique to us. We were blue-collar rock stars. We were always ourselves onstage. We didn't get into costume before a show. Ben often had grease stains on his shirts from working on a car only moments before the show began. As a band, we were held together with duct tape. Our guitars were always great, but none of us were motivated to be the most polished band in the world, or even our industry. We were driven instead by passion, guts, and grit. This is what our fans identified with. They recognized the same in themselves.

The perfect storm for us was big lyrical concepts and musicality bridging the widest demographic. That's the universal language of rock and roll. It's a rallying voice. A way for a generation to identify with each other in a collective experience. The energy of a live concert is built on the exponential equation of strangers meeting and saying to each other, "You too?"

We wanted the Underdog tour to be a chance for kids to hear the message of the gospel. Youth groups came in buses as an opportunity for young believers to introduce faith to their friends in a language their friends could understand. Though I was growing in this area, I was still reluctant to become a real preacher. I felt I could never fill my father's shoes and wasn't worthy to. Later, I'd meet people who'd come to our shows and by the end of the concert made big life changes or started following Jesus for the first time. The truth is, we are all inadequate. That's the point of our faith. The lie is that because we are inadequate, we can't be used. It's exactly because we were not worthy that God showed up so powerfully at our concerts.

To talk myself out of the fear of my limitations before heading onstage, I reminded myself that God is good, he is big, and he is in control. Whatever was about to happen was in his hands, not mine. On that tour, God revealed to me that the platform I'd been praying for my whole life wasn't a stage for me to walk out on. It was a stage for God to perform a live work in me, the band, and the watching audience. Every night, in every circumstance, God showed up. Just completing a set semi-intact was for us a small miracle. Even that didn't matter. Nor did the lights or the opening band or the sound. No matter what, God showed up. *He* was the special effect that people came to see.

It took a while, but *Underdog* found its audience. Our fans carried us. They requested songs on the radio, and in spite of smaller radio promotion, radio discovered and played several singles from the album. First in light rotation. But as requests poured in, *Underdog* singles played on heavy rotation across the country. That album produced more radio hits than any of our other albums. Most of the bands the label promoted at that time never made it. *Underdog* went on to become one of the biggest albums of our careers. Thanks to our fans, we got our mojo back. We wouldn't lose it again.

BILLY

A highlight of our career was getting asked to play a concert for the Billy Graham crusade at the RCA Dome in Indianapolis. My wife and I had recently returned from a trip to Europe. I'd hoped an over-the-top romantic getaway would reignite our first flame of fire. We'd walked terraced vineyards above the Italian Mediterranean and dined in the intimate Moroccan courtyards of Marrakesh. We'd enjoyed the architecture and food, and appreciated our time together the way two good friends might. But there was no flame.

As Billy aged, the Graham Association hoped bands like Audio Adrenaline would help him connect with younger audiences. I'd never met Billy. This was a rare honor that made me nervous. To ease my anxiety, I brought my grandma. She had closely followed how God had used Billy throughout his ministry. She shared stories of his impact with me on the way to the dome, which only made me more nervous. We awaited Billy's arrival backstage to review the program and spend time in prayer. When he arrived, his presence could be felt more than seen. No matter where he stood, I felt like he was right next to me. It was beyond star power. He carried a spiritual mantle that far exceeded his six-foot, two-inch frame. For the rest of my life, I would meet celebrities and politicians, and only once experienced this again.

We played that night to more than fifty thousand people and Billy Graham preached the good news. Over the weekend, two hundred thousand people came to see him and hear that there is a hope beyond any of the circumstances they faced in life. We played "Big House" and a couple tracks from *Underdog*, including "Hands and Feet." While the band played the pre-chorus behind me, I asked the crowd if they would go anywhere Jesus called them. As the question filled the stadium, I wondered if I would do the same. A young man volunteering for security stood in front of me while I sang and smiled as we sang. His name was Bart Millard. I didn't know it then, but our paths would cross again. These were the types of ordinary miracles Billy preached about. He promised God could do even more in our lives if we'd just let him. I wanted more, and prayed for it. For my voice. For my marriage. I prayed for the miracle I needed. That weekend, more than ten thousand people made commitments to follow Jesus. Their lives would never be the same. Sadly, when I got home, neither would my marriage.

TWENTY-FOUR

I Know That Guy!

At its core, Audio Adrenaline was a little redneckish while on tour. We just brought our cars on blocks with us. Literally. On one of our tours, we towed a trailer full of tools and a broken-down Mini Cooper that Ben restored in the parking lots of arenas throughout the US. When he wasn't working on a car, he had something else planned for us daily. Motorized scooter races. Remote-control 4x4 trucks. Rockets. Archery contests. Remote-control airplanes having dogfights in the arena. Flat track go-cart races. Mountain-bike jumping contests. We were daily at Ben's creative mercy. Artistically, he equated his drumming to being a monkey on a stage, so his creative genius unveiled itself between lunch and showtime. We played a lot of shows bandaged.

Other bands caught wind that Audio Adrenaline was the funnest band to tour with. When a festival-style tour launched, including motocross jumping and a circus variety of audience attractions, we were a perfect fit. The tour was called Festival con Dios, and we'd be launching it with the Newsboys. A small rivalry had begun between us on an earlier tour when we opened for them. One of their sound guys had rigged our sound to be much softer than theirs. We'd be playing as hard as we could, and people in the back of the audience looked bored. There were complaints that we couldn't be heard.

Sound is measured and monitored with a dB meter, and dB volumes are carefully negotiated between bands. A band who plays louder is often the preferred band of the night. It's a sound trick that all touring acts know. When we took the complaints to the tour manager, he showed us a dB meter that read exactly as negotiated. It didn't make sense. A couple shows later, we found out why. The Newsboys's sound guy had rigged the dB meter. It was a good prank. Since then, the two bands were always trying to outdo each other, which added some extra energy to the con Dios tour.

Festival con Dios was the first traveling festival for Christian music. To pull off the festival environment, additional attractions had to be towed by the bands. We were responsible for the rock-climbing mountain, a massive forty-foot trailer shaped like a mountain lying on its back. When erected to its full height, it was a big hit and cornerstone for the con Dios experience. Our ball hitch was technically too small to tow the mountain, but the tour production manager told us it was fine and reminded us that contractually, towing it was our responsibility. So, at the end of every night, our bus driver attached the mountain-trailer to the bus, and when we felt it sway in a big wind or climbing a grade, we just prayed it would make it to the next destination.

POPS

Our bus driver at the time was named Pops. Though his age remained a mystery (we didn't ask and he didn't tell), the consensus was that he was in his late eighties. Pops regaled us with tales of driving Elvis and of his involvement with the Masonic lodge, which meant he could've been older. We loved Pops. He was a cranky-yet-lovable grandpa for everybody on tour. The lives of touring musicians are in the hands of their bus drivers. They are supposed to be sleeping during the day so they can drive through the night. We had no idea what Pops did during the day. He just disappeared, then returned when it was time to drive to the next venue.

We were pretty certain this would be Pops's last tour, either because he'd retire or we'd all die in a fiery crash. This wasn't only because of his age or the bottles of heart pills piled around the driver seat. He also stopped noticing things. Like the lanes on a freeway. I'd be asleep in my bunk and wake to the violent sound of bus tires rolling over rumble strips on the far edge of freeway lanes, right before oncoming traffic or a cliff. He was always as surprised by them as I was. We finally resorted to one person staying up with him all night just to make sure he stayed awake. Whosever turn it was would pass the night trying to dislodge secrets about the Masonic lodge and the Knights Templar. Pops never divulged.

On our way home from a show in Colorado, we stopped for gas, and when I went to stock up on Mountain Dew, I noticed something disconcerting.

"Pops, where's the rock mountain?"

"What mountain?"

"The one we are supposed to be towing."

He slowly leaned his head around the gas pump to get a view of the back of the bus.

"Well," he said, "I guess it's gone."

He leaned back and looked at a gas stain on the ground. He had the distinct look of figurin' somethin'.

"Musta come off in the middle of the night."

Pops called the production manager and told him it was his job to retrieve the mountain. They found it six hours back, somewhere in Kansas, in the grassy middle of the freeway.

Shortly after, Pops retired.

CLASS PRESIDENT

In the summer between festivals, we played amusement parks and state fairs. We were paid well as a headlining band, but the real perk was getting an official park escort who took us to the front of the line of any ride we wanted to enjoy. Even better, our friends in other bands, like the O. C. Supertones or Third Day, would show up to the parks as well, and we'd enjoy the rock and roll perks together. In those moments, we were more kids than band members. Other bands relaxed in sophisticated cities or exotic tropical islands. We headed to Silver Dollar City and Frontier World and every Six Flags we could find.

Summer festivals are regional, so between the Midwest and the West or the East and the South, we would plan routes based on what roller coasters we wanted to ride or who had the best pig races or fried-dough elephant ears. Every Six Flags amusement park had an iconic wooden roller coaster. I loved them. The clacking of the wheels on the slow tow up, up, far above the trees and the world, to the unknown precipice, and the fast rumble coming down. My favorite was the Beast at Kings Island in Cincinnati. That was my first roller coaster. I remember feeling completely out of control as the coaster twisted and turned over a crisscrossed scaffolding of stained lumber that felt like it might crumble at any moment. Past the fear and lack of control were complete happiness and freedom. Every band, as they hit a certain level of success, enjoys some indulgences that come with it. Mine was to ride every iconic wooden roller coaster in the country.

We booked a show at Six Flags St. Louis. It was a classic Shakespearean outdoor amphitheater, with the stage at the lowest point. Bleacher benches rose in half circles above the stage that from the band's vantage point looked like a solid wall of people. Summer heat hung heavy. It could grab hold and squeeze the energy out of a crowd several thousand strong. I worked overtime to keep them engaged. We launched into "Big House," and I used the bleachers to walk midway into the audience. There I danced and gave high fives and signaled that we were all in this together. The crowd went wild.

Standing on the bleachers I was taller than the audience, able to see over the crowd that stood to about my waist. Where I stopped, a guy who appeared my age stood right next to me. He looked different from the rest of the crowd, with bold arm tattoos and a sleeveless cut-off shirt. He yelled my name. He looked like a tan, greasy version of Larry the Cable Guy. The girl he was with was not amused. I kept singing, but he wouldn't stop. I could hear him yelling back to her, "I know this guy!"

I kept singing.

"Mark!"

During a concert, I can immediately tell who is a fan of our music and who is there because they were invited by someone else. This guy looked like he had been dragged kicking and screaming. Possibly from jail.

"Mark! Mark!"

He pulled at my pant leg so hard I thought I might fall over. I tried to walk away, but he had a firm grip. I looked for security.

"Mark! Mark!"

I finally took a good look at him.

"Garth?!"

He smiled. Standing in front of me was my high school class president. He looked much older than when he'd passed out cigarettes in exchange for votes. I had stopped singing. The song fell apart.

The mic was on. Instead of listening to "Big House," the audience was now listening to me ask incredulously, "What are you doing here?"

"I'm a Christian now! We're here rocking out, doing the Jesus thing. What have you been up to?"

"I'm singing. This is my band. What have you been up to?"

"Well . . . I was giving tattoos to . . . um . . . dancers for a while. Then I got married again. Then divorced again."

Pointing with his thumb to the girl next to him, "This here's my new wife. She's the best one."

I realized that Garth was still unfiltered and that I probably shouldn't talk to him with a mic on. I invited him backstage after the show, where I got the rest of his story. He'd lived fast and hard after high school, in and out of relationships, finally hitting bottom, where he found Jesus waiting for him. He became a Christian and was driving trucks but was looking for a new job.

"That's great! We need a new bus driver."

TWENTY-FIVE

Summer Festivals

It was amazing to me that God put Garth back in my life after all those years. The constant of rock and roll is the highway, with miles upon miles between shows. Garth sat behind the wheel, and I sat up front beside him. We'd watch the sun dip below mountains or deserts or plains and wait for the stars. They appeared as faint as childhood memories, becoming clearer and brighter as we shared our stories. Constellations appeared in the oversized windows. For hours, there was nothing but me and Garth and the stars above. Together we sailed the vast, empty lands of our northern hemisphere.

Our great American economy is quietly carried on the backs of trucks. Our food and supplies and clothing and pretty much everything else is hauled from farms and distribution centers to our stores and doorsteps. For this economy to run smoothly, drivers follow an unstated code of conduct, which Garth followed faithfully. Though a Christian, Garth still had rough edges, and his deeply held truck driver's etiquette kept them sharp.

One primary rule of driving etiquette is that once gas tanks are refilled at the fuel pump, move the truck before taking care of any other business at the truck stop, such as eating, shopping, emails, laundry, or showers. All drivers are on a tight schedule, so remaining parked under the canopy when not refueling chokes the whole system and frustrates other drivers. It can even be the last straw that throws them off schedule, costing them money from their own pockets. All this to say, it can make drivers like Garth mad. Very mad. I had to talk him down on several occasions when the fuel pumps were blocked. Some drivers would get a middle finger from Garth, but I had a feeling that if I hadn't been there, they would have gotten much worse.

CREATION FESTIVAL

In the 1990s, the biggest gig a Christian band could have was headlining a major summer festival. There were festivals in every region of the country. Ichthus in Kentucky. Alive in Ohio. Jesus Northwest. Creation West. Cornerstone in Illinois. SonFest. Creation Fest. Celebration Fest. TOMfest. Blue Door. Purple Door. Spirit West Coast. And more. The granddaddy of them all was Creation Festival on Agape Farm in Mount Union, Pennsylvania. It was four days of wall-to-wall music on multiple stages.

Throughout the day, the farm was organized like a high school at lunchtime, sliced into the demographics of genre music. There was ska, punk, rock, alternative, rap, folk, contemporary, worship, and even some yet to be categorized. People who loved a certain genre of music found their corner of the farm with their stage and their musicians and held forth in their musical denominations. Up to forty artists played daily. Energy built. As the sun lowered, a great pilgrimage migrated to the main stage, where the headlining band would attempt to unite the tribes and lead them as one body into the presence of God. There were only a few bands at the time who could headline a festival. Audio Adrenaline was one of them.

The job of the headliner was to perform the waning magic of rock and roll and unite the tribes in an age of genre music and its resulting denominational divisions. If the tribes could unite, the power would be transcendent. This required connecting with every single person in the audience. It was a musical tight rope. We had to rock hard enough to not bore the kid who came to hear the latest Tooth & Nail punk band, but not so hard as to offend the parents who were there to hear their favorite contemporary Christian artist. Beyond that, I had to have something worth saying. It had to be a truth that stood on its own, required no apology, harnessed the power of the gathered, reminded them who they were and who they were meant to be, and released the power back to them to fortify their self-doubts and ignite within them that God-flame burning in their souls. There is only one truth that does that: Jesus.

Stepping onto the main stage at Creation Festival was a high-stakes game based on sheer numbers alone. We played to a crowd of eighty thousand. The scale was massive. Only a handful of stadiums in the US could hold a crowd that large and spread over a farm. The stage sat at the bottom of a small valley, with gentle green hills rising up several football fields wide. It was a natural amphitheater. The last of the sun lit the audience with a golden spotlight. Faces could be defined maybe twenty rows back. They watched with anticipation, wondering if we had the goods they came looking for. Beyond that, faces blurred, then bodies, until it was all waves of color and motion, and the crowd appeared as a sea swelling and surging to the cool evening winds descending into the valley. The best speakers in the country went onstage before us. The crowds watched them on TV screens as large as buildings. To those in the back, the stage and its light show appeared only as a small spark. A single candle in a large room. The speaker hyped the crowd, then called our name. It was time to light the fire.

Every band dreams of playing to stadium-sized crowds. We'd played stadiums before, but it was to warm up the audience for national pastors like Billy Graham. At the festivals, other bands were warming up the audience . . . for us! Anticipation built all day, and it was the most pressure I ever felt onstage. To look over an inconceivable assembling of God's people ready to lift up his name was both the most terrifying and the greatest feeling I've ever experienced as a front man. The crowd filling the valley waited for me. For my count. For my cue.

All live shows are fragile. There's a long list of things that can go wrong at any moment, and often do. Tuning issues. Monitors. Lighting cues. Pyro misfires. Sound issues. Feedback. A dead crowd. The crowd is too far away. The security is too uptight. We learned these by experience. A band's best defense is to build an excellent crew. We did this and things mostly went right, most of the time. But every set has something going against it. Every seasoned band knows this. You only hope you find it before showtime. For this festival, I was nervous. Maybe terrified. That was the "something" that could destroy the set. I felt a heavy burden. How was I going to inspire and ignite eighty thousand people when my flame was barely flickering?

If you're in this business long enough, there will be nights when you just don't have it. Or you're just not sure. That night, I wasn't sure. My mind drifted between my marriage and my voice. Meanwhile, the sound of the crowd had become deafening. The time for second-guessing had passed. I had to trust that the songs we'd written would do what they were meant to do. I had to trust the guys I stood next to night after night and the miles and rehearsals and the years of honing our craft. I had to trust that our fans were out there and that they would do what they always did. Ben started on the drums. Frenzy built. Then came the guitar and bass. I said a quiet prayer, leaned into the mic, and brought the greatest conviction I had to the opening lyric. It was time for liftoff.

There was a two-story wall of speakers on either side of the stage. It was the biggest sound setup I'd ever seen. Still, I couldn't hear anything but the crowd. It sounded like the heavens opened and brought the thunder that created the world. First, our fans showed up. They willed the band to be bigger than we were. The calm ocean of people turned to a tempestuous sea. From stage, eighty thousand people looked like a single body, moving together as one, dancing and jumping, repenting and rejoicing. Then God showed up, bringing the greatest special effect for any live performance: changed lives, mine included. There was no limit to how big the night would get. We kicked the set into overdrive and sent the festival into the stratosphere. Those were the shows we still talk about. If you were there, *you were there.*

What we had going for us was that our songs were built for moments like this. Festivals were made for spectacle. Audio Adrenaline specialized in spectacle. Every year we tried to outdo ourselves. We hung Ben's Mini Coopers onstage and drove them through crowds. We hired our own fireman to light troughs of fire onstage. We had the biggest pyrotechnics, the biggest lights, the biggest sound. From the beginning, we built our band for the largest platforms God would give us. Everything from our inspiration to the songs we wrote were built for massive crowds. The songs were anthem songs, written to the widest possible audience. Our biggest songs were simple in the best way. They were loud and raucous and didn't get lost in translation traveling from the stage to the back of the valley. Our lyrics didn't offer debate or insight into subtle nuances of the Christian faith. Instead, songs were penned to the broadest faith convictions: that Jesus is real, that he loves us and would do anything for us to draw near to him, including dying on a cross. We brought this message to youth groups on our tours, teaching them our songs and the power behind them. In the long days of summer, they returned the favor. Youth groups came in loaded buses to festivals, ready to add their voices to the Audio Adrenaline choir.

Beyond the music and the hype, festivals contained the best of summer. People traveled great distances and camped in farms and meadows. It was a summer reunion for friends and families. There were barbecues and games and campfires where strangers would gather to worship together. It was a fun time for bands and fans to hang out. One of our traditions was to create silly festival T-shirts. We played a silly song called "If You're Happy and You Know It, Bang Your Head." We turned that song into a T-shirt and gave high fives to any fans we saw walking around with it on.

On nights we didn't play, I climbed the gentle hills to sit under canopies of hardwoods. I looked over the valley with wonder. Strangers and friends circled around campfires. I heard the singing of hundreds of worship songs all at once. Disparate voices blended into one and echoed in the valley. Those were God's people, gathered to celebrate his music. It was a glimpse of heaven. I imagined singing God's praises for ten thousand years and how that wouldn't be enough. At those festivals, I was blessed to play a small role in some of the best rock and roll moments of Christian music history. You can't recapture a moment passed. But that was a time and place I will never forget. If you were there, it's likely that you won't either.

TWENTY-SIX

"Lift"

I sat upright in the examination chair. The doctor held down my tongue. It tasted like the disappointment of a dry wooden stick after finishing an ice cream bar. He numbed the back of my throat and nose and started the procedure. The steel of the scope was cold. I felt it penetrate through my nostril and past the back of my tongue, into the cavity in the back of my throat. It was difficult to breathe. I couldn't swallow. The doctor scoped inside of me. He was considered among the best in the country, working at Vanderbilt Voice Center in Nashville with the biggest singers in the world. He hoped he would find a vocal node, an abnormal growth on my vocal cords. This would lead to surgery, time away from the band, and a decent chance to continue singing. That was the best case. I hoped he wouldn't probe too deep. He might also find the spot where I stored my fear of being found out as the fraud I felt I was. He removed the scope. No nodes. We'd have to discuss worse cases.

There were tricks I developed to get through our live performances. I could rely more on Tyler. I could get the crowd hyped and turn the mic over to him. I could take steroid shots. But in the studio there were no tricks. I talked to an engineer about tuning my voice. This was now standard studio practice. The engineer took whatever pitch a singer produced, then electronically tweaked it to the note it was supposed to be. He tried with my voice. Whatever was going on with my vocals was producing three different pitches without any control. Like the doctor, there was nothing the engineer could do.

My voice was now regularly cutting out onstage and becoming a topic of discussion in the industry. The band noticed, but we didn't talk about it. Finally, after years of keeping it all inside, I decided to confide in Will. He and I had come a long way together since starting this band, and he deserved to know. When I told him my fears about my voice, he was upset that this was happening to me. He didn't want me to carry this burden alone, so he prayed with me and promised to support me in any way I needed. I knew he would and was comforted by his friendship. We'd fought and worked and overcome the odds to become one of the biggest rock bands in Christian music history. Audio Adrenaline was poised to go even bigger. Since I was a kid, I'd prayed for the largest platform possible, and so far, God had delivered. We headlined every major tour and festival, and our overseas audience was growing. The platform was within our grasp. I decided to manage the decline of my voice through steroid shots. I didn't like the feeling of dependency, but I hoped it could buy time while I figured something else out. I got a shot and prepared for our next album.

The industry was again changing with the emergence of worship music written exclusively to and for the church. The change seemed subtle at the time but turned out to be seismic. It was the beginning of the end of Christian rock. Bands like Delirious? and Sonicflood blended rock and roll sensibilities with hymnlike lyrics. Christian rock, though attempting to glorify God with music and lyrics, was still peer-to-peer focused. It's horizontal music. The purpose of Christian rock was uniting believers into a larger shared experience that created a cultural covering, allowing you to be a Christian and still uniquely express yourself through personal musical preferences. The worship revolution changed that equation. Worship music is the church's modern-day hymns. It blends popular music of the day with words meant to orient our hearts vertically. Worship music is Coldplay meets "How Great Thou Art," a powerful combination.

Accusations arose that Christian rock was chasing money. The industry had grown massively. Millions of albums sold, and lots of people were making money. It's true. Money complicates things in the church, and it can be difficult to draw lines between ministry and paid occupations. Mixing money and religion always elicits strong opinions.

However, the biggest money was shifting to worship music, and there was significant industry pressure for artists to create worship albums. Selling Christian rock albums could be lucrative for the labels and publishers, but creating hit worship songs was a gold mine. Worship music took the industry to higher heights, both in album sales and in the intellectual property of songs sung on Sunday morning. Traditional hymns are public domain, with copyrights long expired. Modern worship songs, on the other hand, are copyrighted and protected. Every time you sing a song in church, somebody gets paid. Other rock bands were moving in that direction. We'd started as a college worship band and felt deeply connected to the music of the church. We felt the pressure as well, but for us, a modern worship album didn't feel like a good fit, especially with the troubles I was having with my voice. However, we did love the idea of creating a more vertically focused rock and roll album, and based on that concept, decided to call our sixth Audio Adrenaline album *Lift*. Something beautiful was happening in Christian youth culture: they desired more connection to God, and we were amped to help move our listeners in that direction.

Thematically, the album follows the arc of our relationship with God from beginning to end. It opens with three big encounter songs declaring our awe and stating our devotion: "You Still Amaze Me," "I'm Alive," and "Beautiful." The album then explores the depths of God's forgiveness with "Ocean Floor," and our response to it with "Rejoice." "Speak to Me" is about our need to hear from God, while "Glory" is about our inability to describe him when we do. "Summertime" describes the pure joy of heaven. "This Is Everything" is a love song written to Jesus, and "Lift" expresses the confidence of why that love is so well placed. At the end of our time here on earth, we will get to see God face-to-face, so "Tremble" is about that moment of realizing just how big God is—his power, his holiness, his glory, and his grace—and how small we are in comparison. One song at the end of the album is outside of this theme. It is called "Lonely Man," and instead of exploring the perfectness of God, it conveys the mess we make of our lives. Specifically, mine.

After the success of *Underdog* and other bands we produced, we decided to again produce our own record. With *Lift*, we also wanted to control the studio experience, so we purchased an old house on Main Street in Franklin, Tennessee, and renovated it into a studio. It was a historic two-story cottage with a stacked-stone face, covered front porch, and period details throughout. The interior reflected the same charm, complete with old-house smells and creaking hardwood floors. We designed the studio around the structural charm, with drums in the dining room and guitars in the den. There was a stone fireplace in the sitting room, where we placed the control mixer and furnished the rest of the room with worn leather couches and romantic lighting. It felt like a second home.

It quickly became clear that we'd have to find a different approach for our vocals. My voice couldn't hold out in some of the vocal ranges the songs required. One of my favorite bands of all time is the Eagles. They essentially had two lead singers with two very different voices, and their best work featured both. I asked Tyler to take over the lead vocals on a number of tracks. He stepped up. There was a purity and youthfulness to his voice that provided a whole different window into a lyric. When my broken voice was placed next to Tyler's perfectly restored voice, something magical happened. Our voices sounded like the gospel.

Even with Tyler doing much of the vocal heavy lifting, I still struggled. It took much longer for me to lay down my vocal tracks, and sometimes I could never get it to sound right. I tried to keep up the positive energy needed to make it through an album. Records are permanent. Bands work on a single track sometimes for days to ensure its sonic perfection before release. But none of my tracks would be perfect. I ran out of positive energy and fell into a deep depression. When I fell, it was Will who held me up.

Will stepped in when I most needed him to produce that record. It was a hard job. He had to produce his best friend, who was losing his voice. He had to confront what no one wanted to talk about, that our future was uncertain. In the midst of that, he had to get the best out of everybody to cover my weakness. Will told me something remarkable in the *Lift* sessions that I'll never forget. He said that people didn't want perfection. They wanted us to be real. Onstage. On our albums. My voice was real. People would respond to it. Will found a way to keep everyone's spirits high in an uncertain time and to produce an artistic breakthrough album for Audio Adrenaline, with two distinct voices. One busted. One beautiful. Both calling vertically to God.

"LONELY MAN"

The record was nearly complete when I heard Tyler playing a new riff. It had a heavy, crunchy sound in the lower register that repeated quickly to build upon itself. The riff never resolved or backed down. Instead of a happy, sonic completion, it launched back into itself. The result was the feeling of piling on and not letting up. I recognized it immediately. It was the voice of desperation. The guitar notes felt angry and exhausted, like they were trying to find a way out of a maze. I suffered the riff from a dark place beyond the doctor's scope. That's also where I found the lyrics.

For the first time in my life, I recognized that I was lonely. Nobody knew what I was going through with my voice and marriage. I couldn't fix it, and there wasn't anybody I could talk to. I felt completely trapped by our success. Our crew had grown, and between them and the band, there were a dozen families depending on my voice. Other members of the crew could come and go. We'd already had different guitar players and drummers. But the one instrument in a band that can't be replaced or swapped out is the lead singer's voice. More than anything, a clear voice defines a band. I couldn't take time off. I couldn't quit. There was nowhere I could go.

At that time, I felt like the Christian music industry demanded from its leaders an image of perfection. Even if it was false. There wasn't space for transparency or failure or forgiveness. There was only judgment and disgrace, along with a quick, rumor-filled replacement for any Christian celebrity who publicly struggled. There was a long line of talent waiting to break in. They had the perfect Christian hair and style and sound and knew the appearance game and were willing to play it in exchange for a song on the radio and the money it brought. I'd stepped out in faith to pursue this platform, and now that it was there, I felt abandoned by God. Helpless with my voice. Hopeless in my marriage.

Neither my wife nor I was equipped to handle the challenges of marriage. Publicly, we put on a good performance. I preached hope onstage, but in my personal life, things were falling apart. I knew talking about it would end my career. Since we lived on the road, we didn't have a home church or pastor. I bottled it all up. I stepped onstage every night as a lonely man, pretending I wasn't. That was the song.

"Lonely Man" began with Tyler's riff, building to the point of explosion, then detonating with pounding drums and bass. The tracks went down quickly. I wanted the song to sound live on the tape, to capture the energy behind it. The band accomplished that amazingly. All that was left was vocals.

In addition to losing control of my vocal register, my range was also shrinking. I couldn't consistently hit the notes required in the song. I'd hit it on one part of the song, and in the next my vocals would slip or disappear entirely. I tried multiple takes and continually landed on the hopeless side of hope. I'd get close enough to think the next cut was the one, only to find that it wasn't. This continued for hours. The rest of the band watched as I struggled to do something that had previously come like breathing. Looks were given, but no one said a word. I was embarrassed. Frustrated. Ashamed. I sent the guys home. They had families waiting for them. I stayed to finish the vocal alone. Going home would be worse.

After everyone left, I wrote lyrics and experimented with arrangements I thought I'd be able to sing. The studio was dark except for a single light near the mixing board, where I could cue the song over and over again. The lyrics were a cathartic spotlight into my life. They opened with great swagger: *"I got some game and I got some style."* Then, as a defense against the pressures of performance, *"My secret's safe, can't read my mind."* Next came the ecclesiastical futility I was experiencing with my stage life, along with my nihilistic response: *"It all comes down so I break it down."* By the end of the song, I'm begging for someone to *"take some time / you can see inside."* But warning, *"You'll never know me 'cause I've always lied."* At the end of it all, the chorus repeats over the angry guitar riff, *"I am a lonely man."*

I punched the track to record the chorus. I tried singing it but couldn't hit the notes. I tried again. And again. Anger built. I yelled it. The tracks were playing through headphones, so all that could be heard in the studio was my broken voice screaming *"I am a lonely man"* over and over and over. All the emotion was there, but not all the vocals came out. I couldn't even voice my anger. I started crying. I couldn't stop. I cried into the darkness. And into the emptiness. Until I felt nothing at all. I erased most of what I recorded that night, but I did leave with the knowledge of just how lonely I was. I changed the lyrics so nobody would know the song was about me. I turned off the light and walked out into the darkness.

I was able to record "Lonely Man" in the following days. With it, we finished Audio Adrenaline's sixth studio album, *Lift.* I was as proud of that album as any other we recorded. It represented the best of who we were at the time. That's all you can ask of art. That's all it needs to be. *Lift* also represented the changing nature of Audio Adrenaline. Out of necessity, it distributed the vocal burden, and we discovered a way to make our songs work between Tyler's voice and mine. The album showcased Tyler coming into his own as a guitarist, songwriter, and singer. He was the whole package. The songs on *Lift* wove through the heart of Will. Without him that album would never have happened. He was the leader of that album, and the best of what *Lift* became could be traced back to him. There was something on that record for everybody. For me, they were songs of desperation. I needed God to show up on the record. He did. It was well received by critics, and our fans loved it. It sold as well as any other album. Plus, the album contained a surprise for us that we hadn't seen since "Big House": a massive hit.

TWENTY-SEVEN

"Ocean Floor"

At some point you have to decide that either everything you sell from stage is a hoax or a truth so big you can't fully understand it. I sang about community but didn't feel like I was in one. I sang about intimacy with God but felt abandoned. I grew lonely and depressed. Every night I sang songs to pull people from their struggles, yet my struggles grew. I was running out of ways to hide my vocal issues onstage and felt an impending doom. At home I felt another kind of doom. I preached answers to others from stage with the full conviction that it was the truth. For them. Not for me. I didn't believe God wanted to do in me what I saw him doing in others. I wasn't worthy of that.

At the peak of my doubt, long before we'd even considered recording the album *Lift*, Tyler had shown me a new song he was working on. Tyler and I often roomed together on tour, and we were alone in a hotel when he strummed the chords and sang through the chorus. The moment he started singing, I felt a presence in the room. It doesn't happen often, but sometimes the birth of a song makes the ground you stand on holy. The melody is carried by the angels, and the song opens a secret door into heaven. An artist's job is to humbly step through the door and write down what they see and feel and hear, then translate it through music so the rest of the world might know it too. At that point, there wasn't much more than a chorus, a guitar riff, and a title. That song became "Ocean Floor" on our *Lift* album. The concept was deeply personal. I couldn't know it at the time, but God would use the two most devastating issues of my life—my voice and my marriage—to help create the most enduring song of our career.

I knew immediately "Ocean Floor" was a big song. It was rooted in a guitar riff, which was our classic formula. The riff itself was haunting and melodic. It felt weightless, like someone swimming in the deep expanse of the sea. Tyler already had the overall concept. The lyrics were about the power of God's overwhelming grace. This showed up in the imagery of the chorus, *"Your sins are forgotten. / They're on the bottom of the ocean floor."*

Once we identified the song's spiritual core, we layered it with the idea of a life going from brokenness to beauty. This is the arc of grace. The opening line, *"The mistakes I've made / that caused pain,"* gripped people immediately. We've all been there. We all have regrets that sit just below the surface. Those regrets are rooted in our sinfulness, and the verses just listed them out in acknowledging our universal struggles. Selfishness. Pride. Misdeeds. Greed. *"All the things that haunt me now."* This resonated with me because it felt like someone had examined my heart and listed what they found. I needed the message of this song more than anybody.

The biggest struggle with "Ocean Floor" was writing it in a way that I could actually sing it. This proved to be troublesome. The recording session was a disaster. I heard the melody of the chorus in my head but couldn't sing it. I was embarrassed and almost killed the song because there was no way I could sing it live. Will loved the song and encouraged me to keep trying ways to pull it off. I skipped the chorus and started working on the verses. After a few hours I got a beautiful, broken take on the verse. As exciting as that was, the song still hung in the balance because I'd taken it as far as I could and didn't know where to go from there. Out of desperation, we decided to have Tyler sing the chorus. After the first time listening to my voice next to Tyler's, we realized what a special combination that was.

The verses of the song were meant to be broken. My voice provided the texture needed to illuminate the struggle and brokenness of life. However, the chorus needed to reflect the miracle of redemption. Tyler's vocals soared with angelic qualities of rebirth and were the answer to my brokenness. The effect was imperfection alongside perfection. Each needed the other for the full power of the song to be made complete.

A MIGHTY, MIGHTY WAVE

"Ocean Floor" connected with people live for the same reasons it worked in the studio. The verses were sung in complete brokenness, and the brokenness was real. I was in an ongoing struggle with God. I couldn't do it anymore. I needed God to cover my shortcomings as a husband, as a leader, and as a singer losing his voice. By then, I'd learned how to put on a good show and get a crowd hyped. I could just mail it in if I wanted to. But when "Ocean Floor" came up on the set list, I reached into my deepest, darkest secrets, where everything I was hiding from the band, from myself, and from God resided. It was a moment when nothing else mattered. Not the band. Not the audience. It was a moment between me and God. The stage was my confession box, and every night that song slid back the window. I would cry singing that song. Other bands and singers would comment on how well I'd "sold" the emotions of "Ocean Floor." The truth was, I wasn't selling anything. It was believable because those lyrics meant everything to me. And because they meant everything to me, they meant everything to others too.

The most important thing a band can do for their fans is be honest with their music and transparent with their performance. In exchange for being all in with their songs, their fans will go all in as well. This is what creates the moments when the music becomes something bigger. God-breathed music is a doorway to our healing. When I experienced an authentic moment of confession onstage, it gave the audience permission to do the same. Their lives felt like the verses. They needed God to show up as much as I did. When we sang it together, honest in our brokenness, he did.

There was a weightiness to the song that was hard to understand. It was the most real thing we'd produced, and the depth of its rawness resonated in ways that none of our other songs did. When we started "Ocean Floor," the audience stopped whatever they were doing. There's an unexplainable reverence in collective confession, when we acknowledge our vulnerabilities and recognize our need for grace. It's a holy moment. I disconnected from everything and went completely vertical. The rest of the show was about me and the audience going somewhere together. "Ocean Floor" broke that pattern. You were welcome to join me, but I was going somewhere different with that song. I was going to spend time with my Father.

God was felt the moment Tyler launched into the chorus. Tyler's melody soared in purity and perfection and was victory over defeat that felt like flying. God's truth washed over me and the audience like *"a mighty, mighty wave."* It was the truth I needed: *"Your sins are erased / and they are no more. / They're out on the ocean floor."*

Every night I felt like Tyler sang that lyric to me. I felt freedom and forgiveness and knew it was real. It was happening in me. But without the broken verses, the chorus would never be as glorious.

Will was right about our fans wanting us to be real on the *Lift* record. "Ocean Floor" worked musically because we were forced into having two different voices on the song. The audible juxtaposition of brokenness and beauty was the secret sauce. My voice needed to be broken to make that song work, and for a moment, my busted voice made us more successful. "Ocean Floor" became a massive radio hit on multiple formats. It was our only other song ever to be up for Song of the Year and propelled *Lift* to become another hit album for Audio Adrenaline. Impressively, this happened when Napster and other free music services consumed the industry. Record sales for the entire industry were going down. In spite of that, *Lift* was going up.

It wasn't lost on me that in my most broken moment we produced what was arguably the best song of our career. "Ocean Floor" won some awards and gave me hope when I most needed it. It was a vehicle where my broken voice worked and gave us a path to keep going with this idea of me and Tyler sharing vocal moments on stage. I felt that "Ocean Floor" was our most complete song. We were seasoned, and everybody contributed at their highest level. There weren't any tricks. Just great songwriting and production, guitars and musicianship, and an honest vocal. We had something important to say and said it in a way that still endures. At the peak of our career, "Ocean Floor" impacted more people than I could have ever imagined. That was the platform I'd prayed for. It took my being broken to achieve it. The song was critically acclaimed and consumer loved. It's now considered a classic, as relevant today as when it was first recorded. That doesn't happen often.

If you're lucky as a band, lightning might strike once, but "Ocean Floor" was our second bolt. With "Big House," our music was youthful, full of optimism and hope. It was a song about the beginning of our faith, when everything is new and exciting. It was forward-looking, heaven-looking, simple, and even a little naive. We were a young band with the whole world in front of us. "Big House" was a party, a song for the mountaintop. "Ocean Floor" was a matured bookend. It looked backward, after life has crumbled and we are dealing with our trials and the consequences of our sin. It was marked with age and struggle. "Ocean Floor" was a song about the hope that always awaits us, even when we feel like the party is over. It was a redemption song for the valleys of life. For Audio Adrenaline. For our audience. For me. It rebirthed our music.

This time around, I knew that music alone wouldn't be enough.

TWENTY-EIGHT

Breakfast with Bono

We didn't do a Lift tour. We instead headlined the second annual Festival con Dios. DC Talk had broken up. We'd seen it coming. What had made them a supergroup was having three very different, yet world-class vocal talents. Ultimately those talents wanted to pursue different musical directions. As a result, TobyMac was now opening for us as a new solo artist. He didn't miss a beat, and with his new musical focus, his show was tight and excellent. He wouldn't be an opening act for long.

Audio Adrenaline was now considered to be living legends in Christian rock, which meant that basically, even though I was only in my late thirties, we were considered the old guys who still rocked pretty hard. One of the roles we felt was important was to mentor and encourage younger artists. Festival con Dios provided a good opportunity for that. A couple of up-and-coming artists opened up the festival. Jeremy Camp had one of the singularly most powerful voices I'd heard. I knew right away he had something special to offer and would enjoy a long career in the industry. It's been a joy to watch that happen. MercyMe made their national touring debut at Festival con Dios as well. I'd known MercyMe for years and tried to get them signed a few times. They reminded me of us when we were in college, a little goofy but with potential. Now, everyone was talking about them and their new song.

Months earlier, our former road manager Scott Brickell, who was now our manager with a new company called Brickhouse Entertainment, had asked me to listen to a demo by the new band MercyMe. The song was called "I Can

Only Imagine." In his office, I sat on the floor and listened on headphones and cried like a baby. It was transcendent, vertical, breathtaking. Amy Grant had already placed a hold on it, requesting to put it on her next album. Later, at a party at Brickell's house, Bart Millard, the lead singer of MercyMe, asked me if they should keep the song for themselves. Although I love Amy Grant, I told Bart that he would be crazy to give that song away. Amy agreed. This wasn't just a career song for Bart and MercyMe. This was a song that would change the industry.

As a headlining band, Audio Adrenaline had some say in who would open for us on tour. We made sure MercyMe was on the bill. It was amazing to stand backstage while they played "I Can Only Imagine." That song held a psalmist's power. You could almost watch the Holy Spirit reach from the speakers and into the audience and deliver whatever healing their hearts needed. No other song in Christian music history has provided as much hope as that one.

"Hands and Feet" from *Underdog* was becoming a fan favorite for our live shows. The song tapped into my missionary experience with my dad and included a strong call to action. Before playing the song, I asked the audience to raise their hands if they were willing to be the hands and feet of Jesus, to follow him anywhere in the world. Every night, thousands of people raised their hands. It was a highlight of the night and a reminder that God could use me in the midst of my struggles.

My voice was worse than ever on that tour, and Tyler was already carrying more than his fair share of the vocals and couldn't do any more, so we hired an additional guitar player who could help with the singing. My life revolved around extra singers and steroids and wondering how much longer I could last. By this point, my marriage also felt as doomed as my voice. I again fell into depression. After listening to amazing vocalists perform all night, I had to come out and close the show.

Audio Adrenaline was built for soaring anthems. I could no longer deliver that. Onstage I screeched and scratched and dropped out and embarrassed myself nightly in front of massive audiences. Backstage, I listened to what seemed like thousands of theories about what was happening with my voice and a thousand more suggestions for what to do about it. People prayed. Doctors experimented. Nothing changed. There was nowhere for me to go and feel complete. Not in the studio. Not at home. Not onstage. The stage was the last place I had.

Once I lost that, I lost my joy with it. I isolated myself, hiding out on the bus and backstage. I was tired and empty, jaded and out of gas. Every show was an introduction to my ending. I hoped I could find a purpose beyond the music.

THEY'LL KNOW WE ARE CHRISTIANS

Our friend and record producer Charlie Peacock was hosting a small gathering at his house with Bono to discuss his efforts in Africa. Like everyone attending, we'd been fans of U2 since the beginning. Will's college dorm had been covered in U2 posters. In Charlie's living room was the A-list of Christian musicians. No one else. Just artists. Everyone in the room regularly commanded arenas, yet there had never been a gathering like this. No one could command this group's attention or our egos. Except for Bono.

Bono is the biggest rock star of our generation. Arguably the biggest in history. He wore all black with a green military-style hat, and with his signature sunglasses off, was modest in appearance. He was also fully present in the room in a way I'd only experienced before with Billy Graham. Like a prophet, Bono carried a weightiness far beyond his size. We all felt it. He walked in purpose and humility and was in touch with something none of the rest of us were. That gifting allowed him to reach into people's hearts with his music and move the world toward the gospel, even when they didn't know he was doing it. Certainly, Bono was not perfect, but he reminded me of King David and what it meant to be a man after God's own heart.

Bono talked to us about his work in Africa. It was during the early stages of the ONE Campaign, and he wanted the American church to step up and engage in the global poverty crisis. At that time, the largest global footprint of the church was in denominationally driven evangelism programs. We could do better. We could love better. We could participate in the restoration and healing of the most impoverished people in the world, and in so doing, become more like Jesus. As Christians, this is our mandate. Bono said that in twenty to thirty years there would be a cure for the AIDS crisis. There would be a cure to global poverty. He then pointed to the room and said something that would shape the second half of my life: "When these cures are found, my desire is that the church had led the way."

Throughout Scripture, God uses music to move the hearts of his people. In Charlie Peacock's living room that day were the most successful musicians of the American church. Each of us had a large platform, and our role in the causes of the poor was implied in Bono's challenge. It's our mantle as musicians. And our responsibility. In that meeting, Bono pushed us to use our platforms for good. He challenged us to write songs that inspired our fans to do more and to push the church to love better. Meeting Bono felt like meeting Billy Graham. They were men tapped into something bigger, and God flowed through them in a different way. I've never met anyone else like them.

When Bono finished talking, there was silence in the room. It felt symbolic of the moment when Jesus commanded his disciples to go, but with the emphasis of a dropped mic. We all looked at each other, wondering what had just happened. Bono had opened some door to heaven in a way I'd never experienced, and the room flooded with the Holy Spirit. In that instant, I knew God was speaking to me. I'd thought about Haiti the whole time Bono spoke. I knew I needed to do something there. I just didn't know what. Many artist-led social movements can be traced to that meeting. Before Bono left, he grabbed Charlie's guitar and sat on the hearth of a fireplace. The biggest rock star in the world sat humbly before us, and with a borrowed, worn guitar he strummed. We knew the lyric. He sang to us, and by the time he reached the chorus, we all knew why we'd come. In that famous Irish accent, these words warmly washed over the room: *"They will know we are Christians by our love."*

TWENTY-NINE

"Hands and Feet"

You never really know why people are fans. At first, it was shocking that we had fans at all. We were eager to talk to them. It was like an archaeologist discovering a lost people group. But after a while the fan-band relationship becomes more complicated. A red flag always goes up when fans approach. It's like a box of chocolates. Most of them are great, but you never know which ones have the nuts.

THE BEST KIND OF CHOCOLATE

After a show at a Louisiana amusement park, we were approached by Arnold Austin and his wife. They were the best kind of chocolate and had been coming to shows since the beginning. We met thousands of people every night, and as much as we tried, it was impossible to remember fans from one show to the next. It was different with the Austins. There was a realness to them and their faith that made them memorable. Arnold asked if I remembered what I'd said during the "Hands and Feet" song the last time we played here. I did. It's what I said at every concert.

Moments before the bridge, I preached to people while the music built. I asked them if they would follow Jesus anywhere, and if so, for them to raise their hands and yell with me, "I will go! I will go!" It was the biggest public reaction in the show. Every night, in every city, people responded. We got

147

letters about how that moment transformed youth groups and mobilized people to go into missions. I enjoyed the letters, but honestly didn't think much more about it. In that moment in the show, we were thinking about how to finish the song and what song was next. Arnold let us know what was really happening in that moment.

"At the last concert we were at, you put out the challenge about who would go."

I nodded.

"Well, God spoke to me and my wife during that song. I'm quitting my job as an engineer, and our family is moving to Peru to be missionaries."

I was stunned. Regardless of where my head was during that concert moment, God had used our song to create a supernatural moment in this man's life. He'd answered the call.

I was humbled to the point of embarrassment because I lacked the same big faith. It was our song, yet fans responded to it more than we did. There's often a veil between the songs we write and the fans who listen to them. I was never courageous enough to accept that the songs we wrote were written for me. Until now. Here was a guy who had given up control. It made me uncomfortable. It was a moment of confrontation. I had to confront the reality of my life and ask myself the same question I had asked Arnold and thousands of others. What would I do? Would I go?

The back of the Audio Adrenaline bus was typically a place for poker playing or songwriting or other forms of tomfoolery. That night a bigger conversation took place. Ben was gifted in noticing the inconsistencies in people, the church, or our band. He felt strongly that we shouldn't be calling others to something that we weren't willing to do ourselves. He pointed out that our fans had raised the stakes on us. As a band, we'd have to match the ante or be called as a bluff.

After the last conversation I had with my dad about Haiti, he started working with a ministry that provided food and education to children who couldn't afford either. He and my mom were living in Haiti part-time, though they wished they could be there more. Between tours, I flew down to spend time with them and see firsthand the work they were doing. Although it was with a different organization, and on the opposite side of the country from their last ministry, I found that I still loved the country just as much. Maybe more. I made financial contributions to their ministry and visited as often as touring life allowed.

Ben said he wanted in on that. He insisted we do it as a band. The rest of the band agreed. It was a moment of total commitment. Like Arnold and so many other fans, we decided to go, and it happened in about ten minutes. Where? My parents wanted to move back to Haiti. When? Now felt good. What? Not sure. Let's fly down and find something that's needed. I asked the guys if they were serious. They were dead serious. Okay. We booked flights, and as soon as we got back to Nashville, we were on a plane with my parents heading to Haiti.

My mom and dad worked with their friend Tina in Jacmel, on the southern coast of Haiti. Jacmel, once a port town, sits in a deep-blue bay, rimmed with coconut trees and white sands and filled with rusted container ships and brightly painted dugout canoes. It's the art capital of Haiti and captures the vivid colors of the country. Walls deconstructed by time and struggle are inlaid with arches of brightly painted doors leading to secret courtyards where wild bougainvillea grow in pink and white, red and orange. The city is connected through a maze of cobbled streets and a spiderweb of electrical wires that seldom carry electricity. The city is French-inspired and has the bare-bones beauty of New Orleans, with ornate metalwork lining buildings and balconies terraced from the sea to tropically covered hills. It's a dark beauty, though, color thinned by poverty and the ailments it brings.

There is no public education in Haiti. For twenty-five years, Tina ran a school so poverty-stricken children could learn to read and write. When we asked her what the biggest need in the area was, she said a good, quality orphanage. Many of the kids she tried to educate didn't have a home, and those who did often went without food, medical care, and other essential ingredients for a child to grow. The largest need she could imagine in the area was to care for the most vulnerable who could not care for themselves. There was little hesitation. That was a problem we could help solve. We settled on starting an orphanage and, with Tina's guidance, purchased a property.

Mom and Dad fulfilled their dream and moved back to Haiti full time. Tina's builder had a brother named Odius who could help my dad. The two of them developed plans for the first building. My dad had plenty of experience leading construction in Haiti. He just needed money. So we went back to the

US, hopped on a tour bus, and started telling the story. Our fans generously gave. At first, we didn't have any idea what we were doing, but it felt good to do something other than just play music. There wasn't a master plan or strategy, and though we were naive, we just went for it. Looking back now, if we'd actually known what it took to build an orphanage in Haiti, we probably would never have started. But at the time, we didn't think of it and it didn't matter. We were a rock and roll band starting an orphanage in a developing nation. What could possibly go wrong?

PART V

"Start a Fire"

So go ahead and light the sky like a bonfire
in the night. Let the fire keep burning
higher, it can never be too bright.
—AUDIO ADRENALINE, "START A FIRE"

"I am the light of the world."
—JOHN 8:12

THIRTY

"Worldwide"

When we started playing music in college, the music was the message and the message was the ministry. It was simple. We wanted to let people know that Jesus loved them. At that time, many of our fans told us that they felt judged by the church. They had the wrong hair. They listened to the wrong music. They had the wrong skin color or lifestyle or ethnicity. A spirit of religion hung heavy in the church and bled over to parents tightly controlling kids through a narrow and twisted belief system that substituted dogma for following Jesus. As a result, these fans associated Jesus with judgment.

Our ministry was telling the truth about Jesus. That Jesus loves you. With no strings attached. No judgment. There is nothing you can do or become to make Jesus love you more or to keep his love from you. In fact, Jesus values your life more than his own. He died for you. He resurrected, defeating the grave for you. He wants you to be with him forever. Our song "Big House" was our attempt to communicate that. Music and message and ministry reflected in a song about freedom, about love, and about a Father's house large enough for all of us.

We signed into the Christian music industry thinking that as our platform grew, this message could grow with it. That's all we wanted. And to play some rock and roll. We got to do the latter on a scale that our college selves could never have imagined. However, the ministry got complicated. Christian rock exploded in the decade after we signed, and the Christian music industry did what all industries are made to do. It made money. Then more money. Then even more. During that time, *Newsweek* reported Christian music to be the hottest genre in the entire music industry.[2] Huge mainstream labels jumped in to buy up fast-growing Christian labels. The industry was opportunistic. Labels looked at trends in secular music and put together a Christian version of it. That's how we got signed. The industry followed every trend. Ska bands. Hip-hop bands. Boy bands. We were put on tour with bands who were supposed to be Christians but offstage lived nothing like it. But their albums sold, and their labels were happy. The industry became formulaic in music and message, and we became jaded to the whole thing.

Our work in Haiti got me excited about music again. We called it the Hands and Feet Project. It was personal. I was the one who spoke from stage most often, and after twelve years, I was running out of things to speak about. At times, it felt like acting. I wanted something real to talk about. There was nothing more real to me than Haiti. Real injustices. Real poverty. Real opportunities to live out the gospel. My talks went from hypothetical to very real. A set list for a live show is filled with small messages of individual radio hit songs. Standing on their own, some songs didn't feel important, and a hype song could lack soul while an introspective song could feel self-indulgent. Uniting these songs in the singular message of serving the orphans and widows written about in the Bible rooted the entire show into something real. We now had a solid platform from which to encourage people to make a difference in the world. Our fans loved it. It was a way for faith to become real to them too.

The Hands and Feet Project more deeply connected us to our fans. Instead of just signing autographs, we invited them to go on this journey with us. There's always a professional distance between a band and the audience. It's an invisible wall designed to protect bands from the messiness of life with fans or from having to do the things they talk about onstage. It became accepted that bands and record labels and the industry were only the messengers. It was the job of the fans to do the work. And buy the records. And pay for the tickets.

Haiti blew all that up. We asked our fans to go on trips with us, and they said yes. On our early trips we had no idea who would be coming. It was scary at first, but all the things I worried about with inviting fans—solicitations for autographs or music advice, or just awkwardly wanting to be near the band—turned out not to be true. They wanted to make a difference in the same way we did. It was a partnership. Together, we built homes for abandoned children and brought whatever hope we had to offer. We truly were being the hands and feet of Jesus, and we were doing it alongside our fans. It was hard. It was messy. But it was a beautiful partnership that brought new life and purpose to our music. It was more than concerts and music. It was us and our fans living out the gospel together.

We had no idea what we were doing. My dad would tell me what we needed; then I would communicate that from stage. Our fans were amazing. They donated. They went on trips. A scrap-metal guy showed up at a show in Michigan. I don't even think he liked our music. But when we started receiving regular donations from Michigan, we tracked him down and he took the whole journey with us, eventually becoming the president of our board. He has big hands shaped by hard work, heavy with grace and love. When things got tough and he put those hands on my shoulders and said everything would be okay, I believed it.

We raised money on the tours, and afterward, we flew down and worked side by side with my dad. Other bands joined in. Hawk Nelson had some of the purest hearts of any band I knew. They, too, were left unfulfilled with the normal music-industry cycle of making records, doing tours, and hitting repeat. They longed for a bigger purpose in their music, and when they heard we needed a van for Children's Village, they challenged their fans to join them in making a donation. They talked more deeply from stage about the purpose of their music, and their fans rose to the challenge. They raised the money and bought the van! The platform God had given us was now connecting us to the whole body of Christ in a miraculous way. It was amazing to see. We were living a big, big life together.

WORLDWIDE

This all led to the concept of the *Worldwide* album. I felt a new freedom in my writing. Previously, pressures had been closing in all around me—to fix my marriage, to write a hit song, to improve our ratings in the charts. Eventually, I wrote to those pressures, and it sucked the trueness out of me and out of the band. Haiti gave us a purity and truth in our music again. This is where the best music comes from. True art doesn't require a defense. It stands by itself and asks the listener to recognize the same truth within them. I knew again what we were pursuing. It was pure and good and big. I wanted to record a whole album about that.

Central to the *Worldwide* concept is the question: Are you willing to go? The where and what can come later, but until our faith is put to action, it isn't much of a faith. Faith is always in the unknown. We wanted the whole album to be about stepping into the unknown and getting our hands dirty. It was a response to a fan who was willing to quit his job and take his family to serve others on the other side of the world. Haiti and the Hands and Feet Project weren't dominant in the album's theme, but they were central to our hearts. We talked about the Hands and Feet Project in radio interviews and in churches. At that time, artists weren't linked with causes, and the industry was confused by what we were doing. But not our fans. They were on the faith ride with us. Some of our fans ended up spending more time with my parents than I did. It was a homegrown, messy, misunderstood, rebellious, audacious, antiestablishment movement. It felt like rock and roll. From that, *Worldwide* was born.

Producing the album was a family affair. We recorded it in our Franklin studio. Tyler's brothers helped with design and his uncle helped produce it, alongside our good friend Charlie Peacock. The record felt true, congruent from the inside out. The music reflected the message: don't be afraid to jump in. Jesus is active and powerful and already on the move everywhere. You just have to find where to get involved. My wife helped with the photos and artwork. The original idea was to do photo shoots around the world, but the budget didn't allow for that, so Kerri came up with the idea of shooting in California. We shot in San Francisco, Chinatown, the Japanese Tea Garden, and a location in Yosemite that looked like Switzerland. We got the look we wanted, and the album art was complete.

Every part of the process felt right. We even found a way to make my deteriorating vocals work. I was bound in range, but by writing in the right key and relying on Tyler to deliver the soaring melodies, I was able to deliver my vocal parts. Between the vocal decay and steroid shots, there was even a brief moment of magical tone where the breaking of my voice provided a sophisticated grit that sounded like a mix of Rod Stewart and Tom Waits. Yet, as excited and proud as I was for the record, I was more excited about the platform. I was reminded once again of my childhood prayers. With the release of *Worldwide*, it seemed like the moment had come for our platform to reach its fullest potential.

It did.

THIRTY-ONE

Rock Star

The *Worldwide* album was nominated for a Grammy Award. It wasn't our first nomination. With previous nominations, we all flew to participate in the event. Once nominated, the Grammy journey starts in fancy hotels. Nominees arrive a day or two earlier to prepare. In my case, preparation meant buying clothes I'd actually be let into the Grammys with. I wasn't the only one last-minute wardrobe shopping. I met Eric Clapton while shopping for a suit.

We put on our fancy clothes in our fancy hotels and got a ride in a fancy car to the red carpet. I'd watched red-carpet events on TV and always wondered what it would be like to walk the red carpet at the Grammy Awards. I mostly felt like a kid unsupervised.

The only job I had on the red carpet was to walk, something I'd been doing since I was about a year old. But all of a sudden, walking made me nervous. We were in the middle of the biggest music stars of our generation, and I was near certain I would trip over my shoelaces (even though my shoes didn't have laces). I met A-list celebrities on the red carpet and at the parties afterward. Paul McCartney glided into the EMI after-party heavily guarded and wearing some sort of robe. He was untouchable, like a king. Even celebrities go to the bathroom, though, and Dwight Yoakam pulled up to the urinal next to me. He had long been a musical hero of mine, and my wife and I had fallen in love while dancing to one of his songs. I didn't stop to think about what to say.

"You're Dwight Yoakam!"

He responded in a dry and measured voice, deep with a slow Southern drawl, "What's left of him."

Inside the event, the level of production and musical talent was astonishing. We watched Madonna give an iconic performance, and Aerosmith was about to do a live version of their massive hit "I Don't Want to Miss a Thing," when Steven Tyler's monitors went out. It was during a commercial break, and there was a countdown for the cameras to go to live TV. Millions of people were watching. Steven was communicating to the sound man, trying to figure out the problem. "Four . . . three." Nothing. ". . . two." Still nothing. Steven was as calm as could be. ". . . one." Aerosmith launched into their performance, and Steven Tyler was perfect, even without monitors. These guys are the best of the best for a reason. That was the same Grammy show where Ricky Martin played his breakout US performance. Nobody knew who he was, and the audience was buzzing with anticipation as he climbed onstage. He launched into "Livin' la Vida Loca" and became a star right in front of our eyes. I'd never seen anything like it.

WINNING THE GRAMMY

Worldwide was our fifth nomination for Rock Gospel Album of the Year. We'd grown accustomed to losing. I felt if we were to have won, it would have happened with either *Bloom* or *Underdog*. My hopes weren't high. So instead of going to the Grammys, we decided to save the money and took a stop on our tour to watch the show at Ben's parents' house in St. Louis, Missouri. We ordered pizza and played pool, and I was hanging out with Ben's dad in the hot tub when Ben's phone started going crazy. Relient K had been nominated for the same award we were, and their singer, Matt Thiessen, called Ben from inside the Grammy Awards.

"Where are you guys?"

"We're at my parents' house in St. Louis."

"You just won a Grammy!"

Over the phone, in the background, the Grammy announcer could be heard calling for Audio Adrenaline.

"Is Audio Adrenaline in the audience? Is there a representative that can pick up Audio Adrenaline's Grammy Award?"

Our pizza party erupted with high fives and phone calls. Audio Adrenaline's first Grammy was won in true blue-collar fashion: on the road, away from the glamour, eating fried cheese sticks.

THE RUSSIANS

It was great to share the Grammy news with Garth. I'd known him longer than anybody in my life, so he felt like family. We both acknowledged the unlikeliness of a guy growing up in our little hometown ever winning a Grammy. I looked forward to our long drives together. He was a steady presence, and my time with him at the front of our bus helped keep me grounded. He shared more with me too, though his stories were more colorful and often started with the phrase, "Mark, something happened . . ." With his stories, names and locations often have to be changed, like they have been in the following vignette.

We were on tour, in an undisclosed location, when this story took place.

"Mark, something happened last night while you were asleep."

As the story goes, Garth pulled into a truck stop around 3:30 a.m. for a quick fueling. The schedule was tight. We had to be at load-in another state away by midmorning. Since we owned our own bus, we got to hire the bus driver. This is not the norm. Tour buses are typically rented and come with an assigned bus driver. We were on a big tour with three drivers, in addition to Garth. Bill was six foot eight, as loud as he was tall, and more aggressive than that. He normally drove for a well-known country music star. Larry was the opposite of Bill in every way. Small, polite, mild-mannered. Wayne was the fourth. All we knew about him was that he seemed crazy.

Our tour's four rigs, led by Garth, pulled into the truck stop behind some long-haul truckers who'd blocked the fuel islands. The truck drivers had eastern European accents, so for the sake of the story, let's call them Russian. They were showering, washing windows, and generally hogging all the space. This broke every bit of truck-driver etiquette. Garth's patience waned. He tightly maneuvered the bus around one of the trucks to get access to the fuel pump. There was only one trucker watching the trucks at the time, and he yelled at Garth, who gave him the international hand signal of complete displeasure. This triggered a quickly escalating series of events.

When Garth got out of the bus, the first Russian came at him pretty strong. Garth used his size to pin the Russian against the truck and started whaling on him. A second Russian arrived on the scene. He grabbed a tire iron and busted out the front lights of our bus before taking a swing at Garth. Bill intercepted the tire iron mid-swing and went after Russian number two. Mild-mannered Larry lost his cool and grabbed the truck-stop window washer, with its extra-long metal washer rod, and started knocking off all the mirrors on the Russians' trucks. Just about the time he finished, Russians number three and four came out.

This was the Russians' moment to get back at the Americans for Ronald Reagan and Rocky, and they were taking it. Words were exchanged in completely different languages that everybody understood perfectly. An international fight was about to go down. By the time Wayne realized what was happening, the brawl had reached a Cold War climax. He pulled out a gun and started firing. *Pop! Pop! Pop!* The Russians, realizing they were once again out-armed by the Americans, scrambled back into their trucks. Alarmed at how serious things were getting, Garth yelled at Wayne to stop firing his gun.

"You can't just shoot at those guys!"

"I wasn't shooting *at* them."

We came upon the Russian trucks about thirty miles down the highway. Rubber fragments littered the asphalt and little pieces were flying everywhere. Sparks flew from the rims of the trucks. Wayne's warning shots had pierced their tires. Our buses passed them by.

The band slept through the whole thing.

THE POPE

When Pope John Paul II visited the US, Audio Adrenaline was among a few Christian rock bands selected to play at a large Catholic youth rally the pope attended. When I was growing up, many, if not most, evangelicals believed Catholics weren't true believers. A great deal of energy was applied to emphasizing our differences. These differences were argued in classrooms and preached from pulpits. It was this issue that largely created the crisis of my faith during college, ultimately repelling me from westernized religion until I discovered Jesus in Haiti and found my way home. Now I was onstage, singing to eighty thousand Catholic kids who loved Jesus too. They knew the words and sang along. Together, we lifted up the name of Jesus, and we asked him to heal our world and unite us in our efforts to make his name known. I became more aware of how big God is, and how small of a box I'd put him in so I could examine him from all sides and make my conclusions. A boxed god can be controlled and understood, not hallowed and worshipped. In reality, God is limitless, expansive, and active worldwide, through different people, different cultures, and different flavors of Christianity all over the world.

SOUTH AMERICA

South Americans are unbridled in their passion. It's seen in their sports, in their dancing, in their lust for life. It's also seen in their love of Jesus. We played to audiences overcome by their emotions, weeping at the goodness of Jesus. There was no shame in their emotions. Those who weren't weeping were banging their heads. No one was banging their heads at concerts anymore. Except in South America.

Almost as much as Jesus, the South Americans also loved American rock and roll musicians and treated us to cultural highlights at every opportunity. For one concert, we were transported in armored vehicles. Before the concert, our host took us to a racetrack. We thought we were going to race him in some nice, friendly, safe-for-the-whole-family go-carts. But we began to wonder, Why did we need fire-retardant suits, helmets, and goggles? We were placed in miniature Formula One race cars and challenged by the host to try and keep up. Our egos were up to the challenge, but our skills left us defeated. Later, we asked him why our transport cars were bulletproof. He told us that he was running for Senate and we were playing at his political rally. And, oh yeah, a lot of people wanted him dead.

AUSTRALIA

Of all the countries we played in, Australia was my favorite. It's one of the most beautiful places in the world, full of amazing people, world-class cities, and natural wonders. The architecture of Sydney is among the most striking anywhere.

We played in Sydney and Melbourne and at a camp with Hillsong Church and at the Sonfest musical festival run by Dale Bray on the Gold Coast. More than ten thousand people showed up to one of our Australian concerts. They sang our songs word for word. It was impossible to take in. In another country, halfway around the world, our music had an impact. Our cultures were vastly different, but we were united in rock and roll and our faith in Jesus.

GREAT BARRIER REEF

Our concert schedule was rigged so we'd have a few days off to take advantage of Australia's natural playgrounds. Ben, Will, our road manager Joel, and I were certified in scuba diving, so we headed to the Great Barrier Reef. The reef stretches for 1,600 miles, greater than the distance between Boston and Miami, and is the largest living structure on earth. We had a section to ourselves. Well, us and the sharks. A blacktip reef shark bumped into Will, and once we were circled by a lemon shark. We saw fish and coral of every imaginable color and swam with dolphins and great sea turtles. To view the Great Barrier Reef is to experience God's pleasure on the fifth day of creation.

After diving, we retreated back to the northern Australian city of Cairns. There we ate local barramundi and mudbug on white-sand tropical beaches, lined with gently swaying palms and overlooking a translucent sea changing from turquoise to green to blue. It was the best meal of my life, after one of the best days of my life. I couldn't help but dream of moving there, as unlikely as it was.

TASMANIA AND NEW ZEALAND

After Australia, our tour took us to Tasmania, where I saw an actual Tasmanian devil, and then to New Zealand, where the craziest mosh pit I have ever seen took place. It looked like a war zone. In the US, that mosh pit would have been stopped for liability reasons. At one point, people were getting thrown to the ground, and I thought I needed to stop the concert before anyone got seriously injured. Before I could say anything, they helped each other up, gave some hugs, then went back to work beating the crap out of each other. Don't be fooled by the demure countryside and endless herds of sheep. The Kiwis are ready to rock.

EUROPE

The night before playing a soccer stadium show in Amsterdam for more than eight thousand people, we went out for some food. We found a local pizza shop. They didn't speak English. Tyler is picky with his food and at times can be as artistic with a food order as he is with a guitar solo. He's the one most responsible for pushing our food-and-drink repertoire beyond cheeseburgers and Mountain Dew. He was excited for a European culinary experience, but the communication barrier prohibited the experimentation he hoped for. He settled for the simplest order possible.

"I'll have a pepperoni pizza."

"A pepper . . . what you say?"

"Pep-per-o-ni."

When Tyler's pizza arrived, it was a thin piece of crust with nothing but peppers on it. He asked what in the world kind of pizza that was.

"You order, pepper-only."

Fueled by his pepper-only pizza, on show night, Tyler's guitar riffs ripped through the stadium, and we played a no-translation-needed set of American-style rock and roll. Our Amsterdam friends were ready to party, and the pond between us was quickly bridged by the cross. Fans sang "Big House" and "Ocean Floor" in Amsterdam, Sweden, Switzerland, Germany, Norway, Poland, and England.

PARIS

After one of our European tours, I vacationed with my wife in Paris, hoping the city of love would help rekindle ours. We visited Montmartre and the Eiffel Tower and walked the banks of the Seine. We even took a Princess Diana tour that ended in the tunnel she never reemerged from. I searched for our love in the lights reflected on the Seine. If it was there, I never found it. Or I arrived too late and it had already passed under the Pont Neuf, making its way to the sea.

We had a show the next day in California. I barely made my flight from Paris and was picked up by a driver at the LAX airport and delivered straight to the back door of Anaheim Stadium, where the band was already onstage. In true rock star fashion, the band opened our set as I was driven across the outfield on a private cart to the wild applause of forty-five thousand people. I didn't even have time to change, so I sang in the same clothes and flip-flops I'd worn along the Seine. My heart was left there too.

There was never a time to catch our breath. Audio Adrenaline had a worldwide platform. Fans filled venues on every continent we played. Our songs were sung around the world. We snowboarded in New Zealand, salmon-fished in Alaska, dived on exotic reefs, white-water rafted in the Alps, raced cars in the Amazon, played in almost every theater and arena and amusement park in America, and rode every roller coaster. We even played for the pope. God took a few corn-fed kids from the heartland and showed them the world. Not because we were any good, but because God is good. We were just willing to sing about it.

Every country reacted differently to our music, but there was something in it that connected everywhere. Though cultures and languages differ, and though vast oceans lie between, God's people are united by something stronger than the differences trying to separate them. It's the love of Jesus, in the hearts of believers, shared through the universal language of rock and roll. Audio Adrenaline was worldwide because God was already worldwide. God is bigger than our borders.

Faith looks different in Australia and Amsterdam than it does in the small, rural congregation I grew up in. I wouldn't have believed God could be found in the differences. But he's there. He's bigger than we could ever imagine. From the faithful flock of Richland, Indiana, to the impassioned believers of Rio de Janeiro, the presence and glory of Jesus cannot be hidden.

THIRTY-TWO

All the Light That Remained

Audio Adrenaline became a staple for massive crusades throughout the country. Crusades (why they were branded with such a historically terrible name, I'll never understand) were large-scale Christian outreach events made popular by Billy Graham that took place in arenas and large public spaces. The largest were held in sports stadiums. The events were massive in scale and typically hosted by Billy Graham, his son Franklin Graham, Luis Palau, or Greg Laurie, who hosted the Harvest Crusades in Southern California. Of all the large events, Harvest felt like home. We were invited back so often people assumed we were the house band.

The main Harvest event took place at Anaheim Stadium, home to the Angels baseball team, for forty-five thousand people per night. The main stage was built over second base, and the event's only real rule was to stay off the outfield grass. Greg was pastor of Harvest Christian Fellowship, and he took us in. He had a comfortable approach to the gospel and gave a genuine invitation to follow Jesus. It wasn't based on guilt or fire and brimstone. It was an invitation, based on love and grace, to come home to the place you were always supposed to be. We were intimately involved, essentially part of the furnishings. Our role was to bring the party. We were good at it.

At one event, Ben dared me to run across the outfield. I started first by running into the audience and getting the packed stadium hyped as we sang and danced to "Big House." Then, as the song kicked into overdrive, I jumped onto the grass and ran from home base, through the infield, into the outfield. Camera guys chased me. I performed my best football jukes to get away from them. I ducked and faked and dodged my way deep into the outfield. The crowd went wild, and it was complete mayhem until the chase scene ended with me collapsing, completely out of breath, somewhere in right field. Our songs were perfect for these events. Not all music holds up at this scale. In fact, not much does. But "Big House," "Get Down," "Ocean Floor"—these were faith anthems meant to be sung in stadiums. From stage I watched tens of thousands of the faithful and new-to-faith sing and dance, and the roar and movement looked and felt like the tidal wave of Angels the stadium was built for. I felt a part of the kingdom fabric in a big way. It was a combination of rock and roll party with a gospel invitation on a massive scale, all seared in the golden light of Southern California.

Our biggest show for the Harvest Crusade was on the Fourth of July, and we were double-booked. Harvest is in Anaheim, just south of Los Angeles, and our following show was in San Diego at a large event with our good friend Miles McPherson, a pro football player turned pastor for the Rock Church. There wasn't enough time between shows to make the drive. The biggest rock-star moments of my life came after finishing our set at Harvest. We were whisked away on golf carts to a pair of helicopters waiting for us just outside the stadium. Will, Tyler, and I jumped into one and Ben jumped into the other with the crew guys so he could film the whole spectacle. As we were lifted above the stadium lights, we could see and hear the packed stadium standing and cheering. Our pilots circled around the stadium as we waved to the audience, and I realized the cheering was for us. They were saying goodbye. The cheering of forty-five thousand people was a roar of heaven that continues to reverberate in my soul.

Our fans lifted us with voices and clapping hands, and we rose in the graces of their goodwill until the stage we played on was a small dot in a green field surrounded by a sea of people lit by the lights of Anaheim Stadium. We flew toward the sun setting over an infinite Pacific Ocean that from this height looked like a mirror of heaven. Lights of Los Angeles were off to the right. I could see the rooftop of the high-rise building where we'd shot the music video for "Never Gonna Be As Big As Jesus." My wife had produced the video, and the concept was about a band trying to climb the rock and roll ladder and the vanity of chasing fame and fortune. It was shot in the days of big-budget videos and required airspace permits for a helicopter cameraman. The penultimate cinematic moment was shot from the air as our band played on top of one of the largest buildings in Los Angeles. The cameraman flew between high-rises to get shots of us and our instruments serenading the slow-fading sunlight. I thought life could never be bigger than that.

I looked over to Will, who was lost in his own thoughts. From dorm rooms of a small college in the hollows of eastern Kentucky to the bright lights of Los Angeles, we'd taken the whole ride together. The last of the sun lit the tops of tall buildings, and they glowed like candlelight. I thought about the video and *Bloom* and my wife and the art we'd created together. I could still see her standing on the rooftop high above Los Angeles; half her face hidden behind a film camera and the rest illuminated by the golden California light filtering through her long blonde hair. The art endured, but the image of her faded into a distance made dark with our secrets. The helicopters turned south.

The sun was well beyond the horizon, and all the light that remained showed in a thin curve of faded gold separating the ocean from the sky. The helicopters lowered to one thousand feet. Twilight outlined the western edge of the continent. Beaches were crowded with families and friends celebrating the Fourth of July, and fireworks reflected on the ocean. The world below was filled with noises of music and love and laughter. In the helicopter, with headphones on, the world was silent. Will looked over. We locked eyes and gave a knowing nod. Together, we'd experienced a life very few ever would. We didn't know what it was at the time, but we knew it was special. We hung in the thin space between dreams and the sunrise, wondering how much longer it could last. Eventually we'd descend and play another show and morning would come and my secrets could no longer escape the light. I was suspended in the dark.

PART VI

"Losing Control"

This is what it feels like to lose control.
This is what it feels like to be left alone.
—AUDIO ADRENALINE, "LOSING CONTROL"

Jesus said, "It is finished." With that, he
bowed his head and gave up his spirit.
—JOHN 19:30

THIRTY-THREE

The Arena, Part 2

In 2003, Audio Adrenaline was nominated for three Dove Awards. The band was up for Group of the Year. Our album *Lift* was up for Rock Album of the Year. "Ocean Floor" was up for Song of the Year. But after the disappointing visit to the doctor's office, I lacked any enthusiasm for the night. I wasn't even sure if my voice would work. I left the greenroom and found the rest of the band. We lined up onstage during the commercial break to perform "Ocean Floor." Camera operators got in position to broadcast the band live. The crowd went silent. Steven Curtis Chapman was on the side stage, awaiting his cue to introduce us to a packed Nashville arena. Millions more watched on TV. To win even one of these awards would be a lifetime honor. But at that moment, I didn't care about any of it. I only wanted to make it through the song.

My recent doctor's visits hadn't brought good news. No one could tell me what was happening with my voice, why I was losing control of it, or why sometimes it didn't work at all. I quietly went to every specialist I could find. Nashville is filled with singers experiencing vocal issues and high-profile doctors who fix them. Those same doctors had no solutions for me. I got a double dose of steroids and a grave prognosis about how the shots wouldn't work much longer. But I already knew that.

The Dove Awards were a celebration of all aspects of Christian music. The concept was originated by Bill Gaither and had grown to become a Christian music version of the Grammy Awards. Similar to the Grammys, the night was filled with winners in all genres, including pop, gospel, rap, worship, and rock.

We were nominated in the coveted rock category. It was the award given to the most impactful rock albums and groups of the year.

The industry itself was riding an all-time high, after a decade of staggering growth. The size of the crowd reflected that. The floor was filled with industry folks—artists, producers, managers, labels, radio—who somehow made a living from those whose art would soon be awarded. Whispered through the floor of the industry was speculation about my voice and what should or would happen with Audio Adrenaline. I felt pressure from our label and other industry execs but remained silent with them. Beyond the floor were rows upon rows of Christian music fans who'd come out of a genuine love of the music. These were the folks we knew best. They lifted me up in my toughest moments onstage. We were about to play one of the biggest songs of the year, live, at the biggest industry event, at the peak of the industry, and I wasn't sure if my voice would work. I hoped the fans would come through one more time.

Tyler started the song with a soaring vocal intro. His voice filled the room with purity and beauty, heralding the core message of the song. The symphony followed. It echoed Tyler's vocal, cellos and violins voicing the song's melody as a chorus of angels. My vocal was next.

"The mistakes I've made, that caused pain, I could have done without."

My voice was a rough juxtaposition against Tyler and the symphony. But it worked. Words formed and met with wind from my lungs and together released into the room with all the tension and fear I'd bottled up with it. For the fans, it was exactly what they wanted. A rock and roll front man, singing his guts out, leaving it all onstage, like I'd done a thousand times before. The crowd responded. They lifted my voice higher, willing me to be better than I was, ushering in the Holy Spirit, like they'd done a thousand times before.

For me, the night was a miracle. There was no reason for my voice to work. The steroids had lost their effectiveness, and there was nothing left. That night, my voice was carried by the love of God. Then, something bigger than the song washed over the arena. It was for me a holy moment of affirmation. I knew my voice was gone, and it was all over, but here we were, doing what we loved, one more time. I looked around at each of the guys, and they smiled, and in their eyes, I knew that they knew it too. But that was for another day. This moment was ours. It was the best we'd ever played that song, and the entire Christian music world was watching.

Mac Powell, the lead singer of Third Day, led the standing ovation. The arena followed. This was a pinnacle moment for us. For the evening. For my career. I forced back the tears. We were ushered offstage to the right, and the clapping continued. The heavens had opened, and in my spirit, it felt like the voice of God saying, "Well done, my good and faithful servant." As we walked past leaders in the industry, Bill Gaither stood from his chair, walked through the crowd, and stopped us in our tracks. He put his hand on my arm, and in it I felt the entire warmth of the night.

"Now that, son, was a song!"

We finished up the interviews and were called back onto the stage, where we learned that *Lift* had won Rock Album of the Year! Once again, the crowd was on its feet. We were floating on air. With the additional nominations for Song of the Year and Group of the Year, we were being recognized as industry leaders. That night, the boys of Audio Adrenaline became men. After leaving it all onstage for over fifteen years, we'd finally arrived at our destiny. Audio Adrenaline was the beloved underdog that won the championship.

The Dove Awards that year was a fantastic blur. I only really remember two things about that night. First is the overwhelming gratefulness that my vocals held up long enough to make it through the song and put to rest the growing industry speculation about my voice and the future of Audio Adrenaline. We earned the right to decide our own fate. The second is that my wife didn't show up.

That was the last Dove Awards held in the arena. Like the rest of the music world, our industry was in the midst of a seismic shift. Music was going digital. Napster and other music-sharing technologies were on the rise. Christian music would never be the same.

There were interviews and after-parties, and then I went home. It was dark. Empty. We'd recently purchased the house, and it was under renovation. I stopped in the area that would one day be our library. I imagined the richness of wooden bookshelves filled with stories that make a life. Pictures of my wife and me, holding hands, watching the sun set over our favorite island. Pictures of future children and friends and family and the grand holiday feasts we'd enjoy in these halls. There, I could see my Dove awards and Grammys among pictures of a love restored and lived, in the hope that this house might one day become a home. I turned from the fantasy, walked through the drywall dust, and found my way to the attic, where a couple rooms were set up to sleep and eat during the renovation. I found a box of my unpacked belongings. In it were the awards representing fame and security. It was all the things I strove for and fought for and thought would make a good life. I added the Dove award to its contents, then sealed it closed. And hoped it would one day find light again.

THIRTY-FOUR

Music City

The day after I graduated high school, my parents moved to Haiti and I moved into my car. I've been on the road ever since. I'd purchased a house with Kerri, but it hadn't felt like a home. The closest thing I had to a home was a tour bus and an open road. I had favorite coffee shops and restaurants throughout the country, even churches and friends. There I dreamed of roots deep enough to withstand the storms. But we were gone before any roots could grow.

I knew there wasn't much left in our marriage. I maintained hope, but I knew we couldn't continue down the same path. Problems had plagued our marriage from the beginning. We were still young, though, so I thought we had the benefit of time. Maybe we did, but that time was slipping between tours and recordings, and the road had been an easy escape. I'd grown up in a good home and knew it wasn't a place you run from when the storms come. It's the place you run to. And I was ready to put down roots. It was the last thing I could think of to save our marriage.

The band had been spending a lot of time in Franklin, Tennessee, south of Nashville's Music Row and just outside the grip of the music industry. It wasn't far from where my wife had been working. I had bought an historic house in downtown Franklin that my wife wanted to renovate, and Audio Adrenaline purchased a house a few blocks away and converted it into a studio. The town had the veneer of the life we'd all seen on TV as kids. It was perfectly sized, with a town square and pre–Civil War brick buildings and a soda fountain and a theater with a vintage marquee that opened the same year as *Snow White and the Seven Dwarfs*. White-painted church spires rose above the canopy of hardwoods that cooled sidewalks in summer and signaled the autumnal changes of solstice. Other Christian musicians were moving there too. But at that moment, it still felt like a secret.

When not touring, my wife and I were going to a church called Christ Community. It was filled with the artists of the day and led by an unassuming Presbyterian preacher named Scotty Smith, who spoke messages of amazing grace. I was secretly broken. I didn't feel like I could tell anyone. I wanted a deeper relationship with Jesus, where I could confide my brokenness and stop the illusion of a perfect life. This message of grace gave me hope that it was possible.

In the early '90s, Christ Community met in a historic chapel not far from Five Points. On Sundays, church overflowed beyond the choir lofts and spilled over into Bible studies and youth programs in adjacent downtown buildings. That grace was felt along the shaded sidewalks of Main Street for the remainder of the week. The church spiritually anchored the town. The best musicians and thought leaders in the world moved to Franklin to experience it. It was a safe place for people like me to build a real life. Coffee shops filled with conversations about art and spirit and grace and the love of Jesus. Within those few blocks of downtown Franklin, a soundtrack to those conversations was written and recorded and shared with the world. I wanted to be a part. I also thought moving to Franklin would save my marriage. We both hoped roots might grow.

My wife had an amazing eye for style and wanted to apply that same skill to renovating a house. We'd found a large place for sale on a three-acre wooded lot in downtown Franklin. The house was registered with the historic society, which was good news, but it also was an absolute disaster, chopped up in unexplainable ways, with nothing updated since it was first built in the early part of the last century. However, the inspector said it had the best foundation of any house he'd ever seen. It was one of the very first residential structures in Tennessee to be framed with heavy steel. He told us that we could rebuild anything on that foundation, so we purchased the house, divided tasks like we'd done on album artwork, and began with the unspoken urgency that this was our last-chance project.

The house had four levels: two main levels, an attic, and a basement. The two main stories were once occupied by two sisters who inherited the house and promptly divided it in such a way that they would never have to speak to each other. Each story was converted into its own separate living unit, with a visible lack of repair. The house was rotting and empty. It looked like a couple of abandoned, spooky grandma houses stacked on top of each other. Which is exactly what it was. Whatever the original design intent, the home was now modified for two separate lives. The basement was a dark, large, unfinished space that still housed a coal stove and the remnants of coal once used to heat the house. Even with the hope of the foundation, the basement was too foreboding. We started in the attic. The attic was large enough to create a couple of rooms for us to live in while the rest of the renovation took place. From there, the primary challenge of the project was taking two dysfunctional houses and turning them into one home.

T-BONE

In addition to the house renovation and the recording studio, Audio Adrenaline was building our management company and new label from Franklin as well. We'd started Brickhouse Entertainment several years earlier with Scott Brickell and watched the artist roster grow. Brickhouse, through the years, added MercyMe, Phil Wickham, Matthew West, Switchfoot, and many others. The guys from Switchfoot had an authentic musical aesthetic that destined them to become one of the most exciting new bands in the industry. Matthew was a new artist with a voice and songwriting skills that were in a different league. All around us, we were watching the music industry shift and grow. Franklin was the epicenter. It was an amazing gift to walk alongside some of these incredible artists.

Our other opportunity to shape the next generation of music was with our record label, Flicker Records. The label was named after our song "Flicker," written with the idea that even just a flicker of light can bring hope to dark places. It doesn't matter if we have a candle or a flamethrower, we are only meant to offer the light we have and let God do the rest. Though Bob was becoming proficient on guitar, his army background and creative gifts were well suited for the business side of music, and he left the road to become the Flicker Records CEO. The first artist we signed was a Canadian singer-songwriter named Riley

Armstrong. After Riley, we signed a dozen other bands, including Kids in the Way, Wavorly, Flatfoot 56, the Swift, and Mortal Treason. Our greatest label success came through two hard rock bands, Pillar and Fireflight, but one artist we signed became one of my closest friends, lasting long after we sold the label to Provident. He has a long list of aliases.

T-Bone, aka Boney Bone Corleone, aka Bone Soprano—or the name I affectionately gave him, T-Bizzle—is a Christian gangsta rapper with a personality that lives up to his many names. I met T-Bone doing the Harvest Crusades at Anaheim Stadium. He had his own interview TV show with TBN and was asking us some questions before our set. I knew of his previous records and that he was esteemed as one of the founding fathers of Christian rap. I asked about his career. He stopped doing records because he no longer had a record deal. *What???* We offered him a deal on the spot. His first album with us, *The Last Street Preacha*, was nominated for several Dove awards and a Grammy. He gained more popularity with *Bone-A-Fide*, and by the time *Gospelalphafunkyboogiediscomusic* came out, T-Bone was a bona fide inspirational rap celebrity in Christian music, and he'd made regular appearances with me onstage, giving our live shows a moment of oversized hype.

Offstage, T-Bone lived the courageous life of faith I was longing for. He had no fear. He'd go for anything and everything he felt God leading him to. Where I leaned on my own understanding, T-Bone leaned on something too big to understand. He connected to Jesus from the deeper places, where life hadn't gone well and Jesus was all that was left. In that well was the courage he lived from. He had a pastor's heart, and I could get real with him. I told him what was happening with my marriage. It was a great relief to finally open up about it. He deconstructed the walls and fears I'd built up, particularly around my relationship with God. He tore them all down and helped me find the truth. It started with him telling me to get real about my marriage.

FINAL RESTORATION

We'd made the decision to buy the house based on its facade and proximity to other things we liked. My hope was that over time we'd be able to do much of the renovation ourselves, working side by side, turning that old broken house into our home. We didn't know anything about what was below the surface. To find out what was true, we had to strip back all the layers accumulated from years of negligence. Beneath the old carpet were original hardwood floors. Behind the heavy drapes was enough light to fill the rooms. There was built-in shelving and paint was stripped to reveal beautiful craftsmanship in the woodwork. The potential was there. We had the right instincts. But once the house was stripped bare, we realized we weren't equipped to rebuild it. To restore it ourselves required a level of commitment, discipline, and expertise neither of us possessed. The house required professional help. Kerri went back to her work and I went back to the music, and we contributed together where time and interest allowed.

The house wrapped up. We restacked fallen stones along the short wall separating our yard from Boyd Mill Avenue and trimmed overgrown oaks so the newly painted facade could be seen from the street. The historical society came for a final approval. In the end, we had torn down walls and reimagined spaces and tested the limits of the footings. Through the entire renovation, the foundation of the house held.

The foundation of our marriage did not. The project was over, and there was nothing left to hide behind. Suspicions, intentions, and words once unspoken were brought into the open. Things unraveled quickly. Our relationship was made clear. We'd built the house she'd always wanted. It just wasn't me she wanted to share it with. I left for a tour with MercyMe.

My voice deteriorated on tour, and I could no longer make it through the show. At the beginning of the tour I could fake my way through half the set and rely on Tyler to cover the rest. By the end of the tour, I couldn't make it through a single song. I snuck away often, isolating myself to call my wife and beg for any way to fix things. I didn't want us to be over. I had tried everything I could think of. Vacations. Church. A new house. I reminded her of everything we'd done, but by the end, my voice didn't even work enough for the phone calls. My desperation went unheard. The only sounds I could make were stuttering, scratchy whispers and the guttural agony that comes before the tears. The band thought I was isolating myself out of frustration that my voice was continuing to fail. It left gaping questions about our careers and the future and how to support our families. They gave me space. I let them think my secrecy was because of my voice. My voice was the least of my problems. The tour was ending.

I walked past the stacked stones and under the oaks and through the newly painted front door of our house. Kerri was gone, having left the place her heart had long abandoned. The house was finished. It turned out beautifully. The historic society gave us an award for the quality of our restoration. We never fully moved in. It would never be our home.

THIRTY-FIVE

"Until My Heart Caves In"

Ben was the first to bring it up. He couldn't let the elephant run loose in the room any longer.

"You can't even talk. How are you going to sing?"

I told the guys about the doctors and the shots, but at the time I had no idea what was really wrong with my voice. The vocal cords are two side-by-side bands of elastic muscle tissue located in the larynx, just above the windpipe. The most common issue for singers is that the vocal cords swell with overuse, or a nodule or polyp grows on them. Swelling can be fixed with rest. Nodules and polyps can be surgically removed. I explored surgery, but the doctors said those weren't my issues; therefore, my vocal cords weren't surgically repairable. They didn't know exactly what was wrong, if it was permanent or if my voice would work again in the future after giving it some rest. The only thing I knew for sure was that my voice didn't work now. It wasn't the best information to make a career decision on, but that's all we had.

In a rock band, the lead vocalist is the only instrument that isn't replaceable without fundamentally altering the band. Busted guitars and drum heads can be replaced. Blown amplifiers can be fixed. But a broken voice is a different thing altogether. We were diminishing. Because of the limitations of my voice, we couldn't be who we used to be. We were becoming a watered-down version of Audio Adrenaline. I suggested getting a new lead singer. The guys didn't like that. For better or worse, we were who we were because of me as the captain. They would rather go down with the ship.

With awards and live shows and album sales, we were on top. Now could be a good time to be remembered as our full and complete band, not just a shadow of it. The conversation felt a lot like a family discussion about putting down the favorite pet.

"He's had a good life."

"This is what's best for Mark."

"It's time."

Audio Adrenaline called it quits.

ONE LAST ALBUM

The guys thought the best way to go was to record one last album, make an announcement upon its release, then do a farewell tour. I wasn't sure about it at first. I didn't have anything left. They promised to step up and cover my deficiencies. They did. Tyler floated the concept of "Until My Heart Caves In." I loved it. I imagined a noble warrior on the brink of his ultimate battle. He has a choice. If he enters the battle, he'll lose everything, even his life. But if he runs, what kind of life will he be saving? The warrior fights because his heart is not his own. It belongs to something bigger. He will fight until the very end, until his heart caves in. I felt that Tyler was writing the song for me.

I wanted our last album to be about loss and doubt and the truth of the difficulties of this life. Only by acknowledging those could we sing about the beauty and victory that comes with faithfulness, the heroic choice to fight all the way to the end, to live this life fully, even if it meant losing it. *Until My Heart Caves In* would be my most personal album.

Knowing this would be my last recording, I wanted to contribute as much as I could, but even with a steroid shot, there wasn't much my voice was able to handle. "Clap Your Hands" is right in the zone of what was left of my voice, and it was a fun release for me to perform live. As the first song on the record it hinted at the theme, but it was mostly the pure rock and roll fun I wanted the band to be remembered for. The title track, "Until My Heart Caves In," is a battle cry to be sung over and over until it was believed: *"I'm a Warrior"* who would *"give it all for you."* We wrote that song at the very moment I felt like giving up. Music calls us to something higher. My heart was fortified by the lyric, *"I won't give up . . . until my heart caves in."* "King" is a declaration that God stands alone in power, and "Melody" reminds us that his grace is even greater, enough to forget our sinfulness. "Starting Over," "Are You Ready for Love," and "Undefeated" are about the different ways life can bring us down. They felt autobiographical. "(Your Love Keeps Lifting Me) Higher" is about God's unrelenting desire to draw us up when we're down, and the power we feel standing next to him. Toward the end of the album are a couple of songs that reflect on a life lived in the presence of the Lord, and that in the end, what will be remembered are the last words on our lips. In "Light of the Sun," Tyler sings, *"The beauty that surrounded me / was like nothing I had seen."* And in "All Around Me," we sing, *"Your wonder, it surrounds me. / You're beautiful. You're beautiful."* Only one song remained to complete the album. It wasn't quite ready.

"LOSING CONTROL"

The band had a few one-off shows. Our bookings were reduced because of my voice. We sat in the front lounge of the bus, ready to pull out for another show in some city I can't remember. What I do remember is that I was frightened. Scared to face the shame of unveiling my failed marriage. I was supposed to be their leader. I got the guys' attention. They thought I was about to offer up the usual prayer for safe travels, but instead I began to share.

I broke down. I told them about my marriage. That it was over. My voice cracked, and tears filled the brokenness. The guys cried too. They'd seen me carry this pain alone. It had hurt them not knowing what it was, or how to help. Now that they did, they stepped in. Though it wasn't their pain to carry, they held me up so I no longer had to support the weight of it alone. These men were brothers to me. We'd been through so much. I felt like I was letting them down. Will put his arms around me. He was angry and upset and protective, yet also filled with grace. I always knew in my head he loved me. Crying in his arms, I now knew it in my heart too. He promised we'd find a way through this. Together. I believed him.

We will all come to a moment when we realize we never really had control over our lives. Control is an illusion brought on by pride. Whether by will or by force, it's when our control is gone that we truly experience God. After a long career, after tours and albums and awards, after youth group rooms and stadiums, after doubting God then believing in him then doubting him again, after bleeding my life on stage after stage until there was no more, and after doing it with the men I loved and trusted most, this was the greatest truth I knew. It was my last song.

"Losing Control" is skeletal in its simplicity. It opens with a raw, stripped-down acoustic guitar, strumming back and forth over two simple chords. My voice comes in. Broken. Honest. Barely heard above the guitar. The lyric is the story of a warrior at the end of his battle, submitting his last breath, finally relinquishing control.

The most intense moment I ever felt in the studio was recording "Losing Control." It was the last song of our last album. The album had already completed its thematic journey from awe to power to grace to beauty. "Losing Control" felt more like an epilogue to the album. And to my whole career. It was the most honest song I ever sang.

Most of our songs were recorded player by player, building the track with one instrument at a time. This song was recorded together, in one moment. Each of us, in different rooms, was only connected by the music we were creating through headphones. We could see each other through the soundproof glass, but the lights were so dim it was hard to make out any facial expressions. By this time in our career, we didn't need to see each other. We could feel what everyone was thinking at the same time. What we were thinking was that this was our last song. Our last moment together in the studio. The producer hit record, and the click track started.

I was known for having one of the most powerful voices in one of the biggest Christian rock bands of all time. My voice once commanded stadium-sized audiences. Here, in front of those who knew this best, my voice was veiled behind loss, reduced to whisper-like utterances of barely audible lines. In those lyrics, after the verse, I found the truth.

God came down
and walked beside me.
God came down.
He sent friends to guide me.

God came down to remind me
this is what it feels like
to be loved.

The producer released the recording button. No one said anything after the song was over. We knew how each other felt.

The album was complete. *Until My Heart Caves In* was as honest an album as we ever made. It went on to win a Grammy.

I received divorce documents before the album was complete. I read them alone in the studio. It was completely silent except for the rustling of papers. The words didn't seem real. In one of our last conversations, I told my wife the band was over. I thought maybe that would change things. That maybe there was hope that comes with the sunrise, after a long journey through the dark. Nothing changed. My hope was as useless as a penny in a well. We came to agreements about the house and our money and our stuff. I entered into a life without sunrises. The band was over. My marriage was over. This was real. Everything I loved and worked for in my life was gone.

THIRTY-SIX

"Good Life"

Kerri wanted to meet at the house. It was December. There were no Christmas decorations or presents under the tree. She had a list of furniture she wanted and walked through the house, double-checking if there was anything else.

"Do you want this lamp?"

"No. You can take it."

I looked around at the furniture. I didn't want any of it. It was hard to breathe. She asked if I was sure. I was sure. It all felt pointless.

She asked about the band. Our last album was complete. We'd announced publicly Audio Adrenaline was quitting. Rumors flew throughout the industry. They needed the distraction. The industry was hit hard by a combination of the digital-music revolution and the rise of worship music. Christian rock was all but over.

I helped load furniture. I remembered the discussion behind purchasing each piece. We'd picked them out based on colors and style and how well it would wear with time and use. Every piece was a part of a puzzle. The interior of the house looked like it belonged in a magazine. We'd produced a great product. Now half the puzzle pieces were leaving. The puzzle could never be completed again.

Some of the furniture was new, some of it was fragile antiques. We were careful not to ding anything while packing the U-Haul she had rented. I watched her red taillights fade away and blur into Christmas lights hung on homes filled with families and joy and the magic of the season. Our house was dark. I turned and walked in.

I felt like a ghost in my own house, hollowed out and haunted. Everything I thought I was and liked about myself was gone. I was humiliated. I felt like the fake I always feared I was. My band, my ministry—it was all pointless. My career was over. People I loved, who counted on me, were now looking for jobs. I didn't know how to support myself. Even if my voice could recover, the industry would move on and the twenty years of Audio Adrenaline would become a small asterisk in music history. I would soon be divorced. A failure with a scarred heart, where I doubted any future love could grow. The fires of God and love and rock and roll were all but extinguished within me. There was nothing left but ash and flickering embers, too weak to provide warmth. I cried myself into the coldness of night. A remnant of a man, puddled on an empty hardwood floor, with no voice to call for help. I was abandoned by any god who could hear me anyway.

Morning arrived without color. It was the first day of the rest of my terrible life. A thick, gray layer of ice had settled during the night, concealing any remaining beauty in the world. After a night of crying, the house closed in on me. I had to get out. I opened the back door. It creaked. The air felt as numb as my heart. Ice crunched underfoot as I walked across the frozen gravel driveway. The cold that had reduced towering summer oaks to skeletons of winter bit at my bones. I buttoned my jacket. It was no use. The cold came from within. My wife had taken our new car, so I scraped ice from the window of my beloved black Ford Bronco. The door was iced shut. I pried it open to sounds of screeching frozen metal. Inside was colder.

My Bronco desperately needed a new battery and barely started on a warm day. It was a decade old and showing signs of age. It was all I had left. Everything I touched felt frozen. The seat. The steering wheel. The ignition. I paused before inserting the key. I didn't know how to move on, or if I wanted to. Everything that gave purpose to my life had come to an end. I didn't know who I was without a band or a wife. I didn't know who I could be. Options are scarce for singers with no voice. Singing in a band was all I'd done since high school. It was my voice that had opened every door in my life. Without my voice, I was nobody.

I took a deep breath and leaned back into the cold seat. I couldn't exhale. I was frozen. There was no sound, no color, no hope. I tried to scream. Nothing came out. The pain, built in my silence and without a voice, could only escape through tears. I had never been so alone.

I stuck the key in the ignition and mumbled a cry of desperation. The words were barely audible.

"God, if you're here, start this truck. I need you to start this truck."

At that moment, I needed to know if God was real. Was he an active participant in this life or did he just wind the clock and let it go? If he wasn't what was promised on that rooftop in Haiti half a life ago, I was ready for it all to be over. I was tired of placing hope in fantasies.

I turned the key in the ignition. Several things happened at once.

I felt the warmth of a lion's breath come over me. The Bronco was no longer cold.

The engine started with a growl.

A song started playing loudly through the radio. I recognized it immediately.

> *This is the good life.*
> *I've lost everything*
> *I could ever want*
> *and ever dream of.*

But it couldn't be. That song hadn't been on the radio for five years. Someone must have put the *Underdog* CD in my CD player and cued it up to encourage me. I looked through the sections of scraped ice on the windows to see if Will or one of the guys was in the driveway, waiting with a smile. No one was there. Who did this? I looked at the CD player. There was no CD.

My eyes were opened, and my heart was pierced. God did more than start my truck. He did more for me than I could ask or imagine. Just like he promised. In one instant, he reminded me that he was my Dad, he was in control, and I was somehow worthy of this romantic, divine, miraculous moment with him.

> *This is the good life.*
> *I found everything*
> *I could ever need.*
> *Here in your arms.*

The song was called "Good Life." We'd written it long ago for my friend Luis, after his wife left him. The first verse starts with the line, *"I've watched my dreams all fade away / and blister in the sun. / Everything I've ever had is unraveled and undone."* The song went number one on Christian Hit Radio, but hadn't been on a playlist for years. I'd never felt more alive. I felt my heart pounding in my chest. The second verse began.

> *Loneliness has left me searching*
> *for someone to love.*
> *Poverty has changed my view*
> *of what true riches are.*
> *Sorrow's opened up my eyes*
> *to see what real joy is.*
> *Pain has been the catalyst*
> *to my heart's happiness.*

My heart raced with the rhythm of guitars, and my tears fell with each crash of cymbals, and my spirit swelled with each chorus as words I'd written for someone else returned in the echo of God's heart and washed over me. I gripped the wheel and lowered my head against my hands. I whispered the next chorus. My broken voice in the Bronco sang harmony with my restored voice over the radio, and for a moment, my voice was complete.

Tears fell from the vault before God separated the waters. He knew me then. From the foundation of the world, he knew about this moment. Since before there was sound, God had known this song. He'd prompted my heart to write it and somehow ordained it to be played on the radio at the exact moment I turned that key of the Bronco. It was God's answer to my question if he was there. Just starting the car would have been enough. The rest was a lavish display of his love, and I knew in that moment, *God had me.* No matter what happened next, I would be okay.

As only God can do, in a split moment, I was healed from a lifetime of hurt. This was my burning bush, where God spoke directly to me. He assured me that my career wasn't a joke and that the song I thought I'd written for a friend so many years ago was really God's song. He held it close, knowing I would someday need it for myself. God told me that the way I felt when the song washed over me was the same way fans all these years felt when the music washed over them. I was not abandoned. In fact, this was a moment of complete awareness. God was there, and I could finally see him clearly. I could see him in the goodness and warmth. I could see him in past and present. I could see him in the band and in my broken marriage and in my empty house. I could see him in my pain. The pain didn't go away. It became God's pain. Only now, I felt it through the filter and purpose of his love. He told me I was not a fake. He told me who I really was:

> *You are Mark Stuart. Not the husband. Not the lead singer. Not the stadium performer. Not the Grammy winner. Not the industry leader. Not the ministry founder. Just Mark Stuart. Period. You are my son. I love you with all the goodness in and beyond this world. I love you when you seek me. I love you in the dark places of your doubt. Even in the silence, when your ears cannot hear, I am busy, loving you.*

Life is a continuous series of deaths made up of losses we endure on the journey. We lose a loved one. We lose our marriage. We lose our jobs. We lose an innocence moving from one stage of life to the next. Ultimately, we lose our earthly lives. I had stepped into the Bronco in death. In there was my baptism, where the Holy Spirit washed over me in song. The warmth was the breath of God resurrecting me deeper into his presence. I was born again—again.

What we are going through is temporary. What we go through does not define us. Death is not our ending. Love is our ending. Because God is love.

PART VII

"Kings & Queens"

Boys become kings, girls will be queens,
wrapped in your majesty.
—AUDIO ADRENALINE, "KINGS & QUEENS"

Yet to all who did receive him, to those who believed in
his name, he gave the right to become children of God.
—JOHN 1:12

THIRTY-SEVEN

The New World

In the early fall of 1492, three ships left the Canary Islands off the western tip of Africa and followed the trade winds to a new world. Leading the expedition was a young explorer named Christopher Columbus. He reasoned this to be the quickest route to the spice riches of eastern Asia and convinced the crown of Spain to sponsor the adventure. The vastness of the ocean was greatly miscalculated. By day, blue ocean rose on a slight and infinite angle until meeting a mirrored sky on the curved horizon. The monotony of blue was broken only by the frothed white anger of toppled swells, hastening a desire for land or a quick return home. By night, inky blackness spilled beyond any reasonable fears, and the mythologies of a flat earth haunted the hearts of the sailors until dispelled by the sunrise.

Sailors slept mostly on deck. They read the night stars and realized their magnetic compasses no longer pointed to the North Star. Adrift at the mercy of the winds, they had to concede that their true north was no longer true. The sailors panicked. Columbus figured out that the compass wasn't actually pointing to the North Star but to some fixed point on earth. Over the span of the Atlantic, even only a couple of degrees off over time could send ships far enough off course to never return. Since Columbus continually checked and tested his compass, he was able to correct his navigation and get back on course before it was too late. They discovered land shortly after. Only, it wasn't the land he expected.

Columbus never made it to the destination he'd set out for. There were no spices or safe passages to the Near East. It was a new world. He bounced around the Caribbean, searching for something valuable to take back to Spain. In December, his men discovered the large island of Hispaniola and found a natural bay from which to explore land at a site now called Môle-Saint-Nicolas in modern-day northwest Haiti. After slipping back into the windward passage, he noticed a small island to the east, rising from the morning mist. It resembled the shell of a tortoise, so he named the island Tortuga. They crossed the channel between Tortuga and the main island of Haiti several times before accepting that their original mission was a failure by their stated objectives and they'd be heading home empty-handed. But first, their ship sank.

TORTUGA, HAITI, 1984

I was fifteen years old, on my first mission trip to Haiti, and sitting in a small wooden boat with my dad.

"Mark!"

I looked at my dad. He pointed to the floor of our boat.

"You better start bailing!"

Dad was sweating as he sat on the wooden plank fastened between the gunwales. Our boat was filling with water. We were four miles from shore, in the channel between Tortuga and the main island of Haiti, and land was only distantly visible when swells rocked the starboard bow. We were heading to the island of Tortuga, one of Christopher Columbus's stops on his first journey to the New World. It has since been controlled by pirates, both seafaring and governmental. These waters were once rumored to be filled with mermaids. Today we know they're only filled with sharks. The famous *Santa Maria* had sunk in these waters and has never been found. I hoped that would not be our fate.

Another swell hit and covered our feet with water. Dad, who's not a fan of swimming, put on a second life jacket. He could barely move.

I was having the time of my life. We had arrived in my dad's beloved Haiti the day before, and I'd sat in the back of a dump truck for a ten-hour scramble through ditches and rivers and over tropical mountain passes until we arrived in Port-de-Paix, the "port of peace." We'd spent the night in a concrete block hotel with no air conditioning. Electricity was intermittent, and the only light was a single bare bulb hanging from the ceiling. When the light went out, in the dark and silence of a forgotten Third World city gone to sleep, I could hear something crawling. I didn't investigate.

In the morning, we arrived at a port containing a handful of locally made fishing vessels pulled onto the sand. It appeared absent of any real, seaworthy boats. There was one that looked like something from a Huckleberry Finn story or a prop from *Pirates of the Caribbean*. It was planked with brightly painted wood, though the paint was chipping faster than the rate of repair. Toward the bow was a hand-carved mast held in place by remnants of plywood and rope. Its sail looked like stitched-together bedsheets. By the looks of the stains, they could have come from the hotel we'd stayed in. There was no motor on this boat, and no instruments. It was a simple schooner, with fewer technical advances than the *Santa Maria*. A couple of carved oars lay on the bottom.

A barefoot man with tattered shorts and no shirt walked up and smiled and exchanged a few words in Creole with my dad. He would be our captain. Accompanying him were a couple of small boys in oversized rain boots. I assumed the boys to be his children. Or grandchildren. We loaded our tents and building supplies and a couple days' worth of provisions and pushed the boat into the water. Halfway through the channel, I realized the boys were not related to our captain. They were hired to bail water, using nothing more than their rubber boots. They handed me an extra. The boot leaked as fast as the boat.

We came to shore on a remote section of Tortuga. A Haitian man appeared from out of the bushes. He was Pastor Octave from the local church. Our mission was to build him a foundation for a church building. He and seven of his men were there to help. There weren't any building instructions from the organization we were working with. Just, "Go find Pastor Octave and figure it out." If we didn't do it, it wouldn't happen. We had five days to complete the task. My dad and Pastor Octave talked to our boat captain. He'd make daily trips to resupply us with building materials and food. We set up camp with our tents along the sand and found a site that looked good for a church and started digging.

I assumed we were there because these guys couldn't get it done on their own. Pride swelled in me. I would show them hard work and American ingenuity. I grabbed the only pickax and started digging. Pastor Octave looked on. I flew through a layer of sand and was feeling really good about my abilities. *I'm going to single-handedly build this church. This country needs me. I'm a hero.*

Twelve inches down, I hit bedrock. The footer needed to be at least twenty-four inches deep. I swung at the rock with a sledgehammer for an hour. Nothing budged. Pastor Octave watched patiently. I felt bad for the guy. We'd have to find another spot for his church. He pointed to the hammer, asking if he could take a few swings. I humored him and passed him the handle. *Knock yourself out*, I thought. *That rock isn't going anywhere.* In three swings the rock busted, and a few minutes later, the footer was finished. I sat stunned.

Just then, one of the other Haitians calmly got Pastor Octave's attention. A scorpion was in the rock, and it stung Pastor Octave's arm. He took out his machete, slit his arm open where he'd been stung, sucked out the poison, and spit it back onto the rock. He then took his shirt off to bandage his arm and revealed who he really was. Pastor Octave was Superman. He had six-pack abs and forearms made of steel. He didn't need me. He didn't need anyone. We were there because that is how the body of Christ is supposed to work, helping each other out, sharing in the grace and goodness of the work set before us.

That night in my tent, I itched and shivered uncontrollably. I had sun poisoning. For the rest of the trip I could do nothing except supply Pastor Octave and the others with water. He was stronger and more gracious than any man I'd ever met. Over the course of the week, I grew to love and respect him and his men and the boat captain and the bailing boys and the locals who helped from sunup to sundown and slept in worse conditions than my tent. From the outside perspective, the country looked broken. I'd gone to fix it. What I learned is that the country isn't broken. It's just poor. The men building that church loved Jesus and depended on him for everything. Even if that meant putting up with an arrogant American who thought he'd come to save them. In their love and dependence on Jesus, their souls were complete. I was the one who was broken. Those men were strong, capable, and overly gracious to me and my dad. I fell in love with Haiti on Tortuga. I knew as a teenage boy that I would be significantly connected to that country for the rest of my life.

JACMEL, HAITI, 2004

With Audio Adrenaline's Hands and Feet Project I was back in Haiti, and I was learning that the key to success is having "a guy," or someone who knows someone who can mobilize the right people—labor, local churches, government—or can simply put the right construction team together. All construction in Haiti is done under a "boss," and sifting through cultural and language differences to find the right one is a needle-in-a-haystack exercise. There are no Yellow Pages or construction trucks driving around with names of companies plastered on the doors and tailgates. Bosses are found through word of mouth, as in, "I know a guy." It's a position of ultimate trust. Accomplishing any major project in a developing nation requires a complete alignment of the stars, and a little luck on top of that. Having the right guy means you have a better-than-average shot at it. Having the wrong guy means disaster. Or worse.

My dad had a guy. His name was Odius. When Dad first met Odius, he was learning the construction trade under his brother and has since become one of the finest project managers in southern Haiti. Once Dad found him, they moved fast. They were a great team. Audio Adrenaline and friends funded the construction, and under Dad's direction and Odius's capable leadership, the first Hands and Feet Project building was completed in less than a year. The building was designed by my dad and my cousin Tracy. Tracy engineered the structural foundation and columns in such a way that the building could be expanded with the growth of Hands and Feet. It was also designed to withstand the worst Mother Nature could throw at it, which she later did. Tracy's design saved many lives. She passed away from cancer not long after the completion of her building, but her legacy lives on with every child who finds a home in it. My dad named the building and had a sign made for it. He called it Big House. It was perfect. Dad's dream was finally fulfilled when he and my mom moved into the Big House full time.

Our first group of missionaries arrived in the summer of 2004. They came all the way from Bel Air Presbyterian Church in Los Angeles, California, to build bunk beds and shelving and to prepare the site for our first children. I couldn't believe they came. They were more beautiful than a cavalry of angels. It was a group of college and early career kids led by a smart young woman named Patty Johnson, who would become one of our first board members and would help us grow into a real organization. The group worked hard during the day, sweating under the tropical sun, with no escape of air conditioning or ice-blended coffee drinks.

At night, we sat on the roof. Starlight to the south reflected silver on the

Caribbean, and the breeze rustled in the palms and blew over us like whispers. We talked of dreams and uncertain futures. None of us had any idea what was next. We were all trying to figure out life and where we fit in it. We dreamed about the kids laughing in the distance and discussed how this place might enable the less fortunate kids to laugh once more. It reminded me of sitting on the roof with Fred twenty years earlier, and it struck me that I was at yet another crossroad. This time I could only smile and lean into the beauty of the night. In the context of this so-called broken country, we were being fixed. Hearts mended and hopes restored. God is a wonder.

I was in Haiti when the authorities arrived on our property with a very young girl in need of care. Her name was Tamara. She was maybe eighteen months old and badly malnourished. The police couldn't care for her. They took her to Tina, the local missionary who helped us get started, and together they brought her to us and asked if we were ready. The short answer was no. God often tells us to do something but seldom tells us how. The best you can do is step into your purpose and ask God to remove the fear. That's the essence of our faith. We said yes. We went to the mayor with Tamara. Since she'd been abandoned to the police, she was in the government's care. The mayor did the paperwork and turned her guardianship over to us. Tamara was the first child to become a part of the Hands and Feet family.

For the first two days, the only thing we could get Tamara to eat was Cheetos. We loved her the best we could and prayed she'd start liking eggs or toast . . . anything but Cheetos. She did. I sat in a rocking chair on the porch with Tamara in my lap and fed her and watched God perform a miracle of bringing her back to health. She stared at me with eyes full of love and trust and wonder. She connected me to hopefulness again. My marriage and my voice were dead. My band and career were over. Yet here something new was being born. The first time I held Tamara, I realized my life had a bigger meaning. She was something I could live for. She needed me. And I needed her. She brought the new life I was looking for.

The first wave of kids came shortly after Tamara. They reinforced the same feelings I had with her. They arrived hungry and scared and abused, but within a few months their eyes sparkled again. Each child reestablished our purpose. More and more, these kids and the Hands and Feet Project became the focus of my existence. But it was also getting very expensive, very quick. The weight of taking on these kids became real. At the time, I didn't have any doubt I was called to do the work. That doubt would come later. But Audio Adrenaline was funding most of the project, and that well was about to run dry. If this was going to work, I needed to go back to the US and find others to join.

THIRTY-EIGHT

Journey

Though I had experienced a miracle in the Bronco, and God had lovingly shown me I was not defined by my divorce, I still harbored some fear of connecting deeply to any church. I'd seen how other prominent Christian musicians were skewered for divorces, and after mine, the church didn't feel like a safe place to go. I distanced myself from others and slipped into isolation. I knew I had to connect back to the church. For Hands and Feet. And for myself. A friend told me about a church meeting in a refurbished factory on the edge of Franklin. Supposedly, it was a new, unpolished church plant. It was definitely unpolished. I loved it. It was authentic and broken. I especially loved that it was dark, mostly lit with candles. The candles created a cool vibe, but I suspected they were there because the church couldn't afford electricity. It didn't matter. The darkness enabled me to slip in and out without being noticed.

In spite of the church's flaws, or perhaps because of them, I felt at home. The place had the distinct feeling of being a makeshift hospital for people hurt by the church over the years. My career had been in Christian entertainment, so I knew the fake from the real thing. This church, called Journey Church, celebrated its flaws. It was real, a ragamuffin gathering of imperfect people succeeding and failing through real-life issues. I fell in love with the church, and in it, finally found a church home.

Eventually I met the pastor. His name was Jamie George. He invited me to join a "small group," where, according to him, the real business of being in a church took place. It was where we could open up, lean on each other, pray, cry, laugh, be real, and be loved for who we really are. I said no. He said he'd start a new one just for me. Not interested. He finally promised that I could help pick the guys. I reluctantly said yes, expecting to quit as soon as we started. I could tell Jamie was genuinely concerned about me. He didn't care if I went to his church; he just wanted me to be in a community. Lots of churches wanted the lead singer of a Christian rock band in their building on Sunday mornings. For striving churches in Nashville, who attends is the quiet marketing. I didn't want anything to do with that.

With Jamie, it was different. He led by opening up with his shortcomings, struggles, and failures. I was stunned. The professional Christian subculture is one of feigned perfection. By sharing his honest struggles, Jamie created a safe environment where I could share mine. I opened up to the men in our group. They opened up too. We cried together. Prayed together. Experienced healing. It was the church the Bible talked about. I never felt judged. I never felt like I had to perform. I was accepted for who I really was. My honest, raw, and real self. I still meet with these men today.

COFFEE AND MOTORCYCLES

Past the candlelit area in the back of the church was a station for coffee that was always my first stop. Usually I was safe from someone initiating unsolicited conversation, but one morning there was a girl who caught my attention. Our eyes met for an uncomfortable moment. We didn't say anything, and I looked away. I couldn't do it. I caught my breath and looked back, but she had disappeared. Her eyes had already unlocked a door I thought was permanently sealed shut, though, and it unsettled me. For the rest of the day, I couldn't stop thinking about her eyes. They were an invitation into a mystery. Whatever it was, wherever it led, I needed to know.

A few weeks later, we talked at church. I was nervous to speak, but when I did, she was patient, listening to my broken voice struggle to get the words out. I learned her name was Aegis and asked her out to lunch. She said yes.

I said, "You have my number, right?"

She squinted and tilted her head slightly. "Why would I have your number?"

I was Mark Stuart, lead singer of one of the most popular Christian rock bands of all time.

"Oh, I thought you knew who I was."

"You're Mark Schultz. Right?"

She had no idea who I was, confusing me with another contemporary Christian singer.

When it comes to girls, a lead singer's biggest fear is to date a fan. The stage and the music and the hype all work to amplify the image of a rock star. It's not real. Fans fall for the guy onstage only to be disappointed by the real version. The fact that Aegis had no idea who I was made her even more attractive. We talked about the church, and I was also pleased that she felt the same way about Journey as I did. She had grown up in a fundamentalist church and loved that Journey embraced the imperfections of people within the church. I immediately felt at ease with her. She was at peace with herself and with her place in the world. She was lighter than air. I asked her how she felt about riding motorcycles. She'd never been on one. I saw my opportunity.

When I picked her up, she wore Vans sneakers, jeans, and a leather jacket that perfectly matched her dark hair. She seemed neither excited nor anxious. Just present. She climbed onto the back of my bike and wrapped her arms around my chest. I hadn't been held by a woman for years. When she slipped her arms around me the cold gap between us filled with a warmth that thawed a frozen portion of my heart. I realized, of course, she was only hanging on for safety. I'd take what I could get.

The historic town of Franklin is surrounded by wooded hills and rolling horse farms and white-fenced pastures dotted with rounded hay bales. The roads are sinuous. They follow creeks and rivers and undulate between valley floors. We turned onto a country road and followed the sun west. South of Leiper's Fork, we joined up with the Natchez Trace Parkway. The Natchez Trace is a national scenic road following a Native American trail from Nashville to the Mississippi River in Natchez, Mississippi. Commercial vehicles are not allowed on the Trace, leaving the natural beauty undisturbed and safe for recreational use. I shifted into fourth gear and tucked my head into the wind. We sped through a corridor of red dogwoods and purple violets. Aegis tightened her grip and settled comfortably against my back. The motorcycle leaned and twirled along the ever-meandering Natchez Trace. The sun dipped below the tallest hickory and oaks, and the highway cooled in the shadows. I'd never felt warmer.

We pulled off the highway at a scenic overview. The last light of sun kindled in the highest canopies of hardwoods that from above appeared as pillowy clouds of spring. The conversations went deeper. They continued amid the worn wooden floors and checkered tablecloths of the homespun Loveless Cafe.

We saw each other regularly, and our feelings grew quickly. The speed at which I fell for her was disorienting. I still suffered from post-traumatic "relationship" disorder and didn't trust my heart. I freaked out, and to protect myself, I had to shut it down. At least I found a nice place to end the relationship. We broke up at Applebee's. When I told Jamie and the guys in my small group, they told me I was stupid.

A MOVING PRAYER

The Hands and Feet Project needed money. We hatched a plan to do a cross-country motorcycle ride and use the Audio Adrenaline platform to connect with churches and radio stations and tell them about the work in Haiti. It would be a long and difficult ride. Garth was in. He rode a motorcycle that looked like it came straight out of a *Mad Max* movie. It had a new paint job and looked amazing, but it was a vintage bike, and I had my doubts it would make it through the whole trip. I rode a brand-new Victory 1500cc. Scott Brickell joined for portions of the trip riding his Harley-Davidson Heritage Softail, and Will joined for sections riding whatever was available to him. Jeff, whom we called "Cheese," joined the ride. He was one of our crew guys and followed with Sam Shifley, our stage manager, in a support truck hauling tools, tents, and whatever bikes weren't being ridden. Other fans and supporters showed up to ride segments with us. It was our own Cannonball Run.

Sometimes God is working in ways you don't know. The ride may or may not have been a very good idea for the ministry, but it gave me time to sort things out with God. My voice wasn't improving. I had to confront the reality that I may never sing again and could possibly lose my ability to communicate verbally altogether. It was one thing for God to allow my voice to fail and my career to end. But now I was also responsible for a children's village full of kids.

How could I raise money to support them if I couldn't tell their story? On top of all that, God had gone and put a beautiful girl in my life. I mean, a really, really beautiful girl. I was confused on all fronts.

I've always been afraid to ride in the rain. I feared slick roads and was discomforted in wet clothes. We came upon a squall in Oklahoma. There was no way around it. We were heading to a radio interview where thousands of people would hear about the Hands and Feet Project and have an opportunity to get involved. If we waited for the weather to pass, we would miss the interview. I was about to call the interview off when Garth stopped me. He reminded me of the kids depending on us to show up and tell their stories. If we didn't, nobody else would.

Garth gave some pointers and told me to follow his lead. His sleeves were rolled up, revealing weathered arms filled with tattoos, and he casually smoked a cigarette as he rode. The storm front approached like an attacking army lined up over the horizon. We were kings on horses, claiming victory for the cause, triumphantly riding into battle. Before we collided with the rain, I looked at Garth and he looked back at me. He gave a confident thumbs-up, then with his middle and pointer finger, made the shape of a hand gun and pointed it at the storm.

"Let's go!"

I tightened my grip and ducked my helmet and throttled into the rain. At highway speeds, each drop felt like a point of an arrow. My chest and arms were pierced. My helmet thundered. Winds blew me off center, and I had to fight against the rain. My knees were shaking, but I was okay. I would be okay. The rain knocked off layers of fear and doubt and washed away some lies. My heart was not permanently damaged. It could love again. Though Hands and Feet was too much for me to carry alone, I would never be alone. I followed Garth through the rain, my heart and soul cleansed by the water.

I'd crossed the country hundreds of times but never experienced it. I'd viewed the land through tinted windows aboard a climate-controlled tour bus. On a motorcycle, I reentered the story of our land. It rolled by like a moving prayer. We rode along shadowy sloughs and gulf swamps, cooled beneath bald cypress and oaks layered in Spanish moss. We continued through the sticky heat of the Delta and its bottomlands and over our great river and into the southern plains, where we followed the dust-bowl migrations into the West.

There we rode through vast deserts and over once-impassable mountains until we came to the last of our great land and a golden sun setting on a blessed and sinful and complex country.

The whole ride I couldn't stop thinking about Aegis. I thought about her through the southern pines and wide deserts, and at night, memories of her warmed the rides along starlit highways. I opened up to the guys about my feelings for her, but they only stated their disbelief that someone so cool and beautiful would actually like me.

"You know she only likes you because you're Mark Stuart the *lead singer*," they said jokingly.

Garth interjected, "Now, that's not true."

I knew the guys were teasing, but I still had my doubts. It was nice to hear Garth stand up for me. He continued, "I think she would also like you if you were Mark Stuart the *movie star* or Mark Stuart the *astronaut*."

We stopped in Red Rock Canyon near Sedona, Arizona, and I called her. I told her I was sorry and wanted to see her when I got back. Garth found me after the call and asked how it went. Before I could think about it, my heart blurted out what I felt but was afraid to say: "I'm going to marry that girl."

Garth smiled and nodded with approval. We got back on our bikes and headed west.

WHO WE TRAVEL WITH

Garth was pulled over in Williams, Arizona, because his handlebars were too high. (And probably because he looked like someone who had outstanding warrants.) Garth talked his way out of a ticket by telling the officer about our mission and how he was riding with a Grammy-winning Christian rock star. The officer was an Audio Adrenaline fan. He let us go. Before we left, we took funny pictures with the officer, who pretended he was arresting Garth. Under an enchanting southwestern sky, we talked and laughed and went our separate ways. There was a time I would have felt guilty for this joy. I would have thought it was too good for God to approve of. Now I felt only his love. When we truly seek God, he wants to give us the desires of our hearts. For our hearts are his heart too.

Back home, bets had been made that I wouldn't make the whole trip. If I'd been riding alone, I wouldn't have. I would have quit before the rain or the excessive heat and loneliness of the desert. Garth came along to make sure that I would make it. He knew I was called to something important. His calling was to make sure I got there. Garth was my angel. A tattooed, cussing, smoking, divorced, motorcycle-riding angel who loved Jesus. He knew of God's grace. He made sure I didn't forget it. God has called each of us to a destination that will require difficult travel. He doesn't want us to go it alone. We all need a "Garth" to travel with.

The motorcycle tour ended in California. We looped through the heavy vines of California wine country and finished with a triumphant crossing of the Golden Gate Bridge into San Francisco, where we found a seafood restaurant and celebrated. Under the spell of the city's romance, I thought more of Aegis. I grew eager to return to Franklin and see where things stood.

THIRTY-NINE

A Night in Franklin

Audio Adrenaline's contract required one more album. We decided to release a greatest hits collection with one last original song written by Tyler, called "Goodbye," and then go on a farewell tour. Before the tour, I asked Aegis out again. She said no. The sting of the breakup had hurt too much. She still couldn't go to Applebee's.

Instead, she invited me to see a new band with her and some friends, so I met them at a local church. She wore her hair differently and was even more beautiful than I remembered. To get a little time alone, I asked her if she wanted to see my new truck. I'd sold the Bronco and bought a new Ford F-150 pickup truck with leather seats and all the bells and whistles. It was used but looked brand-new. It was the nicest vehicle I'd ever owned. I remarked about her hair.

"That's what happens when people break up."

I was confused. She elaborated.

"Girls cut their hair and boys buy trucks."

I told her I really wanted a chance for another date. She was reluctant at first. She didn't want to be hurt again. I finally convinced her to have dinner with me.

We spent a couple of hours trying to find a quiet restaurant where we could talk. Secretly, I was trying to find a restaurant with a romantic vibe. The west end of Nashville is anchored by Vanderbilt University and Centennial Park, which houses a replica of the Greek Parthenon. At night, reflections of soft Parthenon lights ripple over a pond and add a romantic backdrop to a neighborhood made legendary for its Music Row, Tudor architecture, live music venues, and fine dining. We arrived at Maggiano's around 8:00 p.m. The hostess sat us in a half-circled booth tufted with red vinyl. I sat as close to Aegis as I could without pushing my luck.

A crisp white linen was layered over a traditional red-and-white-checkered Italian tablecloth. Dampened light glowed against dark woods and twinkled in oversized mirrors and reflected from framed black-and-white images of the old country. I loved Maggiano's for the music. They played the old standards: Dean Martin, Ella Fitzgerald, and my favorite, Frank Sinatra. His songs transport me to a time and place of boundless romantic possibility. As we settled into our booth, the waitress commented that we were a cute couple. Aegis quickly corrected her.

"Oh, no. We're just friends."

The waitress looked disappointed.

We ordered chicken piccata covered in lemon butter and capers and a large caprese salad to split. We talked about the band we'd just seen. Aegis had interacted with them at GMA week while working for a management company. The band's name was Freshman 15. The name was clever, but I suggested changing it. It would haunt them later to be named after the first fifteen pounds they'd gained in college. Aegis laughed easily and generously. Then she asked about Haiti. We talked about church and our small groups and how things were going with the ending of Audio Adrenaline. I told her about the motorcycle ride and my soul-searching, and how I'd thought about her and wondered where she'd traveled and where she still wanted to go. Conversation ran long, and the waitresses changed. We ordered dessert.

The second waitress brought us a chocolate cake plated in a dark chocolate sauce and told us we looked like a great couple. This time, Aegis hesitated a moment, stealing a glance at me.

"Oh, no. We're just friends."

"That's too bad," the waitress countered.

I couldn't take my eyes off of Aegis. She tried to show me some pictures on her camera. I can't remember of what. I couldn't concentrate. I was mesmerized by her eyes. And her hair. And her voice. And stories that were mine alone for the evening. I was deeply, deeply in love.

The last dinner plates were long cleared, and all that remained was a few bites of chocolate and an intensifying conversation. I laid out my feelings. I missed her terribly. I told her why I'd had to walk away. After the divorce, I'd needed to check my heart and know for sure what I was feeling was true. By the end of the motorcycle ride, I knew I'd never known anything truer than my growing love for her. I told her I was sorry. It had killed me to lose her once. I wouldn't do it again. She was willing to forgive me. The waitresses were right. We did make a good couple. It was effortless. We decided to try again.

The kitchen had closed and most of the guests in the restaurant had cleared, leaving us to ourselves. Frank Sinatra sang softly in the background. We were transported to a place of outdoor music and dancing and crisp white linens drying on clotheslines draped between ancient buildings washed in light. Time slowed. Our hands moved closer and closer, and the energy of infinity hung between them. When our hands touched, skin on skin, my heart skipped and pulses raced to my head and shaking knees. A new universe was created. My gravity was forever altered to orbit her heart. A third waitress approached our table, and seeing the shifting of our bodies in the booth, said, "Y'all make such a cute couple."

Our eyes never left each other's. "Yes. We do."

LIGHT ON THE BAY

The only thing left was for Aegis to meet my parents and for me to introduce her to Haiti. When you've already been married, you know pretty quickly what you want and need out of a relationship. Aegis checked all the boxes. I wanted to be married to her. The only thing left was Haiti. God had put something big in my heart for that country. His calling for me was the only thing that could put an end to our romance. She agreed to come. I was nervous.

Aegis had a passion for international missions. A lifestyle of kingdom adventure was important to her. Most people are shocked and frightened when they first come to Haiti. They cling to their bags and don't stray far from the ministries they stay with. The opposite was true of Aegis. She came to life walking through surrounding neighborhoods and meeting kids and vendors and shopping at the market. My mom took her to town. Aegis jumped into work where needed, and when not, enjoyed the country. I rented a motorcycle. We rode along a coastal countryside with smells of hibiscus and fern and Caribbean mist. I introduced her to my friends and life there. She loved all of it. The kids. The food. The landscape. I thought maybe we were supposed to move to Haiti.

One day we rode to a secluded beach. The weather was perfect. The sea, calm and warm. We swam past shallow rock ledges and reefs and floated in the deep waters of the bay. Swells gently lifted us and provided watery vantage of the land. A narrow stretch of sand gave way to coconut palms and dense orchards of banana trees. In the backdrop, untamed mountains towered in tropical vegetation. There was a band of rain in the mountains with wisped clouds and sunlight refracting in a rainbow. Aegis looked to the mountains, smiling, sun soft on her face. She was hope and beauty and grace. The ocean reflected perfectly in her eyes. Sea-blue and transcendent, outlined with the deep blue of the horizon. In that moment, weightless in the Caribbean, with a woman more beautiful than anything I'd ever seen, I was finally, completely happy. I watched Aegis fall in love with Haiti as I fell even more in love with her.

We had dinner with my parents in downtown Jacmel. My mom loved Aegis from the start. When it was just me and my mom, she gave me a look. It was full of love and certainty, like she knew something I didn't. She'd given me that look once before.

"Mark, honey. She makes you happy, and you haven't been happy like this for a long time. You need to go for her."

That night, my mom and dad helped with plans for a proposal.

ADIOS

When I first met Will, he introduced me to a Welsh new wave band called the Alarm. Our first band had played a song of theirs called "Blaze of Glory." As a tribute to our beginning and to our enduring friendship, we recorded it on the *Greatest Hits* album. It's how we felt we were going out. In the back of my mind, I hoped my voice would come back. I prayed for it. Others prayed for it. I gave it a long rest. It wasn't coming back. I couldn't carry a tour, so we joined MercyMe for our Adios tour. They'd started their career opening for us. It was an honor to end ours opening for them. In addition to saying goodbye to audiences across the country, this was also an opportunity to introduce them to the Hands and Feet Project and invite them on our next journey.

It was hard to say goodbye to our fans. They'd grown up with us, watching us go from underdog to headliner. The tour felt like a long sunset, with colors burning brighter and more beautiful all the way into the darkness. Familiar faces showed up in places like Cleveland and Denver and Orange County. Over the years, we'd watched our faces age in the mirrors of theirs. Some brought their kids to the last tour to say goodbye as a family to their favorite band. Music is personal. It can be a source of comfort, healing, anger, inspiration, and worship. It seeps through the cracks of our hearts where nothing else can penetrate. There it does the magic only music can do. Losing a favorite band is like losing a close friend. Fans held up signs that said, "We will miss you," and told us what we had meant for their marriages and families and youth groups. Audio Adrenaline was one of the last of the youth group rock bands. The era of Christian arena rock, rebellion, and revival was coming to an end.

A NIGHT IN FRANKLIN

The Adios tour generated a lot of support for the Hands and Feet Project. Fans found ways to get involved with the next part of the Audio Adrenaline journey. With our first donors outside of the band, Hands and Feet was able to expand the ministry. God was on the move. Other artists got involved, and more mission trips signed up. We hired our first missionary outside of Mom and Dad. Michelle Meece had lived with my parents when they first moved to Haiti in the late 1980s and fell in love with the country the same way I did. She arrived back just in time. Dad finished the first building, and more kids were coming. So many in fact that he would have to get busy building more homes to house them. It was the honeymoon phase of the ministry. We had no idea how hard things would eventually get. We just focused on providing the very best care for kids who had lost their families. We'd figure the rest out later.

After her first trip to the Hands and Feet Project, Aegis told me that being involved in kingdom work like this was exactly what she was hoping for. With her on board, my life felt complete. After the first leg of the tour, I went to Pennsylvania to spend Thanksgiving with Aegis and her family. Her mom and I had already met and hit it off. She was a complete delight to be around.

I found time to be alone with her dad and asked his permission to marry his daughter. My intentions became obvious to Aegis, and we had fun dreaming about our future.

I traveled to Haiti every opportunity I had. Dad needed the help, and Jacmel was now a second home. In 2006, I was in Haiti over Christmas and New Year's and surprised Aegis with a flight on Christmas Eve. We spent Christmas with my family and the kids, then continued with our explorations of the southern coast. Our favorite place to hang out was the Cyvadier Plage, a small, unassuming hotel and restaurant run by my friend Christoph. He'd grown up in Haiti, then trained as a chef in France. He wanted to bring world-class cuisine to Jacmel and purchased a stunning cliffside property on the innermost bend of a secluded horseshoe bay. I made plans to propose to Aegis there. Christoph reserved the most romantic section of the restaurant, overlooking the cliff by the ocean. My mom and dad took her on some errands, then dropped her off at the entry of the resort. I hoped that my attempts to conceal this moment had worked.

The open-air restaurant connects to a thatched-roof bar and figure-eight pool through a series of terraces descending dramatically along the edge of a cliff. Thirty feet below, the sea rhythmically surges into the rocks and explodes in white foamed spray. The breeze funnels through the opening of the bay and rustles in the palms and thatched roofs of the buildings, and with the highest swells carries the mist of the spray back to the terraces. Two promontories extend in both directions, like two arms reaching into the Caribbean. The terraces sit at the heart. Christoph cued the music of Sinatra and Fitzgerald, and beyond their silky voices were only the sounds of sea breezes and birds and the outgoing tide. Aegis arrived at sunset. The bay filled with cerulean blue and reflected the blushed gold and pink of the sky. She heard the music and saw me standing alone on the terrace. She approached like a breeze.

She sat down across from me at a small café-sized table. I poured out my feelings, and for the first time I said the words, "I love you. I love you. I love you." Neither of us had ever told each other these words before. I wanted to make sure she heard it. I dropped to a single knee. Tears welled from her eyes. I reached for the ring. With Frank and the sea and the wind through the palms, my voice entered the night, broken yet certain.

"Aegis, will you marry me?"

We decided to get married before the last tour so Aegis could come with me. We were excited about the plan. Except it left only a month to prepare a wedding.

We found a quaint chapel a block from the square in downtown Franklin. It was a simple brick building constructed before the Civil War, featuring white arched windows and doors and stained-glass mosaics lighting the chapel. The wooden pews, worn with history, barely accommodated the intimate gathering of close friends and family. I took my position up front as Aegis's favorite song, "Clair de Lune," played. The old wood floors creaked. Will stood next to me as my best man, as he always has. The guys in the band were smiling. Mom and Dad had flown in from Haiti. Garth even dressed up for the occasion. Tyler came up front, picked up his guitar, and started into a song. Then entered my bride, radiant in winter's light. She walked down the aisle and into my arms. I never plan to let her go.

T-Bone performed the ceremony. He was the first I'd told of my broken marriage, and he had walked with me through the darkest days of my life. Now he was there to get me started on a new chapter. He was as close as a friend could be. After the ceremony, the entire assembly walked a block to Puckett's grocery and restaurant. I drove Aegis in my Ford F-150. The reception was one level up from a high school dance party. There were dance-offs and break dancing and who knows what T-Bone was doing. We shut the place down with music and laughter and dancing. It was a dream come true. The next morning, Aegis and I flew to the Caribbean for a couple nights to ourselves before starting Audio Adrenaline's last tour.

FORTY

Live from Hawaii

The last Audio Adrenaline tour was basically an extended honeymoon for Aegis and me, except that it was on a bus with ten other guys. Aegis was once again at ease and jumped right in. All the action on a tour bus takes place in the back lounge, and each tour comes with its own obsession. For this tour, it was the video game *Guitar Hero*. I heard Aegis in the back, trash-talking with the guys. I don't think she lost a single game the entire tour

The Hands and Feet Project was the centerpiece to our set. Getting to talk about what was happening in Haiti with my wife by my side, even with a broken voice, was one of the greatest highlights of my career. MercyMe took the stage after our short set, which was all my voice could handle. I sat in the back of the arena with my wife, talking to fans about our ministry, and listened to MercyMe sing their greatest hits. They even covered "Tremble," one of my favorite songs that Audio Adrenaline had ever written. MercyMe took the song to the next level. It was an amazing gesture for them to cover that song. All was well with my soul.

I took Aegis to all my favorite places in the country. Places I'd been dozens of times before but got to experience again for what felt like the first time with her. We went snowmobiling in South Dakota. In Las Vegas, we rode our 50cc mini-scooters up and down the Strip like an Audio Adrenaline and MercyMe motorcycle gang. We took in museums, hiked national forests, and ate in fine dining and hole-in-the-wall restaurants I'd discovered over a lifetime of touring.

My favorite Italian restaurant in the country is Cucina Biazzi in Ashland, Oregon. Ashland sits in a fold of the southern Cascades and houses one of the country's largest Shakespeare festivals. It's a town filled with bookstores and cafés and parks and shaded sidewalks meant for holding hands, surrounded by mountains lush with spruce and pine and clear, cold waters. Cucina Biazzi is on the quiet side of Main Street, a couple blocks from downtown. It's housed in an unassuming craftsman-style home converted into a kitchen with two small dining rooms. The rooms are walled with honeywood bookshelves that stage collections of fine wines. Outdoors is an intimate courtyard with terra-cotta floor tiles and fireplace and a trellis shaded by grapevines and wisteria that in spring smell like exotic perfumes. Intertwined between vines are small white lights shaded by broad grape leaves that look like stars in a far greener world. We shared a perfectly prepared four-course meal and strolled the Shakespearean streets of Ashland. God does an amazing thing with the scales of happiness. The weight of a single, pure joy can tip the scales of years of pain. And that joy can redeem the whole thing.

LIVE FROM HAWAII

The last show Audio Adrenaline would ever play was at the Waikiki Shell in Honolulu, Hawaii. For three days, friends, fans, and family snorkeled and had a luau and surfed the soft waves of Waikiki. Will, Ben, Tyler, and I convinced my dad, who still didn't like the water, to ride an outrigger canoe with us. We paddled far into the bay over brightly colored fish and shallow reefs with turtles swimming alongside. What we didn't tell my dad is that we'd be surfing in. We picked up speed and a wave built behind us. The canoe shot down the wave while Will, the guide, and I belly laughed as my dad screamed through the whitewash warmly splashing over us.

Our most dedicated fans flew in from around the world to share one last moment of music with us. Arnold Austin flew in from Peru. We caught up on how his family was doing. They'd settled in and were learning the language. He said his family had never felt so close to one another and God. Every moment possible was spent with our fans. They shared their memories with us. We laughed over funny moments of old shows and cried over the goodness of

God through all the years. Fans got a chance to tell us what our music meant to them. We got to tell our fans what they meant to us. Then it was time for a rock and roll show.

I walked onstage wearing all black and my favorite rock-star sunglasses. The band had already started "Clap Your Hands." I pointed to Will and Ben. I smiled at my good friend Brian Whitman, who'd joined us toward the end to lend his amazing guitar skills and to help carry the singing load. I watched Tyler's opening riff, then exploded into the song. My nerves were high that night, and it was good to get it out with some straight-up rock. The song knocked the rough edges off my nervous energy, and we blew right into "Worldwide: One." By the time "Mighty Good Leader" started, muscle memory and musical instincts had settled us into our groove. Though my voice wasn't working, I was completely at ease with it and having fun.

Tyler teed up "Big House." The audience went wild. "Big House" is about our Christian family, so I walked into the crowd to sing it with our family one more time. I shared the microphone with the audience, and we had fun celebrating the song that launched our career. My dad was near the center of the crowd, near the soundboard. I made my way over to him. From first singing with my brother in his church to writing "Big House" on his roof in Haiti, he was responsible for my career in so many ways. He was the first person to tell me that "Big House" was a hit, and in a moving moment, we brought it to a close together. I started the last line and gave the microphone to my dad so he could sing the last words of the song for the last time.

I got back to the stage to proclaim to Jesus that I would never give up, with "Until My Heart Caves In." I meant it. I looked out at the audience. A warm breeze blew through the palms, and the colors of the setting sun reflected on the white concrete shell that covered the stage. I was going to miss this part of our shows the most. I asked the crowd spilling beyond the ticketed section of chairs and into the lawns if they were still willing to follow Jesus anywhere he called them to go. If they were, I asked them to raise their hands up high. I looked out at a sea of hands waving in the day's last light, declaring they would go. Beyond their hands was the endless Pacific Ocean, and beyond that were the uttermost parts of the earth. The band launched into "Hands and Feet." There are a lot of things I love about our fans. What I'm most proud of is that they did go, that they continue to go, and that they inspired us to go.

Tyler's voice soared into "Ocean Floor" to remind our fans, and me, that our sins are completely forgiven, then into "Leaving 99" to remind us that God loves us so much that he'll find us no matter how far away we go. Ben started pounding heavy on the low- and mid-toms, and Tyler disappeared to some other universe to bring back otherworldly washes of guitar tones for "We're a Band." I introduced T-Bone to the stage. He inhaled the energy of the night and multiplied it in a speed rap that singed the hair off everybody in the front row. It was a verbal detonation that left the crowd on its feet. As I watched I couldn't help but think of all the nights I'd spent crying in his arms and the night he told me I could kiss my bride. I was thankful he was with us on this night. Fans rushed the stage on "Beautiful" for a chaotic dance party that only momentarily paused when a young Audio Adrenaline fan got down on one knee and proposed to his surprised and joy-teared girlfriend. The party continued with "Underdog" and "Get Down."

What struck me most about the night was how profoundly our music had moved in the lives of our fans. They'd flown across a world and oceans to hear it one last time. There were fans who had been with us our entire career and many we'd just met for the first time. And many more we'll never meet. As they shared their stories with me and how our music was a part of it, I was truly blessed. I had been a part of something significant. There, for a moment, I wondered if it was all a joke. In Hawaii, I realized that whatever mistakes I'd made, however imperfect a man I was, it had all been used for good. We were lucky to be in a time and a place where this was possible. We were never the best. We just tried to be true.

I worried a lot about what was next. Where the Christian music industry was heading. I wanted to protect it from the formulas and the money that might corrupt it. A while back, when we played in front of record-setting audiences on the Jesus Freak tour, my friend Louie Weber had pulled me aside. He had a word for me. He told me that Christian music would go on, even without my voice. He has since passed away, but his words still resonate with truth. The kingdom of God is bigger than any individual, record label, or band. Music rises above the formulas and the money and the fame and the hearts of those who might corrupt it. Because music starts and ends in the heart of God.

For the encore, we got people to their feet once more with our throwback song, "DC-10." The night was winding down. We quietly moved into our simple worship song, "King." The fans raised their hands in the air once again, this time to acknowledge our King and sing our praises to him. Together, we held hands high in tropical skies, becoming one in the spirit one last time. I felt God's powerful presence, and was reminded of the power that comes from his people setting aside everything to worship him together. Will felt it too.

Then came "Goodbye." At this point, it was all about the guys onstage. It was hard to believe this was it. Will gave me a huge smile, the one that has brought comfort and laughter and joy since he first flashed it in that divine dorm-room meeting. I shared a moment with each guy onstage. My friends. My family. My brothers. The music dropped down. My only job was to sing the bridge. I couldn't get through it. This time it wasn't because of my voice, but because of my tears. I broke down and couldn't get the words out. I was filled with love and joy and gratefulness. I finally pulled it together to sing one last verse with Tyler. Then he finished the song.

Tyler was a kid when I met him. He was now a man. I was proud of who he had become and lucky he'd chosen to stand next to me all those years. It felt like he was singing the song to me instead of to the audience.

> You'll be fine tomorrow,
> the sun will rise again.

It was a personal moment between good friends. He looked at me with the line, *"Goodbye / my old friend."*

Tyler's eyes shut. The last words sung were his. They were truth. And love. And grace. I looked at him. I looked at Ben. I looked at Will. I flashed to scenes across youth rooms and stadiums and foreign countries and award shows. These guys had given me the best fifteen years I could ever ask for. Wind from the ocean blew over the crowd and through my band and into my soul. I felt them all in the last lines of the song.

> You know I won't forget you.
> You know I never could.
> And when I said I loved you,
> you know I meant for good.

I looked at the audience and the stars and felt peace in the breeze. My heart was full. I said my last words from the stage.

"God bless you. Goodbye from Audio Adrenaline."

All you can really ask for in life is an opportunity to love, to be loved, and to do something meaningful with people you enjoy. I am the luckiest man alive.

Some people have argued Christian rock shouldn't exist. That there should just be bands with Christians in them, or there should just be worship music written exclusively for the church. Maybe they're right. The days of rock-filled arenas and Christian rock anthems and parking lots filled with brightly painted youth group buses are over. But for a moment, something happened. Others smarter than me have tried to figure out what it was. What I know is that all forms of rock and roll are built on rebellion, and there is no bigger rebel than Jesus. He went against all norms of politics and religious institutions to lay claim to the most radical idea in all of human history: every single person on this earth is worthy of God's love. Then Jesus died on a cross and rose again to prove they were. That, my friends, is some serious rock and roll. For a little over a decade, Audio Adrenaline did our gut-level best to sing about that. Perhaps Christian rock shouldn't have existed. But because it did, something real and miraculous happened. Lives were changed. Some of those lives were our own.

THIS IS US

After the tour, I was completely and utterly spent. Aegis and I finally went on our real honeymoon, hopping an island plane to Kauai for a resort I'd booked for us there. For the first time in well over a decade, there was no place for me to be. In one fell swoop, one part of my life ended and a new one began. I took a breath. We slept in, and when we woke we drank locally grown coffee in the shade on white-sand beaches. During the day, I rented a jeep, and we puttered around the island. I was disoriented by the slowness. I looked at Aegis. It was just us now. She was at peace, reading and just being. When I slipped into anxious thoughts about the future, she brought me to the present. We drove to the north side of the island and watched the sun set over Hanalei Bay. The sun dipped behind the blue horizon, and the winds shifted. A cool breeze calmed the waters. Moon and stars appeared. My bandmates were flying east. I faced toward the west and watched the pale light of a waning moon shimmer over the Pacific and wondered what was next. That question would soon be answered on another island, on the other side of the world. I slipped into the arms of a woman who loved me. For now, I was home.

FORTY-ONE

The Day the Mountain Crumbled

My voice was worse. I was hungry and tried ordering a chicken sandwich at a drive-through when the words I'd dreaded came over the microphone.

"Could you repeat that please?"

I tried to repeat it. Nothing came out. I concentrated and pressed my thumb and index finger against my vocal box, holding it in place while the air from my lungs passed between my lips, trying desperately to form the words.

"I'm so sorry. I still can't understand."

I drove on without placing the order. Then I parked in the corner of the lot and dropped my head into my hands and cried.

A GROWING FAMILY

Twelve months after the Hawaii show, Haiti was rocked by three back-to-back hurricanes and a massive tropical storm. Michelle Meece called in a panic as a river from flash flooding roared through the campus. I heard children screaming in the background. They were frightened. I tried to calm Michelle. She struggled to hear my voice over the phone. I flew down with my dad between storms to help dig the campus from the rubble, only to see the next storm cover the campus back up with mud. The country was devastated. I couldn't understand why God would allow such comprehensive damage to an already frail nation. We barely made it through the hurricanes. I couldn't imagine making it through anything worse.

After the floods, Haiti's orphan crisis continued to grow. Not necessarily from the deaths of parents, but because orphan care was becoming a big business in Haiti. Elaborate scams popped up everywhere in the country, where corrupt operators convinced impoverished parents to place kids in their orphanages, promising at least three meals a day and an education. Then these operators would reach out to churches in the US to sponsor orphans for twenty, thirty, even forty dollars per month. They even invited churches to come down and see the children for themselves. The money rarely went to the kids. The children were barely fed and slept in horrifying conditions. Older boys were abused and older girls were sold. Hands and Feet was asked to take the kids from one of these corrupt operations. We agreed and got to work raising money to build these beautiful children a comfortable, safe, and permanent home. The Hands and Feet family was rapidly expanding.

Aegis and I were ready to grow our family too. God placed adoption on our hearts. We sought the advice of our good friend Steven Curtis Chapman, who'd started an adoption ministry called Show Hope. He gave us a frank assessment of his adoption experiences and warned of the many challenges we'd face. But he also promised God would grow our hearts in ways we never imagined possible. After much prayer and consideration, we felt the Lord leading us to adopt from Haiti. Aegis dove into the difficult process. In 2009, God introduced us to a Haitian boy and girl with amazing birth stories that one day they may tell. We knew adopting them from Haiti was next to impossible, but we applied for adoption anyway. Time passed. And passed. My desire for a family grew. We prayed for a miracle.

THE DAY THE MOUNTAIN CRUMBLED

Aegis and I flew to Haiti to spend Christmas and New Year's with my parents and the kids at the Children's Village. The plan was to spend January in Jacmel, preparing for the new year and visiting agencies to accelerate the adoption. Winter months are my favorite in Haiti. Humidity and stifling heat give way to perfectly warm days, cool night breezes, and clear skies; and winter birds are busy with their homemaking. When the work for the day was finished, we cooled off by swimming in the bay near the Cyvadier Plage hotel, and together, we dreamed of parenthood. New Year's Eve arrived. Streets filled with music and optimism. The country was rebounding from the flood and starting to feel hope once more.

Aegis rocked a baby on the shaded porch, and I stood atop the newly constructed second-floor apartment of the depot. My parents returned a day early from the Hotel Montana in Port-au-Prince, and we took in the stunning views together, thanking God for the blessing of Haiti. Mountains covered in lush shades of green rose dramatically behind our property. To the front, all hues of blue gathered to form the Caribbean Sea. The afternoon sun, on its shallow winter's arc, cast flattering light on the mountains and the sea and our campus.

I was shooting videos of different boys and girls saying hello to sponsors when the rumbling announced itself with the sound of a freight train. The building vibrated with a quick staccato. I thought a semitruck was driving by. I looked. I didn't see a truck but saw buildings moving. Vibrations intensified until chattering gave way to wildly swaying earth. The ground swelled and dipped like open ocean. Distant buildings evaporated. I heard a deep cracking rumble as if thunder and lightning had struck simultaneous blows. I looked to the mountain. It was splitting apart. Massive cracks appeared, and it began to crumble. Boulders the size of Volkswagens hurtled from newly formed fissures and plunged at gravitational speeds toward our property. The sight barely registered.

"*Earthquake!*"

"*Everybody out!*"

There were thirty to forty seconds of warlike chaos and then, nothing. It was complete stillness. There was no music in the streets. There were no birds singing in the trees. We stood in awe and disbelief.

Dad's voice boomed like the mountain and shook me from my shock. All the kids and staff had cleared out of the buildings and were standing in the courtyard. Our caregivers and the older children began to cry. Although we were okay, they knew something horrific had just happened. Our buildings had held up, just like they were designed to. But we weren't so sure about our neighbors'. Odius rushed through the gate to make sure we were okay. He was on the phone. He hung up. His face was lifeless.

"Port-au-Prince is flat. Jacmel has tumbled."

We stared at each other, then at the mountain, then at our kids screaming on the campus. We did a quick inventory. Everyone was there. No damage. We'd be okay. For now. Dad sent Odius and me to see how our neighbors were doing.

The street filled with glazed-eyed people wandering without purpose. There was crying and wailing and confusion. People were covered in blood and dust. Others were dead. Bodies deformed by collapsed concrete lay near the road or partially covered by the buildings that consumed them. Information flew. The school had collapsed. Children were in there. The hospital had collapsed. Patients. Doctors. The road was gone. There was no way out. Which meant there was no way in. We walked farther, helping where we could. Some were saved. Some were not. This scene continued as far as I could see in any direction. I'd never felt so small. I rushed back to the Hands and Feet Project to report what I'd seen.

"Dad, it's really bad."

I drove as far as I could toward Jacmel but was stopped by impassable rubble, so I walked the rest of the way into the city to assess damages and see what news I could find. The town was mostly vacant. Everyone had made their way to the airport to receive food, water, and shelter. Sticking out from under a slab of concrete, I saw the legs of three small children near a man's legs. A family killed while eating dinner, not even a chance to escape. A block away a man did try to escape by jumping off his front porch, only to have the shredded steel of a collapsing building impale him mid-jump. His corpse hung in midair, rebar sticking through his chest, face frozen in fear. People dug feverishly through rubble, trying to locate people crying below. Others dug even though the crying had stopped. Above the town hung the acrid smell of decomposing bodies and the wailing of death and destruction and lost hope. It was a humanitarian crisis of generational proportions. It was impossible to know what to do, or where to start.

There were more than forty aftershock earthquakes, and each brought back the terror of the first. Nobody returned home. Concrete homes that had once provided a sense of safety now felt like a death trap. People slept in streets, on pavement, in cars. Aegis and I slept in a van. Jacmel needed shelters. Fast. Worse, Jacmel's already undependable infrastructure was further damaged and could not provide safe drinking water. Local ministries had stockpiles of rice and beans, but food supplies wouldn't last. The damage to the only road between Jacmel and the aid arriving to Port-au-Prince could take weeks to repair. We were completely shut off from the country's capital and the pipeline to the rest of the world. We faced the immediate challenge of food and water and medical supply shortages.

We met with the mayor. He put us in charge of getting US support, while his teams worked to recover lives and bodies, establish a communication system, and clear the roads.

In the US, one of our original band members, Bob, was serving as the executive director of Hands and Feet. His military training helped him to quickly organize and execute an international relief effort. Somehow I got connected to CNN and provided the first on-the-ground reports from Jacmel. I became one of the voices (scratchy and broken as it was) connecting the church, the media, and the needs of Haiti. Through CNN and the church, I was able to tell the outside world what the mayor of a now very isolated Jacmel needed for recovery. I've sung for thousands of churches. They knew me. This made it personal for them. Help quickly poured in. Within the first twenty-four hours, we could tell the church response was going to be massive. However, all roads in were buried. Help could not arrive from the ground.

The first outside help came from our friends at Go Ministries. They arrived by boat from the Dominican Republic, where they were setting up a supply chain to help. Though the first delivery was small, it was enough to let us know we were not alone. That same day, a Hands and Feet supporter, Steve Schapanksy, called us. He was a pilot who lived in Santa Barbara, California, more than five thousand miles away. He didn't hesitate. Neither did his friend and copilot Glenn Miller, who offered his twin-engine Piper Mojave airplane to fly over a continent, a gulf, and a sea, to help people they'd never met. They removed seats, and after finding a faulty part that would have caused a catastrophic failure, left with an empty cargo area. Steve had faith that God would provide what was needed. Glenn, someone who wasn't looking for God's hand, was amazed that such a minor yet critical element to the flight was discovered only minutes before departure.

Churches from everywhere called to help. I got a list of needs from the mayor and gave them to Bob. He coordinated with the churches, then called Steve, who was in midair, and told him to land at a little airport in Texas and look for Jim, who was there with a load of supplies. Another load was coordinated for south Florida. All of this happened seamlessly within hours. Glenn couldn't believe what he was witnessing. It didn't make sense. An initial load of batteries, baby food, rice, and medical supplies filled the cargo area, and they headed to Haiti. They flew under five hundred feet in altitude to stay below radar. That morning, they'd left the beauty of Santa Barbara with an empty plane, and by the afternoon, were flying over Haiti with a plane full of supplies. From a few hundred feet above Port-au-Prince, they were among the first to see the effects of the earthquake.

The enormity of the destruction was unfathomable. What we didn't know at the time was that we'd experienced one of the top ten natural disasters in history. Between two and three hundred thousand people died. Bodies lined the streets to be picked up and buried in mass graves. Nearly four thousand schools were damaged or destroyed. Orphanages were demolished. Hospitals and hotels and churches, all in ruins. The port and government buildings, devastated. Hundreds died in the same hotel my mom and dad had left only hours before. Hardships for the living magnified. Three hundred thousand suffered injury. Five million were displaced. Starvation and outbreaks of disease were still to come. Mountains crumbled. Entire villages disappeared. From the air, towns appeared completely flattened. There was no movement. No life. Between Port-au-Prince and Jacmel, 90 percent of Léogâne was completely leveled. Seventy percent of the homes in Jacmel were wiped out or damaged. These belonged to our friends and staff and the community we were here to serve.

I met Steve and Glenn at the Jacmel airport. We unloaded the supplies, and my dad organized a supply depot. A woman who'd just had a baby showed up. They were without food and shelter. We gave her starving baby some of the baby food that had just arrived. It was a small sign of hope, but hope was overshadowed by the evil and destruction of this world. Not far from the runway, near downtown, a school had collapsed with children trapped in the rubble. We didn't know if they were alive or dead. Locals dug with bare hands. Steve wanted to stay and help, but we needed them to fly, to evacuate those who'd die without immediate medical support and to bring lifesaving relief for those who remained. We loaded badly injured Haitians onto the plane. They were strapped down in the cargo area. There wasn't even time to check weights and balances. The plane bounded down the runway, filled with broken bodies and the goodwill of men and Steve's faith that it would fly. They lifted and banked toward the Dominican Republic, where our friends from Go Ministries waited with another load of supplies.

For nearly a week, my dad and a couple other missionaries ran the airport. I became a fixture on CNN, reporting to news anchor Wolf Blitzer. I called in prayer requests to churches. More churches and more pilots got involved. Bob did an incredible job organizing a massive relief effort. Steve made three to four trips a day between Jacmel and the supply chain Go Ministries had set up in the Dominican Republic. The mayor brought us the most critically wounded and handed a slip of paper with names to Steve as his official documentation, and for several days straight, Steve and Glenn flew out bodies and flew in tents and water and food and medical supplies.

An invisible hand coordinated a heroically undocumented relief effort between multiple countries and languages and faith-based organizations. Churches rose up and believers prayed and people got off their couches and out of their pews to love their neighbors, and as a result, thousands of lives were saved. I thought back to Bono's wish for the church. I had a front-row seat to the miracle of the body of Christ working unselfishly and relentlessly to cast back the shadows with the light of God's hope.

I was at the airport when a massive Canadian C-130 military plane landed and unloaded military vehicles and supplies. The big boys arrived and sent us home. On their way back to Santa Barbara, Steve and Glenn were detained in Florida and given a list of fines that totaled over $60,000 for all their undocumented flight activity. In the middle of their conversation with customs and an

FAA representative, the representative's attitude suddenly changed. He asked Glenn to put out his hands. Glenn, at that moment, thought he was getting handcuffed. Instead, the representative slapped him on the wrist and told him that a directive just came through providing allowances for individuals doing humanitarian aid in Haiti. He thanked them for their work and said their story was already well known, and that they would be getting some help on their way home.

Steve and Glenn were given unprecedented flight path priority, passing through each air traffic control area with a verbal high five and a thank-you for what they did. Glenn reconsidered his belief in God. He'd seen enough miracles to make him believe Someone up there was pulling some strings.

I went back to our campus. The first wave of international relief workers arrived to the area and used our campus as a base. They were a motley crew. Adrenaline junkies from all over the globe, chasing destruction and bringing hope. Every afternoon, an Irishman with red head and beard appeared on the second-story balcony. He wore Coke-bottle glasses, and his cargo pants and shirt were stained from the day's efforts. His voice was classically trained. He could have had a career as a traveling opera singer, though that was far too tame. From the rooftop of the Big House, he looked over the destruction that lay before him. Then he stepped into the spotlight of a setting sun and began to sing. From the Hands and Feet rooftops and decks, scenes from one of the greatest tragedies of our lifetime unfolded to the melancholy opera of a lone baritone facing the sea.

If you believe this life is all there is, that there's no heaven or afterlife, it would be hard to find meaning in any disaster. It would be hard, in fact, to find any meaning in life at all. Haiti as a country has dramatically changed my view of this life. Haiti's people have suffered unimaginable losses. After the quake, they had every reason to walk away from God. Instead, churches that still stood overflowed with people. There was struggle, sorrow, and yet, joy amid the suffering. Prayers were more urgent and worship more intense. It felt like a revival. Even missionaries came together.

It's when the illusion of our control is shattered that God becomes most real. In Haiti, all of life is a struggle. They are not in control. They depend on God for everything. As a result, they are the richest, most joy-filled people I know. I'm trying to become more like them.

FORTY-TWO

"Kings & Queens"

Are you Mark Stuart? From Audio Adrenaline?"

Oh, great. Now I have to talk over the noise of an airplane.

The airplane had taken off from Port-au-Prince for a short flight to the Dominican Republic, over the mountains and, hopefully, around the coming storm. It was a regional prop plane, not much more than a tin bucket with twin engines. The smell of oil and gas fumes filled the cabin. About a dozen people were aboard, and it was hard to hear above the din of voices and engine noise. The flight attendant couldn't hear my voice, so I just pointed to my in-flight snack choices. She set a corn muffin and coffee on my fold-down tray table. I was opening the muffin wrapper when the guy next to me asked the question. I applied pressure to my vocal cords and scratched out a "Yup" the best I could. He worked for the Luis Palau organization, and Audio Adrenaline had played at some of their largest outreach events. He asked why we retired. I told him about my voice. He'd seen many miracles in their work throughout the world and believed God could heal my voice.

"Do you believe in miracles?"

I used to be a skeptic, but I've seen God do too many things beyond my reason to maintain disbelief.

"Yes. Yes, I do."

He was so convinced God wanted to heal my voice that he asked if he could pray for it right then and there. I wanted my voice healed too. I was lost without it. Hands and Feet struggled without the Audio Adrenaline platform.

I'd recently bumped into one of my childhood heroes, Russ Taff, who said he'd suffered from vocal issues that sounded similar to mine. He took a year off and his voice came back. It gave me hope that maybe mine would too. If my voice was healed I could put the band back together. We could raise money. Or I could start a solo career and regain control of my life. Although my voice had been prayed over many times, this one felt special. I said yes, he could pray for my voice. Maybe our closer proximity to heaven would help God better hear it.

He put his hand on me and started into prayer: "Dear God . . ."

At that exact moment, our plane hit the outer band of the hurricane Hanna. It felt like we'd hit a mountain. Or something bigger. We dropped like a rock. I opened my eyes, and my snack and drink hovered midair. The plane was falling. The cabin filled with screams. I called out to Jesus, but no one could hear my voice. Passengers freaked out. Those who weren't buckled were lifted from their seats. The plane listed. It was out of control. This was it. The plane slammed into an air pocket and jolted to the side. It felt like a hard landing without landing gear. Baggage and snacks and drinks bounced everywhere. I couldn't see land or sky out the window, only the darkness of storm clouds. Then, just as quickly as the plane had dropped from the sky, it was perfectly calm. A Haitian man thought we'd crash-landed. He bolted from his seat to the door and tried to open it. We were still ten thousand feet above the Caribbean. He pulled the door lever and started pushing on the door. A flight attendant tackled him. The man was in shock, screaming in Creole. It took a couple more passengers to restrain him. The inside of the plane was a scene of mass chaos. Also, my voice wasn't healed.

As the airplane recovered, my first thought was that I should not have let that guy pray for my voice. Not only because we nearly crashed when he did, but because of something my pastor had recently said. There are three idols that drive us: comfort, control, and approval. When left to our own devices, the decisions we make in our lives reflect our need for one or more of those idols. My focus on my voice reflected all three.

Once our plane settled, I sensed God telling me he didn't need my voice. He needed my attention. After the airplane incident, he had it. Up to that point, all my attention and prayers and the prayers of others were that God would perform a miracle and heal my voice. I wanted it fixed so I could regain control over my life. And comfort. And approval. When you pray for healing and don't get it, it doesn't mean God isn't working on what you asked him to. It means he is working on what he wants to, and that is something bigger and more beautiful than we know to pray for. The miracle wasn't that God was going to fix my voice. The miracle was that God was going to use me with a busted one.

A few months later, I was back with the Vanderbilt voice doctor, and she finally came up with a diagnosis. I suffered from spasmodic dysphonia, an incurable vocal disorder caused by muscle spasms interrupting the pathways between the brain and vocal cords. It affects singers, coaches, and other professionals. She gave a few recommendations. Some people improved with Botox shots injected in the muscles around the vocal cords. I tried. It didn't help. A doctor at UCLA was having limited success with a complicated surgery involving incisions through neurological pathways and letting them grow back and heal themselves. It sounded risky. I passed and just thanked the doctor. I appreciated the closure. I talked with others who had the disorder, and through research and practice came up with ways to improve my speaking voice. I started by holding my throat when I spoke, putting slight pressure on my vocal cords. The support helped the spasms to relax, and over time, there was enough healing that I don't always have to hold my throat. I'll never be able to sing again. But I can at least order a chicken sandwich.

The prayer on the plane was answered during a conversation with the chairman of the board for the Hands and Feet Project. Steve Fair and I were talking through the growing struggles of operating Hands and Feet without the platform of Audio Adrenaline. Steve was a scrap-metal guy from Michigan who was dragged to one of our concerts and felt moved by God to help. He's become one of the most important people in the life of the Hands and Feet ministry. As an organization, we were floundering. After floods and hurricanes and the shutting down of corrupt orphanages, more kids came through our doors. Our facilities and staff needed to grow, but we didn't have any money, and my voice didn't even work well enough to ask for it.

Although I was a cofounder and the main visionary, I led from a comfortable distance. I no longer wanted to be in the mix. It felt like Haiti's orphan crisis was too big, too messy. Too riddled with challenges I had no idea how to fix. My voice felt like a handicap. I told Steve all the reasons I wasn't qualified and why we needed to find someone more equipped to lead the ministry. He stopped me from talking any further. He placed his hand, full of grace and the power it contains, heavily on my shoulder and leaned close to make sure I was listening.

"Mark, these children don't have a voice in the world. You are their voice. Step up and lead this ministry. Be the voice for the voiceless."

FINDING MY VOICE

The earthquake expedited our adoption. Miraculously, God gave Aegis and me a son and a daughter from Haiti. We named our son Journey, after the epic path that led us to him. Our daughter is named Christela, "Christ was there."

When the adoption idea first came up, I wasn't sure about it. I knew of the difficulties of adopting from Haiti, and even after that, the difficulties of adopted kids transitioning into families. I talked it over with my mom, who had provided and overseen the care of Christela and Journey since they were newborns. There was a prophetic, generational longing in her. She gave me that look. We brought our kids home to Tennessee and tucked them in their new beds. I said good night to Aegis. Our house became a home. My love has gone full circle.

My experiences with divorce and Haiti, remarriage and adoption, reshaped my heart. Family became everything to me. Every day, because of Christela, Journey, and Aegis, I'm an eyewitness to the gospel. God is in the business of placing the lost in families. I desperately wanted every kid in Haiti to feel the same love from a family that I was feeling.

Around that time, First Company Management, which had successfully relaunched the Newsboys with Michael Tait as the new singer, pitched Will and me the idea of relaunching Audio Adrenaline with a new front man. At best, we were skeptical. Our buddy Juan Otero brought us a potential track for the new Audio Adrenaline record. The song was called "Kings & Queens." Juan had grown up as an orphan in foster care and connected deeply with our passion for the children in Haiti. In talking to him about the concept and lyrics of "Kings & Queens," it became clear this song could be an important psalm for children everywhere who needed the love of a family: *"Boys become kings, girls will be queens . . . when we love the least of these."* With this beautiful new song, and with our longtime friend Kevin Max, one of the singers of DC Talk, as the new vocalist, Audio Adrenaline was ready to hit the road again and tell the story of Hands and Feet.

The song needed a video as big as its message. I didn't want another sad orphan story. The visual narrative had to be about hope and the promises God has for every child. It needed to be majestic, calling viewers into bigger versions of themselves. We envisioned the video filmed in Haiti with the Hands and Feet children. When completed, "Kings & Queens" became everything we'd dreamed of. Even more. It became an anthem of hope for anyone who's ever felt abandoned. It hit a nerve because it was about the family of heaven. It was about sonship and daughtership and the ways we are connected. Not only for the orphans but for all of us. For the orphan story is our story. It's a picture of the gospel. In Jesus, we've all gone from lost and forgotten to being found. To being loved. To being made abundantly whole and complete.

The concept of the video was to depict children transitioning from being forgotten or abandoned to being a part of a royal family, bathed in purple, the color of majesty. At the end of the day, the kids celebrated their roles as kings and queens of heaven with an epic sunset scene along the ocean shore. We showed purple footprints where they ran through the dirt and purple hand-prints where they touched walls. On-screen, the children looked the way *we* see them—poor, lost, helpless. The purple remnants of where they'd walked showed their true identity, as *God* sees them. It was the contrast of earthly poverty with heavenly majesty that made the video work. Because of Jesus, they've become sons and daughters of the Most High God. It's as true of the orphans in Haiti as it is for all of us.

For most of my life, my voice was bound by my vocal cords and limited by my fear and need for control over my life. That voice is gone. A new one has emerged. It's unlimited. It's the sum total of who I am and who God is, and it's colliding with the rock and roll rebellion of taking up the mighty causes of the kingdom. My voice, and yours, is a melody in the heart of God, sung in harmony with all those who desire to make him known.

As I watched Kevin sing the final scene of the video, I felt an indescribable peace come over me. It was an echo of earlier memories. Singing with Fred on the rooftops of Saint-Louis-du-Nord. Opening for Kevin and DC Talk in the biggest rock and roll stadiums. Meeting God in the frozen cab of my Bronco. Singing "Ocean Floor" with my best friends at the Dove Awards. God was always in control. Instead of anger or sadness or jealousy as I watched someone else sing for the band I'd led for years, I felt complete joy. In that moment, with purple powder flying and kids' hearts exploding with happiness, I was complete. I was no longer a guy with a busted voice. I, too, was a king.

I looked beyond the party happening on that beach in Haiti and up to the mountain backdrop of our Children's Village in Jacmel. Clouds reflecting the color of water hung low over the mountains, and the angled light of the setting sun highlighted emerald ridges against coral-hued sky. Scars remained from when the earth had given way and crumbled toward the sea, though I no longer fear the shaking of the world. Above the mountains hovers the voice of God. He spoke to the earth and put those mountains in place. He reflected those mountains in the sea and in the eyes of the woman who houses my heart and in the family he's given us. Below those mountains is the land of the children I love, running with joy, purple powder in hand, getting ready to tackle Kevin. Haiti has given more to me than I could ever return.

As we wrapped the final video scene, the kids were covered in majestic purple. We are sons and daughters of the King. Our Dad runs the universe. I want to live my life like I believe that. I want you to as well. "Kings & Queens" grew to become one of Audio Adrenaline's most beloved songs. It won awards and became the theme song of many organizations caring for children all over the world.

My voice has never been bigger.

Epilogue

To answer the question I'm asked most often: *Yes, I miss it!* I miss being the lead singer of Audio Adrenaline. I miss the thrill of a perfectly lit rock and roll stage and connecting with thousands of believers in city after city. I miss inspiring people with gutsy guitar anthems and living a larger-than-life, Kingdom-focused adventure with my best buddies Will, Barry, Ben, Tyler, Bob, Brickell, and Garth. It was an unbelievable ride. A dream come true. But I wouldn't trade my story for anybody else's on the planet.

Losing My Voice to Find It was the publisher's suggested title for this book. I love it now, but it wasn't my favorite when it was first presented. It seemed too small. I didn't just lose my voice, I lost everything I thought I was in control of. Some people use a metaphor of jumping off a cliff to discover that Jesus is holding the net somewhere down below. Just trust him. Let go. He will catch you. Well . . . Jesus pushed me off the cliff and, yes, the net was there, but it was more like a flying carpet. When you finally realize that you're not in control of your life and that your Dad is running the universe, you release the tethers of fear and doubt and finally take flight, living your biggest and best life with God.

It's been years since we filmed the "Kings & Queens" video in Jacmel, Haiti. And to say that God used that moment on the beach would be a gross understatement. Those profound lyrics and majestic images of Haitian children unlocked the hearts and imaginations of people around the globe. As the executive director of the Hands and Feet Project, I was contacted by countless people from all walks of life who wanted to be a part of something audaciously hopeful. People were caught up in the wonder of God's economy, where the

235

afflicted and the forgotten become royalty. Hands and Feet Project's impact, through so many new partners, grew exponentially.

Although my career as a lead singer was over, God planted a new song in my heart. My creative and entrepreneurial energy shifted from making records to fighting the orphan crisis in Haiti. We would go on to build multiple Children's Villages and develop job creation initiatives to help alleviate Haiti's poverty-driven child abandonment epidemic. We launched Haiti Made, an artisan and manufacturing business that now employs nearly one hundred Haitian employees. We built IKONDO, a mission-trip hosting facility that introduces a new way to visit Haiti, focusing on providing sustainable, dignified hospitality jobs for Haitian people. We saw God do more than we could ever imagine. It became apparent that music was just a chapter of my life that led to the next chapter—all perfectly authored by our Creator.

I do feel forgotten from time to time as I watch the bands I toured with continue to make hit songs and sell out arenas. But as the Kingdom of God unfolds around me, I step into the new adventure fully aware that what will resonate through eternity won't be our chart-topping songs or award show trophies, but a life totally surrendered to Jesus. In God's economy, boys become kings, girls will be queens, and those of us with broken voices, failed marriages, and busted dreams are often the ones God chooses to speak through the most.

Today I'm back on the road again, but I've traded the old tour bus for our family RV. Aegis, Journey, Christela, and I broke the mold of a normal family existence and chose instead to live life together as full-time road warriors, exploring creation, road-schooling, partnering with ministries, and reminding others that God can use each of our voices, no matter how big or how small, to tell His great story.

Thank you for joining me on this erratic and extraordinary rock and roll adventure. Now it's time for you to live yours. Find your voice, pick up the microphone, and sing.

Mark

To learn more about booking speaking engagements, partnering in ministry, or simply connecting with Mark, visit markstuartmedia.com.

Acknowledgments

A special thanks to my friend and coauthor Roger Thompson.

I've only met a few people in my life who consistently deliver beyond expectations. Roger Thompson always delivers. He is an old-school, salty, surf-loving, trout-fishing, adventure-going family man. And the dude can write. This book would have never happened without him. He took the time and made the effort to go beyond getting the history on the page. He helped find my voice.

Roger has also been instrumental in crafting the vision of the Hands and Feet Project, Haiti Made, Ikondo Guest Village, and numerous other God-sized dreams. I see him as fearless and wise, funny and thoughtful, but mostly, I see Roger as one of my closest friends. Thank you, Roger, for bringing this story to life.

Mark

Notes

1. Justin Sarachik, "Former Audio Adrenaline Guitarist Barry Blair Wishes 3.0 'Success' & Is 'Proud of the Legacy They Are Carrying On' [INTERVIEW 2]," BREATHEcast, June 8, 2015, http://www.breathecast.com/articles/former-audio-adrenaline-guitarist-barry-blair-wishes-3-0-success-is-proud-of-the-legacy-they-are-carrying-on-interview-2-28508/.
2. Lorraine Ali, "The Glorious Rise of Christian Pop," *Newsweek*, July 15, 2001, https://www.newsweek.com/glorious-rise-christian-pop-154551.

About the Author

Mark Stuart, perhaps best known as the lead vocalist for the Christian rock band Audio Adrenaline, is a songwriter, singer, speaker, missionary, and advocate for vulnerable children in Haiti. Although he calls Franklin, Tennessee, home, he travels full time with his wife, Aegis, and their two children, Journey and Christela, in their family RV.

Roger W. Thompson is the author of *We Stood Upon Stars* and *My Best Friend's Funeral*. When not working (even when he should be), he can be found surfing near his home or fly-fishing in Montana. He lives in Ventura, California, with his wife, two sons, one Australian Shepherd, and seven productive chickens.